THE
CAMPER'S
BIBLE

THE CAMPER'S BIBLE

REVISED EDITION

DOUBLEDAY & COMPANY, INC.
GARDEN CITY, NEW YORK

By Bill Riviere

ISBN: 0-385-05475-0

Library of Congress Catalog Card Number 60–9677
Copyright © 1961, 1970 by William A. Riviere. All Rights Reserved
Printed in the United States of America

15   14   13   12   11

Contents

CONTENTS

THE
CAMPER'S
BIBLE

Chapter 1

UMBRELLA TENT WITH CANOPY   *Eureka*

TENTS AND THEIR VARIATIONS

Tents have become rather specialized shelters, so much so, in fact, that it's no longer feasible simply to "buy a tent for a camping trip." Camping interests have broadened. We now travel by car, pack horse, canoe, snowmobile, trail bike, power boat, plane, and afoot. Each type of camping, each mode of travel places limitations on equipment. The choice of a tent particularly is rigidly governed by the use to which it will be put. To make a suitable choice you'll need to know a little about all tents.

The Umbrella Tent

Along with the Cottage tent, the Umbrella tent is the most popular all-fabric shelter used by family campers. For them it is ideal; large enough to house an entire family and easy to erect and dismantle, even for the relatively inexperienced. Being practically storm- and insectproof, it appeals to women who might otherwise be somewhat timid about "sleeping out." Too, it provides ample headroom, has a sewed-in floor and, except for anchoring the canopy, it needs no guy lines. Most models are equipped with at least two screened windows for ventilation, and these are invariably protected by storm flaps.

The center pole with its four radiating arms, from which the tent derived its name, has virtually disappeared except in a very few low-priced models. Instead it is now suspended on a sectional frame of tubular aluminum alloy fitted either inside or out.

The interior-type frame has several drawbacks, the worst being that a camper must struggle in semidarkness inside the tent while setting up or dismantling the frame. Under a hot sun, the experience can be likened to remaining too long in a sauna bath! Also, such a frame is usually "spring-loaded" so that it will "give"—expand or contract longitudinally—as the fabric shrinks or stretches with changes in humidity. Because of this flexibility, a constant wind from one direction will warp the frame and cause the tent to lean crazily, placing undue strain on the fabric. The lower ends of the corner poles, even when fitted with rubber tips, tend to puncture the fabric floor on which they must rest. All in all, the interior frame is less desirable than the exterior type.

This, on the other hand, can be assembled in the open. First, the sewed-in floor is squared on the ground and corner stakes, when required, are driven in. Some models have eliminated stakes but, nonetheless, the floor must be squared. The spreader arms of the upper frame are then

BASIC UMBRELLA TENT   *Coleman*

UMBRELLA TENT WITH   *Johnson*
SINGLE SIDE EXTENSION

UMBRELLA TENT WITH LARGE   *Laacke & Joys*
SIDE EXTENSION

attached to the peak and corners of the tent. Following this, the short sections of the corner poles are inserted, thus raising the tent gradually and easily. Fabric shrinkage or stretching is accommodated by means of elastic shock cord with which the tent is attached to the frame, thus providing automatic adjustment for changes in tension on the fabric.

Early Umbrella tents had a square floor, usually 9′×9′, but with the recent addition of sideroom extensions, the rectangular shape prevails. Extensions are available on one, two, or three sides, each adding about one-third to the floor area. These formerly required guy lines, but modern exterior suspension systems have eliminated these. In the event of a strong wind, however, guying is still advisable. With sideroom extensions, Umbrella tent dimensions range from 9′×12′ up to

10′×18′ with weights, depending on fabric, running between 30 and 70 pounds. The larger Umbrella tents, obviously, are bulky and heavy, but this is not a serious drawback to most campers who will rarely tote it more than a few feet between the family car and the tent site. To older campers and to women, such weight and bulk is a decided handicap. The solution to this, of course, is a smaller tent or one made of lighter fabrics.

Taking a cue from campers in the tropics, some manufacturers equip their Umbrella tents with a fly, or second roof, fitted atop the exterior frame, to repel the sun's heat and unusually heavy rains. So far as the sun's heat is concerned, the effectiveness of a fly atop the frame is questionable. Tropical flies are effective because they are generally used on Wall tents whose sides can

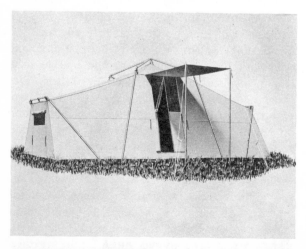

UMBRELLA TENT WITH   *Johnson*
DOUBLE SIDE EXTENSIONS

UMBRELLA TENT WITH FLY   *Eureka*

COTTAGE TENT WITH EXTERIOR RIDGEPOLE IN SLEEVE

Coleman

SLOPING-WALL COTTAGE TENT WITH INTERIOR RIDGEPOLE

Hettrick

be raised for the utmost in ventilation. Also, they cover the entire tent, not merely the top. With an Umbrella tent, this is not possible.

Nearly all Umbrella tents are provided with a door canopy, shading the entryway. Generally, this must be anchored with two guy lines attached to stakes.

The Cottage Tent

The Cottage tent, also known as a Cabin, Bungalow, Chalet, or Lodge tent, is basically a Wall tent whose normally low sides have been raised to a height of four to six feet, this to provide headroom throughout the floor area. There the resemblance ends.

Although certain models utilize an interior ridge-

pole, nearly all are suspended on an exterior frame which may include a ridgepole fitted into a ridge sleeve. Cottage tents invariably feature large windows, screened with Fiberglas or nylon netting, and these may be closed off during poor weather by means of fabric flaps. Most Cottage tents are rectangular in shape with sewed-in floors ranging from 8'×10' up to 9'×16'. Some makers describe their 6'×9' shelters as "Cottage" tents, certainly a loose application of tent terminology. A 6'×9' tent can hardly qualify as a "cottage"!

Due to their great size, Cottage tents can be equipped with rather large canopies, and to these may be added netting or fabric side walls to provide a "second room" or outdoor living space sheltered from the sun and rain.

Because of the vertical walls, double-deck alu-

COTTAGE TENT WITH LARGE WINDOWS

Hettrick

CANOPY DOUBLES LIVING AREA OF COTTAGE TENT

Eureka

COLORFULLY STRIPED COTTAGE TENT *Hettrick*

minum-framed bunks can be used, thus doubling a Cottage tent's normal sleeping capacity. For a family of six to ten persons, it is an ideal choice.

Like the larger Umbrella tents, however, a Cottage tent is generally bulky and weighty. This has to be considered, since most models require more than one person to erect them, to say nothing of loading and unloading. In the case of most family campers, though, there is generally plenty of willing help at hand.

The new exterior frames have pretty much eliminated the need for guying a Cottage tent, but because of the large, flat panels of fabric that make up such a shelter, the tent is susceptible to strong winds, and campers should be prepared to rig emergency guy lines. Too, because of this susceptibility, it's wise to buy a Cottage tent made of high-grade fabrics.

The Cottage tent is usually purchased by large families who need the space it affords, or by campers who like plenty of interior elbow room. Be sure, therefore, to check the specifications before ordering a Cottage model that you cannot personally inspect before purchasing. Don't place too much stock in the apparently ample proportions illustrated in the catalog. One of the tricks of merchandising is to make a tent appear much larger than it really is. Recently, I scaled the catalog figure of an adult standing by a Cottage tent, crediting him with 6-foot height. According to this scale, the tent appeared to be about 15 feet wide. The specifications indicated nine feet!

The Wall Tent

The Wall tent comes near to being the ideal shelter for a semipermanent camp or for one which will be moved by car or boat. It's also the favorite of the pack train outfits.

It offers the greatest variety of sizes and incorporates a good combination of usable floor space and headroom. The better models are easy to ventilate and all of them lend themselves well to heating in cold weather. Also, it's one of the few tents with which a fly can be used as a double roof.

Camp furniture is easy to arrange in a Wall tent—cots along the side walls, a table at the rear, and folding chairs wherever they're most wanted. A lantern can be hung from the ridgepole.

The Wall tent has drawbacks, however. One of these is weight and another is bulk, but these are not likely to create a problem if you're traveling by car.

Of course, the canoeman or hiker will want a lighter and less cumbersome tent. Too, the Wall tent requires many stakes to peg it down and it's not easy to erect unless you have a model with a sewed-in floor.

A number of suspension methods are available with the Wall tent. If you are traveling in the wilderness where weight and bulk are factors to consider, you will not want to use factory-supplied poles. On the other hand, if you will be camping in state and federal parks where cutting poles is illegal, you will want the simplest and most effective rig.

For use in organized campgrounds the most uni-

COTTAGE TENT WITH FLY *Hirsch-Weis*

versally used rigging consists of a front and rear pole with a horizontal interior ridgepole between them. An improvement is the set of poles which are assembled by means of metal ferrules, much like a fishing rod. Just be sure that the ferrules are rugged so that there will be no play in them, causing the poles to buckle or sag.

The poorest rig of all is the rope ridge, which cannot be drawn taut enough to prevent sagging. A tent that sags is more susceptible to high winds, insects get · in more easily, and leaks are more likely. Except in the case of certain tropical tents, where a rope ridge is almost a necessity, it's best to steer clear of it.

The tape ridge, on the other hand, comes close to being the perfect rig for use where you can cut poles. The tape ridge consists simply of tent material, doubled, and sewed to the outside ridge. The tapes, in turn, are sewed or riveted to the doubled ridge and these are then tied to an outside ridgepole. Sometimes rope ties are used. This is one of the rigs favored by professional outdoorsmen in the North and it's generally used with shear poles.

Another rig popular with professionals is the inside ridgepole set on shears. This calls for a Wall tent with holes cut into the front and rear walls, at the apex of the peak. The ridgepole, cut at the campsite, is slipped through the holes and lifted into place by pushing the shears together, scissorslike. With this arrangement, and with the tape ridge model too, side bars can be lashed to the shears and the tent eaves tied to these.

Frequently, a Wall tent is used on a permanent wood platform and this presents no problems. Here, the two vertical poles and inside ridgepole are best, with the eaves guyed to side rails or bars set permanently to each side of the platform.

If you decide in favor of the Wall tent, choose a model which can be opened at the rear, or one which has a netting window in the rear wall, for the sake of ventilation. Some have long narrow windows in the side walls but a rear wall opening is even better. The matter of insect pests, of course, is best taken care of by having nettings over all tent openings, including the doorway. A sewed-in floor will keep out crawling pests as well as moisture.

Going a step further toward good ventilation and protection from insects, is the tropical tent. The sides of this tent, which lace or snap together at the four corners, can be rolled up and insects are kept at bay by full netting sides which admit a breeze. A sewed-in floor helps keep out pests and a double roof turns back the sun's rays. During the cold of night, the sides can be dropped. Drawbacks to the tropical model are that the large areas of netting are susceptible to snagging or tearing and the tent is likely to prove expensive.

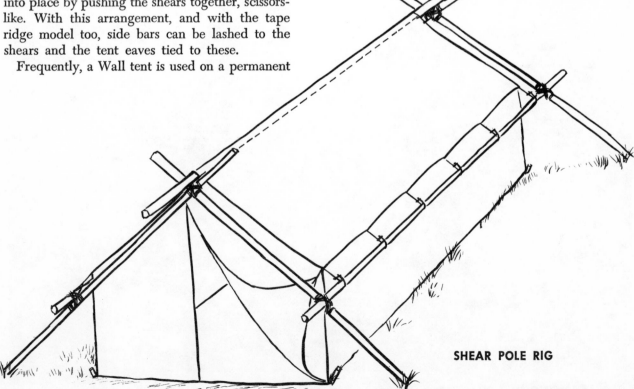

SHEAR POLE RIG

CAMPING IN A WALL TENT, STONY LAKE, ONTARIO

The Quonset Tent

This is shaped much like the World War II temporary building known as the Quonset hut. The design, however, antedates even this, being patterned somewhat after the more-than-50-year-old, and now discontinued, Ross Alpine tent with its interior frame of steam-bent wooden ribs, further proving that there are few, if any, truly "new" tents!

Aptly dubbed the "Prairie Schooner" by its maker, the tent has a sewed-in floor and is avail-

Ventilation is provided by a screened section in the door and by a window at the rear. One Quonset-type tent has a ventilator in the top; another had a divider curtain which converts it into a two-room shelter. Weight is not unreasonable for a tent of this style, ranging from 36 to 48 pounds.

Another curved-top tent is the Avis, invented by Bill Moss, who devised the well-known "Pop" tent. The Avis has the look of the future about it, with its gracefully arched fore and rear peaks so rigged that the fabric is always under some tension, neatly taut but never straining unduly.

BILL MOSS WITH SMALL AVIS TENT
OF HIS DESIGN   *Avis*

LARGER AVIS TENT   *Avis*

able in two sizes, 7'×9' and 7'×12', with 6-foot height. It is suspended on Fiberglas rods which fit into four outside sleeves. Four short guy lines stabilize the tent, and two more hold canopies in place, one at each end.

My family and I used a similar tent through an entire summer, a full 90 days in fact and, although skeptical at first, we grew to enjoy the roominess and headspace it afforded. Particularly, I was impressed by its stability in high winds. In extreme blows the fabric billowed and the curved Fiberglas rods "rolled with the punches," but the shelter always resumed its true shape and position when the gusts died.

Erecting the tent isn't a speedy process. The Fiberglas rods must be fitted together, like a fishing rod. Although requiring more time for erection than some other types of tents, the chore is not difficult.

Since poplin is used in the walls and top, with waterproof vinyl-coated nylon in the floor, this tent is relatively light for its size—the 10'×14' model weighing 48 pounds. Two smaller sizes are available, a two-man shelter and another with a floor area of 8'×10'. These weigh 13 and 30 pounds respectively. The two larger styles have full headroom, averaging between six and seven feet.

Stakes are not required, and guy lines are used only on the canopy which hoods the door. The curved sections of the exterior frame, which fit into sleeves fore and aft, are of Fiberglas to provide tension. Angled uprights, which fit into the Fiberglas sections, are of sectional aluminum alloy tubing.

Not having actually used this tent, I can't vouch for its stability in the wind or its general resistance to storms, but it certainly appears that it will withstand a severe blow, especially if emergency guy lines are rigged.

The Pop Tent

Probably every outdoors-minded person in America is familiar with the "Pop" tent, an igloo-shaped shelter available in 7′ and 9′ diameters. Made of 8-ounce dry-finish drill, it is suspended on sectional Fiberglas rods in exterior sleeves and requires no stakes or guy lines, although the latter are needed to hold the canopy in place. There is a sewed-in floor, a screened window at the rear and another in the door.

During some 180 days' use to which my Pop tent was put, it proved remarkably stable in high winds although once, while it was empty, a gale-like gust rolled it over. It collapsed partially but was not damaged. We simply set it back "on its feet" again.

The 9-foot model is ideal for a couple or as an auxiliary tent for a family with several children. The smaller 7-foot style is more limited but excellent for a single person and suitable for two, providing they are moderately friendly toward one another.

The Draw-Tite Alpine Tents

These, like the Pop and Avis tents, cannot be described in generic terms such as Umbrella, Wall, or Wedge. They are the unique product of a single manufacturer. Devised by Robert L. Blanchard, noted tent designer, the Draw-Tite tents also are suspended on exterior aluminum frames with fabric tension automatically adjusted by shock cord hangers. The fabric, like that in

DRAW-TITE ALPINE TENT IN CAMP   *Eureka*

most of the larger but lightweight tents, is poplin. No stakes or guy lines are required and, in fact, once erected the entire shelter can be picked up and moved without dismantling which, I suppose, might prove an asset on some occasions.

These tents, too, have earned an enviable reputation for stability in high winds. If I seem to overstress this matter of wind resistance, it's only because wind—not rain—is a tent's greatest enemy, the risk compounded by campers who almost invariably prefer camping on the exposed shores of lakes rather than seeking the shelter of the forest where there is less wind, but no view!

The Draw-Tite Alpine tents are available in five sizes, ranging from one-man hiking or canoe shelters up to family-camping-size tents housing six persons. Weights run from 8 to 33 pounds.

The Lean-to Tent

This is the woodsman's tent, probably because it is a simple, uncomplicated, basic shelter. From the standpoint of portability, ease of erection, and general efficiency, there is none finer.

Although it is available with a sewed-in floor and insect netting, it is usually not equipped with these and thus is not a shelter for summertime use. It's at its best in the spring and fall when insects are absent and when heat is required. A campfire built in front of the Lean-to will cast its warmth and glow throughout the tent.

DRAW-TITE ALPINE TENTS IN FIVE SIZES *Eureka*

PRAIRIE SCHOONER TENT (LEFT); POP TENTS (CENTER AND RIGHT)   *Thermos*

THE AUTHOR WITH HIS WHELEN LEAN-TO TENT   *Riviere*

BAKER TENT   *National*

The basic Lean-to is little more than a sloping back wall with vertical sides. The finest of all is the Whelen model, named after the late Colonel Townsend Whelen, who first encountered it in British Columbia some 40 years ago. The Whelen version has side walls which splay outwardly and a 3-foot hood attached to the ridge and overhanging the front opening to ward off rain. When not in use this hood can be tossed backward over the ridge. When you buy a Whelen tent, you get only fabric—no poles or sectional framework. It's designed to be suspended on a horizontal sapling strung between two trees or set in forked uprights. Four stakes hold it in place, and two short uprights keep the hood in position.

The Whelen tent is truly a woods tent, for in the thick timber, high winds are rarely encountered. In an exposed position it probably would not withstand long buffeting. Nevertheless, this is the only old-time tent which has not, in some way, been "improved" by modern tent technology. For use in the woods during cool weather, none of today's tents can match it for comfort, ease of erection, or adaptability to terrain. My own will accommodate two adults comfortably and still provide ample room for gear. I wouldn't trade it for a farm down East!

The Baker Tent

The Baker tent is another Lean-to type that is widely popular and for just reasons. Some models are quite large, easily sleeping four men. It is available as a basic open-front tent, or with sewed-in floor and netting front, and a canopy which can be turned into an extra room by the addition of curtains. It's available in sizes that range from 6 feet square and 5 feet high up to 7′×9′ and 6 feet high. The Baker is an excellent tent for park camping since the front can be closed off for privacy, or opened wide for enjoyment of an evening campfire. The canopy can also be rigged to your parked car in which much of the duffel, not immediately in use, can be left.

The Wedge or "A" Tent

Extreme modifications, complete redesigns in some instances, of the Wedge or "A" tent have resulted in unusual and quite serviceable shelters, some of these attaining Cottage tent size. Adding a pitch roof and blending this into the sloping walls to attain a gambrel roof effect have resulted in greater headroom than was possible in the original version. The end walls, too, have been sloped in some models, adding to the tent's ability to resist wind. With the addition of a sewed-in floor, netting doorway, and windows, an exterior frame and, in at least one instance, a roof fly, it is difficult to recognize some of these ingenious adaptations as a Wedge or "A" tent! Where the original shelters were rarely larger than 7′×9′, sizes now run up to 9′×12′ and 10′×11′, which might qualify them for Cottage tent classification.

MODIFICATION OF THE "A" OR WEDGE TENT   *Coleman*

THE AUTHOR WITH HIS EXPLORER TENT   *Riviere*

The Explorer Tent

Traditionally this is the tent of the canoe camper. It is an easy shelter to set up with a single interior pole and short T-ridge or by means of exterior shear poles cut at the scene. One of the most stable of all tents in a high wind, its steep sides will shed a deluge and, among modern versions, a sewed-in floor and netting door make it virtually bugproof.

For an entrance, early Explorer tents were equipped with a round "crawl hole" elevated above the floor a foot or so. This was supposedly protected against insect invasion by a pucker string closure, which succeeded only partially. The crawl-hole entry also made it nearly impossible to heat the tent with an open fire. Modern versions have a full-front opening or, at least, a full-length door which can be tied back.

In order to combine light weight and durability, poplin is used extensively in the Explorer tent. Sizes vary somewhat but generally are 7′×7′ or

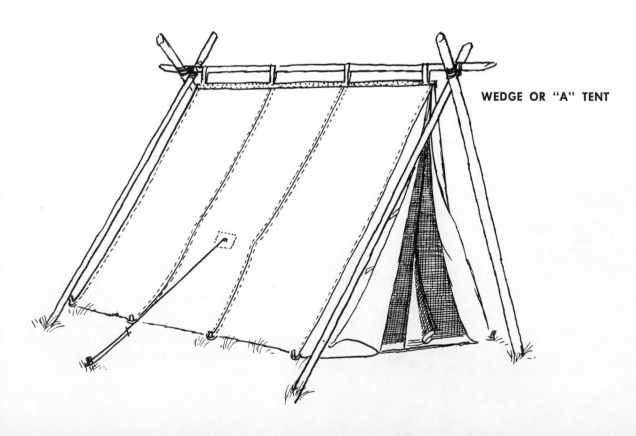

WEDGE OR "A" TENT

8′×8′, usually with a 6-foot ridge height. Some firms make smaller versions, known as Cruiser or Canoe tents, but these are basically Explorers.

One little-known version is the "tropical" model, minus floor and netting. This style is made of Army duck and the one which I have has been used extensively for spring and fall work in the woods. The full-front opening makes heating with a campfire feasible and pleasant, yet this can be closed for privacy. Occasionally I use the tent not only as a shelter but also as a wrapper for other packs when canoe travel gets sloppy in heavy seas. The rugged fabric seems to withstand this abuse well.

The Miner's Tent

Some outfitters are calling this tent a Canoe model and one writer refers to it as a Teepee type —adding confusion to already existing confusion. However, it's likely to remain the Miner's tent.

Except for one drawback, it's an excellent design. It goes up quickly and easily either with a single pole, with shears, or merely hung from a limb. Its steep sides shed water or snow well and it's stable in a high wind. It can be set up with as few as four stakes. It's a popular tent in the West and is one of the few two-man tents affording full headroom in most sizes. It's available in sizes from 6′×6′ with 7-foot height up to 10′×10′ with 8-foot peak height. The single drawback lies within the type of front opening which slants back to the peak. In a rainstorm this must be

kept closed. Most models of the basic Miner have overlapping door flaps which are closed by means of tie tapes. Some have a sod cloth and there is still another style which has a slide fastener running from the threshold to the peak for closing the doorway.

A modernized version of the Miner's tent has a sewed-in floor, full-front netting and side parrels for "ballooning" out the sides, and this is the only model that is really suitable for park camping. The original basic model is excellent, of course, for use in arid areas of the West.

The Canoe Tent

Most so-called Canoe tents faintly resemble the Explorer but are actually adaptations of Horace Kephart's favorite but now outdated Compac tent* and the more recent but equally extinct George tent. Generally, the Canoe tent includes a vertical front wall which can be opened wide for campfire comfort or closed tightly for privacy. It has no horizontal ridge but, rather, a peak from which the walls slope to the sides and rear. Some manufacturers describe their Canoe tents as "hiker's models," which strays somewhat from fact, since these rarely weigh less than 15 pounds. However, most are fine shelters for two-man canoe trips. My own, made of drill, is seven feet square with a 6-foot peak and is nearly 30 years old. Although a weary-looking shelter after seeing service on canoe routes in Maine, Minnesota, Wisconsin, and Ontario, it is still serviceable in a pinch.

It can be erected quickly, requiring only four stakes, two guy lines, and a single pole. The latter can be eliminated by using a tripod rig or by hanging the peak from a tree limb.

The Trail Tents

These are most generally known as Mountain tents, and I suppose I'm compounding confusion by terming them Trail tents. Since they are not limited to use by climbers—flat-land hikers and canoe cruisers use them, too—I think Trail tent is more appropriate. Some manufacturers agree.

* Horace Kephart, *Camping and Woodcraft* (New York: The Macmillan Company, 1917, reprinted 1966).

**MODIFIED EXPLORER TENT
RESEMBLES "A" OR WEDGE TENT**   *Hirsch-Weis*

THE AUTHOR AND HIS 30-YEAR-OLD CANOE TENT

Riviere

FIVE-POUND MOUNTAIN TENT OF COATED NYLON WITH FLY

Trailwise

It is my belief, too, that any two-man tent weighing more than six pounds cannot justly be called either a Trail or Mountain tent, despite claims to the contrary by some makers whose sole experience at packing has been toting a briefcase to a sales meeting. Most of us overrate our packing capabilities. However, a four-mile uphill grade soon restores our perspective. Within this, there is no room for a bulky or overly heavy tent.

Last summer, for instance, I packed loads weighing 40 to 80 pounds into my woods camp from the nearby Jeep trail. These were short hauls over level ground, and they were not unduly tiring. Yet, at the end of the summer, when I climbed New Hampshire's 6280-foot Mount Washington with my son, it was four days before my muscles ceased to cry out! My pack on that trip was a mere 12 pounds! Obviously then, climbing or extensive hiking calls for light loads which eliminate excessively heavy and misnamed "Trail" or "Mountain" tents.

Tents suitable for this type of work are made of nylon weighing a little over two ounces per square yard with a tear strength of seven to eight pounds. Over-all tent weight rarely exceeds five pounds. However, while this fabric will turn a light shower—and the wind—it will not protect against a heavy downpour since it is not sufficiently water-repellent. Coating the fabric is necessary, usually with polyvinyl, butaral, neoprene, vinyl, or polyurethane. This solves one problem but creates another.

An adult daily gives off about 1½ pints of "insensible perspiration,"* which must be permitted to escape the tent by passing off into the atmosphere through the fabric. However, if the shelter is truly waterproof, this moisture cannot escape and, upon striking the cool surfaces of the fabric, condenses, resulting in dampness, even puddles, within the tent. Manufacturers have circumvented this problem, however.

The tents themselves are made of "rip-stop" uncoated nylon which permits the passage of moisture through its weave. This fabric, as I pointed out, is not substantial enough to ward off heavy rain so, for protection against this, a separate fly of *coated* nylon is rigged over the tent. Thus, moisture escapes the shelter and is

* Gerry Cunningham, noted Colorado mountaineer and designer of lightweight mountaineering equipment, mentions this in his booklet *How to Keep Warm.*

NINE-POUND, FOUR-MAN TRAIL TENT   *Gerry*

dissipated between the tent and the fly, while the latter repels rain and snow. A suitable Trail or Mountain tent, then, is actually a two-piece shelter—tent and fly.

There are exceptions to this. One of my Trail tents weighs a mere one pound, nine ounces and is made of coated nylon. No fly is needed. Interior condensation is offset by ample ventilation through netting openings at each end. This tent, however, is of limited usefulness. It would not be adequate protection against the elements at high altitudes or during extremes of winter weather anywhere else.

Another exception is a two-man Trail tent of urethane-coated nylon with ventilation provided by two four-foot vents under canopies along the sloping sides, plus another vent in the peak.

True Trail or Mountain tents roll compactly into bundles barely larger than a loaf of bread. Suspension is usually by means of sectional aluminum alloy tubing, each section seldom more than a foot long. Because such tents are frequently exposed to high-altitude winds, guy lines are necessary and are generally of nylon cord. Practically all, too, are equipped with *waterproof* coated-nylon, sewed-in floors for protection against ground moisture and snow. Insect netting, too, is provided, although this may be omitted from certain models designed primarily for use in cold weather or at extremely high altitudes.

For those who prefer a Trail-type tent where weight is not a factor, there are somewhat heavier versions made of drill or duck. These are considerably less expensive than the specially designed climber's or hiker's models.

SEVEN-POUND, THREE-MAN TRAIL TENT

Gerry

FOUR-POUND, ONE-MAN TRAIL TENT

Eureka

The Expedition Tent

Today's expeditions tend toward Alpine regions —apparently there's nowhere to go but up—hence tent designs are aimed at sheltering against extreme winds, cold, rain, or snow. Fabrics which go into Expedition tents are much the same as those in Trail or Mountain tents. In fact, the latter are used on some exploratory and climbing trips. A true expedition tent, however, is usually larger but with a surprisingly small corresponding increase in weight. One six-man version, for example, is a two-piece shelter weighing slightly over 17 pounds.

All such tents are equipped with exterior frames since in high-altitude snow fields there is no growth from which to cut poles. Often, too, expedition-type tents incorporate a storage vestibule, an integral part of the tent for protection of supplies and equipment, yet separate from the sleeping quarters. Such a vestibule also serves as an entryway where crew members may shed clothing and equipment which would otherwise crowd the tent's interior.

The Pup Tent

Pup, shelter half, or field tent, call it what you will, it's an atrocious shelter whose only saving

FIVE-POUND, TWO-MAN TRAIL TENT OF COATED NYLON

Eureka

THE AUTHOR'S TRAIL TENT *Gerry*
WEIGHS 1½ POUNDS

up the walls all around the shelter, thus eliminating the possibility of moisture seeping in, or rain runoff soaking through. Too, this eliminates a common problem with many American tents, the slow rotting of the walls along their bottom edges. Another innovation is an enclosed alcove where equipment may be stored, thus preventing the crowding or cluttering of sleeping quarters. Ample canopies over doors and windows are usually standard on European tents. All in all, most imports are well-designed, sturdy, roomy, and attractive.

grace is its usually low price. Woodsmen call it a "canvas doghouse" and you'll "have to go outside to roll over" if you sleep in one. This, to my mind, pretty well sums up the Pup tent.

I am writing, of course, from an adult viewpoint. Actually the Pup tent will serve well as an auxiliary shelter, particularly for youngsters who want to "sleep out" but whose parents prefer the comfort of a trailer or truck camper. The relatively low price of the Pup tent makes such an arrangement feasible for most camping families.

Modern Pup tents, unlike the G.I. shelter halves so fervently cussed by Army veterans, offer fairly snug sleeping quarters for children, with sewed-in floors, insect netting, and zipper closures contributing to comfort.

The Teepee

Mention the Teepee of the Plains Indians to most campers and you'll be met with snickers. For a stationary camp, however, it's a difficult shelter to improve upon. For autumn use, when insect pests are gone, it's a delightful shelter, with its interior open fire pit and smoke curling up to the peak and out the smoke hole. Headroom is plentiful and it takes quite a few campers to crowd one.

It has drawbacks, of course, just as most tents have. It's heavy, bulky, subject to invasion by insects and difficult for amateurs to erect correctly. A full sized Teepee requires 12 to 16 poles ranging in length from 20 to 24 feet.

Only two Teepees are available commercially, as far as I know. One of these is 16 feet high and 15 feet in diameter. Made of 10-ounce duck, it has a smoke flap and weighs about 35 pounds. How-

European Tents

Until recent years imported tents were invariably small, not much larger than our Trail or Mountain shelters. Nowadays, however, tents from Europe, particularly those from France, have grown to proportions approaching the dimensions of our Cottage tents. Gay colors are characteristic of imported models, too, with reds, blues, and yellows not uncommon. Fabrics are tightly woven cottons, similar to so-called balloon silk or, sometimes, duck. Workmanship is equal to or better than that found in American tents.

Europeans have developed clever innovations, too. One of these is the "tub bottom," a sewed-in floor of rubberized fabric which rises a few inches

TRAIL-TYPE TENT OF DUCK *Coleman*

EXPEDITION TENT   *Bishop*   **EXPEDITION TENT WITH DOUBLE WALL**   *Bishop*

ever, it lacks a door flap, something which can be added. The other Teepee model is 14 feet high and 14 feet in diameter and made of 7.68-ounce drill, weighing about 18 pounds. It has both a smoke hole and a door flap. Neither model is supplied with poles.

The Hammock Tent

The Hammock tent, sometimes called jungle hammock, is a practical application in tropical camping. It is simply a sleeping bag designed to hang between two trees, over which is permanently attached a canopy or fly. Between this canopy and the sleeping bag is insectproof netting. Using a jungle hammock is usually done through necessity, not for love of hanging between two trees. It's difficult to get into until you're accustomed to it and you'll have to undress while exposed to the insects the Hammock was designed to avoid. All in all, it's hardly a shelter for pleasure camping.

One outfitter offers a Hammock tent that is really a netting tent, with water-repellent roof, of which the hammock is an integral part. The tent is pitched by means of a ridge rope between two trees. Two ropes also support the Hammock so that the sleeper's weight is not directed against the tent fabric. This type of Hammock tent offers protection both from rain and insects while the camper dresses or undresses. This model is a decided improvement over the simple jungle hammock.

The Tarp Tent

This is not a particular tent but rather a flat material which can be draped in various ways, the number being limited only by your imagination. It is, however, usually an emergency shelter, since it does not afford the complete protection given by standard model tents.

Draped between two trees it can be made into a Wedge tent without ends, or a simple lean-to. Rig it with shears and you have a modified Forester. One end draped over an overturned canoe, with the other end staked down, will make a good overnight shelter for two people. It can be hung over a picnic table for shade or protection from rain and it may, of course, be used as a fly over a regular tent.

A tarp designed for these uses, however, should be more than the simple flat cloth sold by most outfitters. It needs sturdy grommets at the corners and along the edges, and parrels, or tie tapes, sewed to its surface on one side. The more grommets and parrels there are, the greater the variety of shelters you can make with the tarp.

Most tarpaulins are quite heavy, being made of rugged fabrics to withstand abuse. However, lightweight materials are available which the canoe camper may carry, and some of the ultralightweight fabrics make possible tarps which the hiker can tote.

Tarps are usually made of duck and these are likely to be heavy, suitable for the car camper, but out of the question for the "back of beyond" canoeman or hiker. You can buy tarpaulins made of nylon, plastics, Egyptian and Pima cottons which will add little weight to your load. Some rubberized fabrics are good, as are those coated with a plastic material.

The Tent Trailer

As a compromise between roughing it and luxuriating among the posh appointments in a travel trailer, the tent trailer has won a large following. This is understandable. Most city-bred families, now camping, would not have adopted the sport had they been required to bivouac on the ground in a tent. Too, there are those who want the mobility of a trailer for efficient campground hopping, and those whose family cars would be seriously overloaded if traditional camping gear *and* passengers were jammed aboard. Still farther along the line of reasoning, many like the fact that camping gear—stove, sleeping bag, lantern, etc.—can remain loaded in a tent trailer between trips. This permits a quick getaway for weekend excursions. The tent trailer makes all of these possible while its owners still literally sleep "under canvas."

The most popular type has cover panels which fold out over the ends or sides of the trailer to form beds, at the same time raising the tent on metal bows. Another style has a Fiberglas top

EUROPEAN TENT WITH ALCOVE *Klepper*

which rises vertically, the power supplied by a hand-operated crank or a small electric motor energized by the car's battery. This one, too, unfolds beds as it rises into position.

The smaller of these rolling tents will sleep four persons and can be towed even by small foreign cars. The larger units, up to 20 feet long when opened, sleep up to 10 persons with the use of auxiliary double-deck cots.

Interior appointments are a matter of choice. Most makers offer basic models which serve simply as sleeping quarters, with cooking done on

PUP TENT

USES OF TARP CLOTH

a regular campstove out of doors and dining enjoyed under the trees. Campers who use this type of tent trailer have merely substituted it for their tent. All else is traditional camping.

More luxurious models, however, make "living aboard" possible, a decided asset in bad weather. These may include full kitchen units with sink, running water and water heater, refrigerator, electrical outlets (for plugging into campground systems), dining area, storage chests, and cupboards. One even has a shower! The "rough it" faction among campers may look with scorn upon such luxury in the wilds, but the fact is that tent trailers are steadily growing more luxurious. We are a nation of comfort and convenience lovers, and this is becoming increasingly reflected in our choice of outdoor equipment!

One of the most desirable features of a tent trailer is the ease with which it can be handled in traffic and on our superhighways. Behind the car, it tracks like a shadow exerting little drag on the car's engine and, because of its low profile, there is no swaying or weaving which sometimes accompanies the towing of a travel trailer. Parking is not difficult, since the driver can see over the

THE TENT TRAILER *Vesely*

unit through his rear window. Many are light enough so that they can be positioned by hand, and most of the heavier units are equipped with a dolly wheel on the tongue which makes it easier to maneuver the unit among trees or other campground obstacles.

CAMPING IN FUNDY NATIONAL PARK, NEW BRUNSWICK

Canadian Government Travel Bureau

Chapter 2

HOW TO BUY A TENT

Few sporting goods stores have room enough to display more than one or two tents, and none can afford to stock all types, sizes, and grades. Catalog firms can, of course, list a greater variety, but they are likely to describe only the best sellers—which are not necessarily the best tents—and certainly, the shortcomings of various shelters won't be pointed out to you. It will be up to you then, before buying, to determine what makes a good tent—or a poor one.

The factors which govern tent quality include the fabric, type of seams, color, number and type of windows, netting, canopies—to name only a few—and these should be examined with a knowing eye before purchasing. However, since you will want a tent to fit the needs of your camping group, your first consideration will probably be size.

Size

The standard method for indicating tent size is by width and length of the floor area, such as 7′×9′ or 9′×12′—almost always given in whole numbers. This is known as the trade size and is not necessarily the actual size.

If you measure a 7′×9′ tent, for example, you may find that it is only 6′8″ wide and possibly 9′3″ long. Manufacturers don't like to cut tent materials lengthwise, as this raises labor costs, removes the strong selvage edge, makes for a poorer seam, and creates general waste. As much as possible, uncut widths are used, which, when seams are sewed, may produce a tent not exactly according to specifications. Also, some shrinkage may occur.

Most important, at any rate, is the percentage of the floor area that is actually usable. In a Wall tent, for example, you can set a folding table and chairs, or a cot, along one of the side walls. In an A or Wedge tent, however, these can't be placed close to the outside walls without bulging the sides outwardly. Therefore, an 8′×10′ Wedge tent, while it has the same floor area as an 8′×10′ Wall tent, won't give you as much usable floor space as the latter, especially if camp furniture is used. Obviously, then, the *type* of tent will

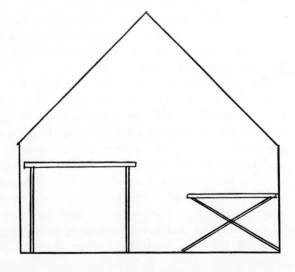

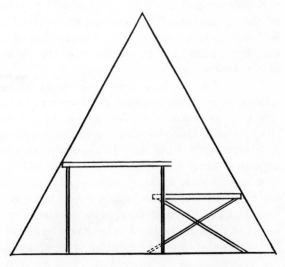

have to be considered as well as its *size*.

Actually, any tent you buy is going to be a compromise and there can be no hard and fast rule governing the choice. The nearest thing to a rule is the suggestion that you plan on floor area ratio of 27 square feet per person. This, of course, applies only to a tent that will be carried in a car, trailer, or boat where weight is not a prime factor.

My family and I use a 9′ × 12′ Umbrella tent for our car camping trips. This gives the four of us 108 square feet, or 27 square feet each. Even this seemingly generous ratio calls for some compromise. My daughter and wife sleep on cots, while my son and I use sleeping bags on the ground. During the day, the sleeping bags are rolled under the cots to allow use of the floor area for other purposes.

On a hiking or canoeing trip, however, this ratio is overly generous, since it will require a tent much too heavy to be carried easily—unless expensive ultralightweight materials are used in its construction. For this work, 18 square feet per camper is about the maximum allowable. Although some Lean-to models offer more floor area per pound, this type of tent will expose you to mosquitoes and black flies during the summer months.

A 5′ × 7′ tent, or 35 square feet, will best serve the purpose for two campers who need an enclosed tent. If more than two campers are going along, it's far better to use two small tents, than to struggle with a larger, heavier one. A well-designed small tent can be surprisingly comfortable, as my wife and I discovered some years ago, when we outwaited a three-day northeaster while camping in a 5′ × 7′ canoe tent on an island in Mooselookmeguntic Lake in Maine. We pitched the tent so that it opened into the lee of the wind and kept a small fire going immediately in front of the open door. We were not uncomfortable, and our cooking was done with some degree of ease by reaching out to the fire from the shelter of the tent.

To visualize tent size more easily, mark off the floor of your garage to match the floor area of the tent you are considering. Set up cots or lay out sleeping bags, arranging them as you would in the tent, keeping in mind that the doorway must be kept free. Or if you're handy with a pencil and rule, make a scale drawing, with cutouts for sleeping bags, cots, tables, and camp stools. Many tent manufacturers suggest floor plans in their catalogs, but these are inclined to be overly optimistic.

Another dimension to consider is headroom. I once owned an Umbrella tent which had been advertised as having 6-foot headroom at the eaves and 7 feet at the peak. The manufacturer, however, forgot to mention that the spreader arms radiating from the center pole locked into position at 5′9″. I'm 5′11″.

When checking on headroom, remember that this will vary, even within a particular tent. For example, a Wall tent listed as having 6-foot headroom has this only under the ridgepole. Headroom will diminish as you move toward either side wall. An Umbrella tent probably offers the most headroom, along with the more recently developed Cottage tents, which usually have full 6 feet of height at the eaves.

Fabrics

The variety of tent materials available today is wide and includes duck, nylon, drill, sheeting, poplin, plastic, combinations of nylon and cotton, and a number of lightweight materials under private brands.

Cotton fabrics which go into most of today's tents must be treated to make them water-repellent—not waterproof. This permits them to "breathe" or to pass off interior moisture as explained in Chapter 1 with regard to Trail or Mountain tents. Tightly woven cottons, even if untreated, will fend off moderately heavy rain unless capillary action is started by touching an inner surface during a rainstorm. Once started, such a leak cannot be stopped until the rain ceases and the fabric dries. Since it's virtually impossible to use a tent to any extent without touching its inside surfaces, fabrics must be treated to preclude a capillary action leak.

In addition, cottons are treated to make them mildew-resistant. Note that I have used the word "resistant," not "proof." Only synthetic fabrics, such as nylon, are mildewproof.

Two types of treatments are applied, these popularly known as "wet" and "dry." The wet finish is usually a paraffin solution with an oil used as carrier, applied after weaving. It is easy to identify. The fabric surface is slightly tacky, and there's a characteristic "tent smell." Wet or paraffin finishes have been described as inferior to dry finishes and, admittedly, these do have shortcomings. Wet finishes will stiffen the fabric in cold weather and permit softening or sagging under a hot sun. Particularly when the tent is new, dirt tends to cling to the fabric. Every few years, too, depending upon the use to which the tent has been exposed, a wet finish will have to be renewed, although this is a simple chore which can be done in the backyard.

The wet finish is generally applied to drills or twills and to less expensive textiles used in the manufacture of low- or medium-priced shelters, never in the better, more expensive grades. During summer-long tests that I conducted in 1961, 12 tents of various types and fabrics were exposed for a full 90 days without being dismantled, to determine their susceptibility to mildew. All of the wet-finish fabrics showed signs of rot, some of them literally disintegrating. None of the dry-finish tents appeared to have been damaged.

The weight of fabric is increased by the application of a wet finish, sometimes up to 40 percent. In reading tent catalogs you will note that the weight of drill, for example, is often given as "7.68 ounces before treatment." This is the weight per square yard before the wet finish was applied. A seven-ounce, *wet*-finish fabric may, then, actually weigh more than a ten-ounce *dry*-finish cloth.

This isn't to say, however, that a wet-finish tent is to be avoided. Given reasonable care, which includes thorough brushing and drying before storage, such a shelter may well last 20 years. Too, wet-finish fabrics are usually less costly than such materials as duck, which usually are given a dry treatment. The latter is usually applied to duck, poplin and, in some instances, to the better grades of drill. Such a finish is not tacky, won't rub off, has no odor, and usually lasts the lifetime of the fabric. The material does not stiffen in the cold, nor soften especially in the heat. Since a dry finish adds no weight, the stated weights in catalogs are actual.

In shopping for a tent you will encounter textile terms which may puzzle you. Among these are:

Warp: The threads which run lengthwise in the material.

Fill: The threads which run across the fabric.

Sizing: Sizing is nothing more than starch, usually made from potatoes, corn, wheat or rice, through which a fabric is drawn. Some sizing is necessary to facilitate weaving. However, excess sizing, which can be detected by rubbing the goods briskly and tightly, is sometimes used on shoddy material to give it a more substantial appearance.

Once wet and dried again, this poor fabric will lose its starchy stiffness and bulk and reveal itself for what it is, a limp, possibly fragile, fabric.

Carded: When a tent manufacturer advertises "carded" cotton material he is reaching for adjectives, because all cotton is carded. This is simply a cleaning process which removes foreign matter from raw cotton.

Combed: Combing is a process whereby short cotton fibers are removed. "Combed" cotton is made of the longer fibers only and is, naturally, of a better grade.

Count: This is the number of threads in a square inch of cloth. The higher the count within a particular type of fabric, the better the material. A high count contributes to waterproof qualities, durability, and waterproofing. Threads may be counted in one direction, either crosswise (warp) or lengthwise (fill); or they may be given in total, such as 120×120 or 240.

Among the tent materials commonly in use today are:

Army Duck: An old material but still one of the best for larger tents and those subject to rough use. Both the warp and the fill are doubled and twisted, greatly increasing strength and durability. The weave is tight and no sizing is necessary to give this fabric bulk or body. Army Duck is available in 8, 10, and 12 ounces and fractions thereof per square yard. The larger the tent and the rougher it will be used, the heavier your choice of fabric should be.

Single Fill Duck: This is an excellent tent material, though not as substantial or long-wearing as Army Duck. It gets its name from the fact that the fill is single, not doubled as in Army Duck. Nor is its weave as tight. Often referred to as S F Duck or simply Duck, it is available in 8, 10, 12 and 14 ounces per square yard weights.

Some Single Fill Duck may weigh as much or more than some Army Duck, and this is due to the heavier and coarser yarns which may be used in its weaving. Single Fill Duck, however, will prove very serviceable.

Drill or Twill: This is also called such names as Forest Drill, Sail Drill, and Boat Drill, all of which mean exactly nothing. Drill is drill. It is a mediumweight cotton, woven with coarse yarns. It is tighter than Single Fill Duck, the weave having a count of 100 to 130 threads per inch and it can be identified by its diagonal weave pattern. It is a good material for small tents or larger tents which will not be subjected to rough use.

Sheeting: This is a material to be avoided, even if it bears such suggestive names as Tent Fabric, Shelter Sheeting, or any other implication that it is a suitable tent material. Actually, it is nothing more than heavy sheeting, not unlike bed sheeting woven with heavier yarns, and doctored with sizing to give it bulk and substance.

Poplin: This is a tightly woven material with a thread count of 160, and fine ribs running across the material. Quite windproof, it ranges in weight from 6 to 7½ ounces. A good material for tents which will not be subject to extremes of wear.

Under a recently passed federal law, tentmakers are required to identify the fabric used and you will find a tag attached to all tents bearing this information. Although nothing is said about wearing quality, tensile strength, or seam construction, it is a step in the right direction toward protecting the unwary buyer from unscrupulous tent dealers.

Seams

Many tents are advertised as having "double-stitched" seams, the exception being among the high-quality shelters where such a stitch is taken for granted. Actually, what copywriters say is true —for I have never seen a tent whose seams were single stitched. However, there is a difference in double-stitched seams.

Some tents have flat seams. This is simply an overlap of ½ to ¾ of an inch, sewed close to each selvage or cut edge. This seam is neat and it lies flat, as the name implies. Its advantages, such as they are, end there. The strain caused by tightening of tent fabric is applied directly to the sewing thread in a flat seam and, in a short time, especially if the seam has been chafed even slightly one thread will break, causing the seam to part.

A better sewing job is done with the lap-fell seam, in which the selvage edges of the fabric are folded over and interlocked. The lap-fell seam,

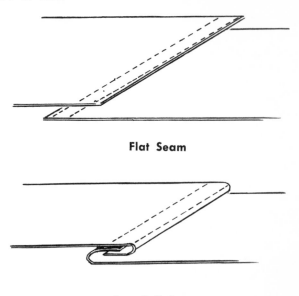

Flat Seam

Lap Fell Seam

after this folding, is double stitched through the *four* layers of fabric. This seam may look slightly bunched and ridged, but its strength far exceeds that of the flat seam.

Color

When a choice of color is made by most tent buyers, it's usually on the basis of eye appeal. However, there's more to color than good looks.

Colors should not run, nor should they rub off on the clothing or skin. When buying a tent, rub your fingers firmly on the material to test it. Nearly all colors used in tent fabrics will fade. No one has, as yet, come up with a dye or color process that will withstand constant exposure to the elements.

White tents are popular in the tropics as that color reflects a greater percentage of the sun's heat. However, after a few weeks afield, they will invariably turn a dirty gray, to which you might ask "Who cares?"—and I would agree. Under a bright sun, a white tent tends to produce an interior glare which is hard on the eyes. This trouble can be alleviated somewhat by using a fly over the tent.

If a lantern is used inside at night, the white walls become screens on which are projected sharp shadows, giving your neighbors an activated silhouette of interior activities. Of course, in the wilderness, this won't matter, but in a crowded campground, where your neighbor may be no more than spittin' distance, you will feel that your privacy is being invaded. You may have noticed that Hollywood invariably uses a white tent for the heroine to retire into!

Dark green is probably the most popular shade sold today and I like it, if only because it's a fitting color to take into the woods. It creates no problem of glare or shadowing.

Some bizarre color combinations are showing up in campgrounds. One, which I call "signal yellow," is so bright it can be seen around corners and there's even a barber pole striped model on the market!

All factors considered, color is pretty much a matter of taste, although I would suggest sticking with the darker shades such as khaki or green—or if you will be camping in a warm climate, white.

Windows

These are especially important in all types of closed tents and I would never buy an Umbrella tent without at least one window—and preferably two. Without these, good ventilation is impossible.

If there is only one window, it should be at least 24 to 28 inches square—slightly smaller if there are two. See that they can be closed snugly from the inside. Window flaps are usually operated by means of a pair of endless cords, attached to the lower edge of the flap, and running through small grommets in the tent wall.

Further, be sure that the storm flaps overlap the window opening adequately—at least two inches on both sides and on the bottom. Some of the better tents have storm flaps whose sides ride up and down in sleeve-like channels, eliminating completely the possibility of rain entering.

Certain smaller tents, such as the Mountain and Explorer models, are not large enough to have windows, in which case, be sure the tent is equipped with ventilators that will allow the passage of air without admitting rain.

Netting

Naturally, the windows should be equipped with netting to keep out insects. At first glance, all netting may look alike to you. Even shoddily made tents are equipped with what appears to be suitable netting, although like tent fabrics, they may vary in quality a great deal.

Plastic Screening: This will absorb considerable abuse by punching and it is very difficult to tear. However, a bulge is likely to be permanent. Its greatest drawback is that both the fill and the warp are inclined to slide together with the result that gaps are created.

Nylon and Fiberglas: These are generally considered best, with Fiberglas possibly having the edge in firmness of weave. At any rate, look for the finest mesh possible. A weave having 16 to 18 threads per inch will stop most objectionable bugs.

Door Flaps

Most tents, if equipped with screening, come with two door flaps, one of netting and one of duck, drill, or other tent material. Sometimes the netting is supplied only in the upper half of the inner door while, in other models, the inside door may be made entirely of netting except for the hem. Naturally, the greater the area of netting, the more ventilation is possible. However, door flaps having tent fabric on the bottom half offer ample ventilation and, at the same time, are less susceptible to damage.

At any rate, a heavy duty slide fastener should close the flap. A door which has only snaps or cloth ties will develop gaps through which insect pests will quickly find their way. It should be possible, of course, to tie the netting back when not in use.

Awnings and Canopies

These are usually found on Umbrella, Cottage, Explorer, and on some Lean-to models. An awning keeps the sun and rain from entering a tent doorway and acts as a sort of front hallway or porch. Its length is usually equal to the height of the door.

On most Umbrella tents, and on certain other models, the awning serves as a storm flap, to be lowered against wind or rain, thus shutting the door opening completely. While this arrangement is common, it's a poor rig, since a canopy is most desirable during a storm. It is better, by far, to have the awning up during a storm so that you can then stop under it to remove rain gear before entering the tent. A fabric floor can become an unholy mess if wet clothing and muddy boots are worn into the tent, even if only long enough to remove them.

A few of the better Umbrella tents get around this problem by supplying a fabric door that is separate from the awning. When not in use, this door rolls up and is tied over the doorway. In the event of wind-driven rain, it can be dropped to close off the door. With this arrangement, you can have a storm-tight door *and* the convenience of a sheltered area for removal of wet clothing and shoes.

If you plan to add side curtains to your awning, it's best to choose one that has a valance. Side curtains are usually attached to the awning with tie tapes or snaps. Without a valance, gaps will develop between the ties through which rain will be driven by the wind.

Sewed-in Floors

A sewed-in floor helps to make a tent bug- and snakeproof (although snakes generally invade tents only in Hollywood outdoor epics), keeps ground moisture at bay, and makes it easy to square the tent prior to setting it up. The sewed-in floor is reassuring, too, when camping in heavily used campgrounds where the tent sites may be none too clean. Also, when the tent is being rolled for transportation, the floor section can be used as a wrapper, protecting the more essential sides and top. All in all, the sewed-in floor is a decided advantage. At one time I questioned this, but the overwhelming acceptance of it can't be denied.

Most family camping tents are equipped with a sewed-in floor of cotton fabric and, since this cannot be made mildew*proof*, constant exposure to ground moisture eventually results in mildew or rot. Clever campers often use a ground sheet of plastic under the floor to protect it, but care should be taken that this does not protrude beyond the edges of the tent. If this occurs, rainwater running down the walls will be gathered in by the plastic and directed under the tent, where permanent puddles will form. These cannot be dried out without dismantling the shelter.

Most Trail or Mountain tents, as well as the better grades of larger shelters, are equipped

with a sewed-in floor of coated nylon, which is impervious to moisture and mildew.

For the stationary or semipermanent camp, however, I'd give serious thought to using a ground cloth in place of a sewed-in floor. You can always roll this up when it needs cleaning and deposit the accumulation some distance from the tent. Some campers use both the ground cloth and the sewed-in floor, thus capitalizing on the desirable features of both.

When camped in areas where fresh campsites are available, I see nothing wrong with a dirt floor. A natural forest floor is more desirable underfoot than a canvas floor constantly crying out to be cleaned. I spent the entire summer of 1933 in the New Hampshire woods, camping in a floorless tent, with my sleeping bag on a small ground cloth that measured only 3′×6′. My housekeeping problems were negligible.

Sod Cloth

The sod cloth is fast disappearing from the camping scene, except among more experienced, or professional tent users. This is the result of the advent of the sewed-in floor which has caught the fancy of vacation campers.

The sod cloth is simply a wide hem along the bottom of the tent walls. It is made of fairly heavy material and treated to resist dampness and wear. It folds into the tent so that the edges of the ground cloth overlap it. In some cases, it can also be used outside the tent, folded outwardly, with stones, logs or even soil placed on it to seal off the lower tent walls. If used in this manner, wall stakes cannot be used.

Chances are, if you want one of these for your tent, you will have to have one attached, as the selection of tents having sod cloths as standard equipment is quite limited. Some of the larger outfitters offer Wall tents equipped with sod cloths, but you will rarely find such a tent in a local store, nor do I know of any mail-order firm which stocks them.

Ropes and Guys

Ropes and guys that are sewed into the peaks or ridges of tents should be examined closely before purchasing, as these cannot be replaced easily. The best quality Manila rope should be used for this work. Cotton rope is poor stuff as it lacks strength and rots quickly. Nylon has great tensile strength and will last for years, but it will stretch considerably under constant tension. Sisal and jute are merely cheap substitutes to be avoided. Most ropes which come supplied with tents are usually too short. Buy 100 feet of ¼-inch Manila rope when you purchase your tent and you will always find plenty of use for it.

Stakes

Whenever wooden stakes are supplied with a new tent, they too, are generally short. Twelve-inch stakes are next to useless unless set in well-packed earth. Eighteen inches is a better length, while 24″ stakes will guarantee that your tent will stand erect in any blow. However, you will probably have to make these yourself. Choose lumber that will not split easily such as box elder, elm, sweet gum, honey locust, yellow birch, sycamore, or tupelo. Stakes made of these woods will last for years.

More and more manufacturers are supplying steel or aluminum stakes and invariably, they too, are short. However, they are ideal for penetrating rocky ground or heavy gravel. Naturally, if you are toting your tent on a hiking trip, or across canoe portages, leave the stakes behind and cut new ones each day.

Strain Points

The points at which a tent is hung or pegged are subject to great strain and these include the ridge, peak, corners, eaves, and the hem. Strain is applied to a tent wherever beckets, grommets, and parrels are attached.

The peak in an Umbrella tent, for example, bears much of the weight of the top and walls, plus considerable downward pull when the fabric shrinks during a rain.

The ridge of a Wall tent, and the eaves, where the guy ropes are attached to grommets, are subject to the same tension. Such strain points exist in all tents. Be sure, then, that these points are well reinforced with double layers of fabric and multiple stitching.

Not many tents are so constructed, but a length of ¼- or ⅜-inch rope sewed into the eave or along the bottom of each wall, will add years of service. Be sure, too, if you buy a Wall tent using an inside ridgepole, that the fabric along the ridge is doubled in order to counter the chafing which is inevitable.

Grommets

These are simply metal-edged holes in the fabric where ropes and ties are attached. There

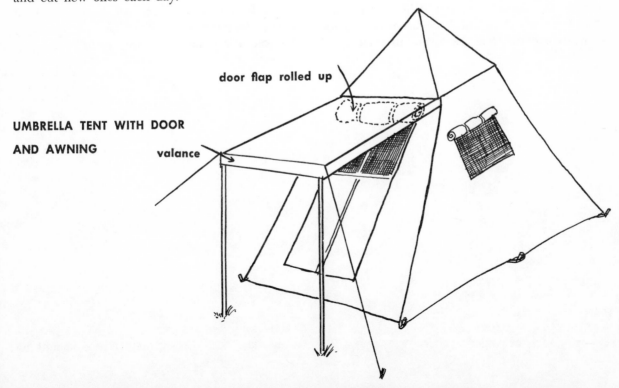

door flap rolled up

UMBRELLA TENT WITH DOOR
AND AWNING   valance

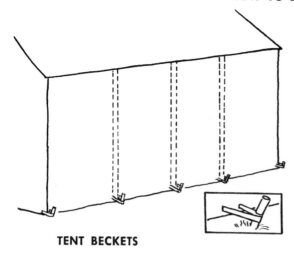

TENT BECKETS

and stitched to the hem. Here is the first source of trouble with a tent. There is little you can do about this when buying a tent. However, there are suggestions in Chapter 4 for improving these.

Recently a few tents have appeared with small wire beckets, barely two inches long. Those that I inspected were anchored in a rope hem, and were not large enough to admit a wooden stake, having been designed for use with thin metal pegs supplied either from the point of view of strength or size with the tent. I didn't consider them adequate.

Parrels

These are tabs, sewed into the sloping walls of some tents, such as the Wedge, Mountain, and Explorer, by means of which guy lines can be attached to pull the walls outwardly, thus increasing the usable space in a small tent.

Most tentmakers attach a metal D ring to a fabric strip stitched to the wall. The point of stitching should be reinforced with an extra layer of material and it should, naturally, be well stitched.

Unless your tent is made to order, you're not likely to find all of the better features I have pointed out in any one shelter. However, since the tent is a basic piece of equipment, around which you will build your outfit, buy the best you can afford, forgoing other equipment if necessary. You can always add the luxury items later.

are two types commonly in use. One of these is a two-piece unit, usually of light brass, which interlocks by means of prongs piercing the fabric which are then folded over snugly. These are machine inserted and only fairly satisfactory. Much better than these are metal rings laid around the hole in the fabric and held in place by a continuous over and over stitching with heavy thread.

Beckets

I know of no popularly priced tent that is equipped with adequately rugged beckets. These are the loops, along the lower edge of the walls and at the corners, through which stakes are driven to anchor the tent. They are usually made of waste material from the cutting room, doubled

Chapter 3

CHOOSING A CAMPSITE

There are approximately 450,000 individual campsites in the United States, enough to accommodate roughly two million campers. However, a conservative estimate of the number of campers places the figure at 30 million! Obviously, then, there is crowding, and many are turned away from overflowing camping areas, particularly during the peak vacation months of July and August.

To some, however, a true wilderness experience is not their aim. Family campers especially are a gregarious lot and don't mind being jammed into bulging camping areas. They enjoy the companionship, the neighborliness, the bustling activity. If there are children in the family, parents want other families close by.

However, the lover of solitude who enjoys the quiet and serenity of the outdoors, whenever he can find it, isn't likely to be happy in such surroundings. Under provisions of the 1965 Land and Water Conservation Fund Act, millions of dollars are being distributed among the states by the federal government, a substantial part of which goes into the building and enlarging of campgrounds. Unfortunately, as soon as a new camping area is completed, word spreads among campers, and there is a rush to it. The crowding continues.

Most beginners at camping visualize an azure lake, tall evergreens, towering mountains, and themselves lounging about an attractive clearing. What happens, then, to a camper who drives into an organized campground and is confronted with a vast clutter of tents whose guy lines seem intertwined and where there seems to be scarcely enough room to pitch a tent? Disillusionment sets in, bitter and hard to swallow. The majority of campers, coming upon such a campground, assume that this is all there is available, or why else would everybody be jammed in here?

The fact is that you can often find much less crowded tenting areas in more pleasant surroundings simply by asking. They generally are not large, nor will they likely have hot and cold running water, showers, laundry, and daily milk deliveries, but you will be able to enjoy camping as you had planned.

The best place to inquire about these lesser-known campsites is at a park office or ranger station, or from the caretaker of larger, more populated camps. Tell the ranger you're the type who likes to get off the beaten path and, chances are, he'll be delighted to send you to another, less well-known camping area. The crowded conditions of some of our popular campsites are not the fault of the local rangers who run them, so don't belittle them for the crowds that are camped tent peg to tent peg in their front yards. Approach the ranger with a friendly attitude and he might surprise you with a little bit of Paradise he knows about and which is still comparatively unspoiled. It's worth a try.

Another good source of information regarding local and lesser-known campsites is at a chamber of commerce information bureau. Also try gasoline stations, game wardens, fire wardens, and sporting goods stores. In many instances, natives of small towns in resort areas have pet camping spots which are not advertised but nevertheless are highly desirable. A friendly approach could lead to the disclosure of the location of one of these, along with permission to use it.

In order to facilitate the search for campgrounds in keeping with your tastes, you should understand the basic philosophy of the various state, federal, and private agencies that offer camping facilities. Particularly, you should know the difference between a national forest, a national park, a state park, and a privately operated recreation area.

The National Parks

Basically, a national park encompasses some wonder of nature which is to be preserved for all time, for all to enjoy. In order to make it accessible, certain man-made structures are necessary: roads, lodges, interpretive centers, and campgrounds. The goal of the National Park Service is to supply these necessities without infringing upon the park's initial purpose, the preservation of its beauty. Thus, the National Park Service is limited as to how far it can go with construction. This applies to campgrounds.

Even so, the Service operates some 570 camping areas in 78 different sectors of the park system, with a total of more than 28,000 individual campsites. In some parks, construction of camping facilities is still going on; in others it has reached its limit. Overcrowding exists in certain parks, so much so that noncampers complain that the National Park Service operates tent and trailer slums. To the extent that it is possible, this condition is being remedied by added construction and by limiting the number of campers and their length of stay.

Nonetheless, many of our national parks are not a good choice for a camping vacation, except during the off-season. The parks can still be enjoyed, of course, simply by rigging a camp in a nearby privately operated campground and making day trips into the park.

The National Forests

A national forest, on the other hand, is simply a government-owned forest from which timber is cut periodically under controlled methods of sound forestry. Unlike the National Park Service, the Forest Service is not in the tourist business. There are no lodges or hot dog stands in most of our national forests because the Forest Service maintains the view that these should be enjoyed for what they are, not for what man can bring with him or build therein.

National forests attract little publicity, for who wants to read about trees? However, the Forest Service encourages the use of the forests for recreational purposes and makes available its roads to car campers and tourists who want to enjoy the forests *as they are.*

There are more than 150 national forests in our 50 states and these include some 180 million acres. As to the number of campsites within the limit of this vast acreage, I doubt if the Forest Service itself can tell you how many there are. Usually they are scattered along forest roads, on the shores of lakes and streams, or at some particular scenic spot. Rarely, too, are they very large, seldom having facilities for more than a dozen tents.

These are campsites consisting simply of a cleared tent or trailer pad, a fireplace and, usually, a picnic table. There will be a water outlet nearby and toilet facilities. The latter, in larger, busier Forest Service campgrounds, will be of the modern flush type and electrically lighted. In more primitive, or remote camping spots, toilet facilities will be relatively crude but sanitary.

Few are aware that in certain sections of many national forests, you need not confine camping to established areas. With a special fire permit, obtainable from a ranger or from the forest office, you may camp in remote areas less accessible to the mass of campers. These areas are somewhat restricted, naturally, and whether or not you will be granted a permit depends upon the current fire hazard in the spot of your choice. On the whole, however, it is possible to get away from crowds in a national forest.

The office of the Forest Supervisor has a map for each of the forests, showing the location of campsites. You can secure the address of each forest headquarters, where these maps are available, from the U. S. Forest Service, Department of Agriculture, Washington, D.C. 20205.

State Parks and Forests Campsites

State park and forest campsites range all the way from excellent to extremely bad and if you spend enough time car camping you'll probably run the gamut from exhilaration to downright disgust. Here, too, the secret is to avoid the bigger, more well-known state campgrounds, unless, of course, you don't mind having your neighbor peering into your stew pot. Before starting on a camping trip to another state, write to the state capitol, and inquire about the lesser-known campsites. Be sure to state that you don't want to camp in the larger more crowded areas. There's a complete list of officials to whom you can write in the Appendix.

FISHERMEN AT BOWMAN LAKE, GLACIER NATIONAL PARK

Bill Browning

CAMPSITE IN LAKE ARGYLE STATE PARK, ILLINOIS *Illinois Parks Division*

Private Campgrounds

Privately owned and operated for profit, these are open to the public for a fee usually slightly higher than those charged in state or federal areas. As a rule, facilities are somewhat better developed than those in public campgrounds and may include such luxuries as hot showers, running water at every site, electrical and sewer outlets for recreational vehicles, automatic laundries, recreation buildings, and supply stores.

Private campgrounds are increasing rapidly in number, in the face of a 15 percent annual increase in campers which state and federal campground officials admit they can never contend with. Private campgrounds are *necessary*. They may not always be located in as scenic an area

as a national park, but many are beautifully situated. Standards vary, of course. State laws, in most instances, govern the quality of sanitary facilities, waterfront protection, and the size of sites. However, this is a highly competitive business, so that campers benefit from the owners' zeal in matching their competitors' facilities.

One outstanding advantage of the privately operated campground is that advanced reservations for a campsite may be arranged, usually with a small deposit. Thus, a camping family is assured a campsite, without fear of being turned away or being kept waiting at the gate.

Names and addresses of private campground groups are included in the Appendix.

Another alternative, which many campers are coming to, is the leasing or purchase of a small plot for a private campground. This, of course, does away with the high adventure of travel to distant points, but it does have a charm of its own which shouldn't be overlooked.

Land may be leased in some national forests and, in some instances, timberland companies will lease small plots to responsible persons. Even a nearby farmer may have a woodlot on the shore of a lake or with a stream running through it that he'll be willing to sell or rent if he likes the set of your sails.

This is a possibility which offers the chance for many long and pleasantly undisturbed vacations. Getting to know an area, exploring lakes, valleys, and hills, can become a source of endless joy. Also, you can develop an efficient campsite for use time and time again, knowing that when you arrive for a few days' fun, you won't be beset with a horde of neighbors or a shortage of firewood. If you can't afford trips to distant wilderness areas and you get discouraged with crowded public camp-sites, the idea of a personal campspot, either pur-chased or leased, is well worth investigation.

In the meantime, however, there'll be occasions when you will stay at some of the larger, more well-known campgrounds, in which case there are little tricks which will help you get a better camp-site.

Keep in mind that three to five in the afternoon is "fill up time." This is the time of day when motor campers, on the road since morning, head for the nearest campground. Many of these are transients, or "one nighters," and a late arrival at almost any popular tenting park will find you competing with them for tent space. Plan, then, to arrive as early as possible.

If you're planning a lengthy stay at a particular campground, you may have to accept a second-rate campsite for the first night, particularly if you arrive during a weekend. Get permission from the ranger, if it's necessary, to shift your camp to a better site as soon as the transients pull out in the morning. Oftentimes, too, if you tell the ranger that you're planning to stay a few days, he may allot you a more desirable spot than he would if he thought you were a "one nighter."

In the event that the campground is not crowded when you arrive it will then become a matter of *which* campsite to choose. At nearly all campgrounds, you will first be required to register at the office and then, chances are, you'll be told to "take your pick." If, as is the practice in some areas, you are assigned a tent area by number, ask the ranger if you can look the tent sites over

first and, if he's good natured, he'll probably al-low you to do this.

For an overnight stay, you need not be overly fussy, of course, but for a stay of a few days or more, the location of a campsite will have a bear-ing on how much you will enjoy being there.

Of course, you will want to be fairly near the water supply and the woodshed and, especially if you have young children along, you'll want to be reasonably near toilet facilities. If there is a camp laundry and a shower house you may want to be near these too.

Keep in mind, however, that the closer you are to these for your own convenience the more you will be exposed to a constant stream of passers-by bent upon using the same facilities. I've found that many people, who wouldn't think of taking a short cut across a lawn back home, won't hesi-tate to walk through an occupied campsite on their way to using the area's facilities. No matter how friendly you are, you will, after a day or two of this, resent having other campers parade through your tenting site. Therefore, choose a site at least a short distance from campground points where traffic is heavy.

Also, look your neighbors over before settling on a tent site. Most campers are fine people, but a noisy group next to you will be a nuisance and, if there are young children, chances are you'll be awakened shortly after the sun peeps over the hills. I like children, but not when they set out to play at six in the morning.

Avoid a tenting site that sets directly beside a gravel road, especially if it is the main route through the campground, otherwise you will be eating dust much of the time. Try to locate a site some distance from well-traveled roads.

If there's a pond or lake within the campground where swimming is permitted, don't pitch your camp too close to the swimming area, for this is bound to be noisy and traffic will be heavy during hot weather. On the other hand, if you have young children you may prefer to camp as close to the swimming area as possible, in order to keep an eye on them. Your point of view, here, will vary depending on the age of your children and their ability in the water.

The same thing applies to a boating dock or launching ramp. Traffic around such installations is usually heavy and noisy. However, if you're also a boating enthusiast, you may prefer to be in the thick of things.

If possible, choose a tent site that has trees on

its southwest and west sides and pitch your camp fairly close to them. This is so that you will have shade during the afternoon when the sun can be unpleasantly hot. Inversely, avoid trees on the east side of your tent so that the early morning sun can strike your tent when it's needed to dispel the morning chill.

A thick stand of trees or a clearing of deep grass will harbor mosquitoes and black flies, or other local insect pests. Needless to say, a nearby bog or swamp, or even a damp low spot, will be the base of operations for swarms of insects. If you have a choice between a knoll or hillside and a low area, choose the high land. You'll get more breeze during the day and you'll find such a position warmer at night, since cold air settles in low places.

Check the fireplace, too, for sometimes the grates are missing or broken. Look over the picnic table and benches as these are occasionally rickety or even unsafe. Park authorities are usually diligent about these but, once in a while, poor equipment is allowed to remain for "one more season."

I have tried to point out, with some honesty, the conditions you may find in organized campgrounds. Writers have always painted our well-known tenting areas in glowing terms with some disregard for the facts. Some of these are hopelessly crowded and such campgrounds are little fun to use. You can, however, with a little planning avoid these and search out lesser-known areas which will provide more camping pleasure.

However, even some of the crowded areas can be fun if you will show the same thoughtfulness that's to be expected of others. The informal living that goes with camping out presents a good opportunity to make new friends, and to exchange camping tips and area information. Also, some of the evening campfire experiences will long be remembered after you've forgotten other phases of your trip. I recall one dismal rainy night in a campground near Ely, Minnesota, when everyone in camp near us seemed to be in a mood to sell the camping outfits and take up stamp collecting. I rigged a large tarp as a shelter, built up a roaring campfire, set the coffeepot on the edge of it, while my family got out marshmallows and chocolate bars for "Samoas." We then invited the neighbors in. It was well after one A.M. when we finally allowed the campfire to die out. The conversation that night among comparative strangers—the exchange of tales, the swapping of ideas, the expressions of opinions, could not have taken place anywhere else but around a campfire on a rainy night in a Northwoods campground!

Wilderness Camping

Many campers, after a couple of summers of campground outings, decide to graduate to wilderness camping, traveling either by canoe, pack horse, or car. Don't for a moment think that wilderness areas cannot be reached by car. Take, for example, the Alaska Highway. The roadway itself represents civilization, but step into the bush to either side of the road and you will be in as primitive a wilderness as you can find in North America.

Different problems present themselves when it comes to choosing a campsite, for here you will have to consider those factors which were decided for you at public campgrounds.

Despite the frequent suggestions, no set formula is valid regarding what time of day you should start to pitch camp. Many experts advise two or three hours before dark; others will insist that four to five P.M. is right. Actually, if you come upon a campsite which appeals to you shortly after noon, by all means stop and enjoy it. Don't strap yourself to a tight schedule that calls for travel most of the daylight hours.

On the other hand, don't wait until too late in the day, perhaps searching for that dream campsite. Such sites are rare and, like tents, they often require compromise with perfection. Remember, especially if you are a beginner, that it will take you longer to pitch camp, cook the evening meal, and clean up afterward than it will an old hand who can put up his tent, cook and eat a hearty meal, and hit the sack within an hour. Keep in mind that a camping trip is supposed to be fun and to be enjoyed in a leisurely manner.

In those areas where daylight saving time is in effect, you'll get an extra hour of daylight after mealtime, during which you can prepare the camp for the night. Remember that, as the season progresses, however, daylight length after the supper hour decreases.

If you've had some experience, there's no harm in traveling late and making a simple bivouac for the night. Occasionally, on canoe trips, you may have to hole up on shore during a high wind and travel late in the evening after the wind drops. If you do this, planning on a late camp after dark, stop en route while there's still daylight and pick up some tinder and a few sticks of firewood. These may be difficult to locate at a dark campsite. As a matter of fact, I do this on canoe trips regularly, stuffing a few sheets of birch bark up into the bow deck of the canoe, along with a few sticks of dry kindling. It speeds up the evening meal a little and, in case of a sudden shower, starting a fire is no problem.

During the normal course of looking for a camp-site, keep in mind that you may have to examine three or four before finding a suitable one, so start looking during the middle of the afternoon. Once you've found one that is moderately good, stick with it. Don't go traipsing all over the country looking for that picture-book campsite which doesn't exist.

As your experience grows, choosing a campsite will become almost automatic, but, until then, learn to look for certain features that make up an ideal overnight stop.

Traveling by boat or canoe, you'll need a safe place to draw up the craft out of reach of the wind, waves, currents, or, if you're camped on the seashore, the tide. If you're traveling by car, seek a parking space where your car will be out of the way of other cars going by. Don't leave the car in a country lane or backwoods road, thinking that, because it's remote, "no one will pass here." Also, don't leave your car on a grassy slope during the night. If it rains, the wet grass will give you mighty poor traction and you may have trouble getting out. The same applies to a low spot where there's dry, hard baked mud, for a rain will turn this to goo which will bog the car down when you try to move it.

For the tent site itself, however, look for a small knoll or gentle slope where, if it should rain heavily during the night, your tent won't be flooded out. Never camp in a hollow, dry wash, arroyo, or gully. A sudden shower, while you're sleeping, may send your outfit floating downstream on a newborn creek. In the West, these dry washes are dangerous, for even a distant storm in the mountains may send down a solid wall of water powerful enough to carry off everything in camp, including yourself.

Drinking water, of course, is important. Many springs in national forests and state forests are marked by signs. On private timberland where logging is being carried on, you can often spot a spring by the tin cup or inverted can propped on a bush by the spring. Safety precautions regarding drinking water are discussed in detail in Chapter 13.

Much has been written regarding camping above the "dew line." This is a level above which moisture carried by night air cannot reach you. To avoid this, you may have to climb halfway up a substantial hill, particularly if you're camped on the shore of a large lake or river. The closer you are to the water, the damper it will be, so try to get your camp set a few feet above the water. If there's a little dew on your gear in the morning, don't worry about it—it's not malignant!

You may have an opportunity to camp near a substantial waterfall. If you do, try to get upwind of it, for you'll find that a light mist will drift over your camp, wetting everything.

Disregarding the matter of dew, you may want to build your camp close to the water's edge if the forests are particularly dry and forest fire danger is obvious. This is good campcraft, if you kick the fire into the water when you're finished with it, making sure that no sparks or glowing coals remain when you retire at night, or leave after breakfast.

Another consideration when looking for a camp-site is firewood. This, like water, can be carried some distance if necessary, but it's more convenient to have it close at hand. Look the immediate area over for standing as well as down wood which can be burned.

Exposure, too, may be critical. On a quiet, warm summer night when black flies and mosquitoes are buzzing about, choose a clearing where the breeze, if any, can strike your camp. A breeze won't keep insects away completely—it takes a minor gale to do that—but it will hamper them somewhat. During this kind of weather, keep away from thick timber or tall grass.

On the other hand, if the weather is wet, windy, or cold, choose a campsite within a stand of *thick young timber*. The woods will shelter you considerably, especially from the wind. Be sure, though, that there isn't a large tree nearby which might blow down on your outfit. All trees have to fall down sometime and the off-chance that your camp may be under one at the right time is not impossible. Even if the tree looks solid as a rock ledge, it may have a "turkey" in it. A "turkey" is simply lumberjack language for a broken limb, waiting for someone to fall on.

During thunderstorm weather a thick stand of young growth where none of the trees are much taller than the others is a safe place so far as light-ning is concerned. The matter of lightning is dis-cussed in the chapter on Camping Safety.

As you examine a possible tent site, be sure that there's a suitable area large enough for you to pitch the tent in, with no immovable rocks, stubs, or heavy roots which may gouge your backbone during the night. The area should not be abso-lutely level as, in case of rain, it will not drain well. Make certain, too, that stakes can be driven into the ground, or that there are rocks or trees to which tent ropes can be attached.

If there should be a large boulder or a ledge, so much the better, providing other factors are fav-orable. You can build your campfire at the base of this and have an effective reflector which will drive warmth into your tent. Even during the sum-mer, nights in the North are cool and a night fire is often welcome.

Even in the deepest wilderness, you may occa-sionally see small clearings along canoe routes. In-vestigate these and you may thereby locate a campsite used by the professional woodsmen in the area. They have a sharp eye for campsites and chances are, if you find one of theirs, it will be as good as you can find in the region. If you also find a wood supply, already cut and covered with birch bark or part of an old tarpaulin, go ahead and use it. However, before you leave, replace it, leaving a few sticks more than you found by way of saying "Thanks." Be sure, too, that it's well cov-ered.

Many campers on their first adventure into the wilds may be a little timid about wild animals. One writer, in a recent issue of an outdoor maga-zine, didn't help the feelings of such campers much when he suggested that they wear a small tin can full of pebbles. Strapped to a camper's belt, the pebbles were supposed to rattle in the can and frighten away bears! What this country needs is something to frighten such writers out of our magazines!

Wild animals are rarely a nuisance, and this is especially true in the deep wilderness. In the Su-perior National Forest, my family and I once had a visit from a large black bear who perched on our camp table, some fifteen feet from where we slept and were awakened by his stomach rum-blings and pawing at our duffel. However, he did no harm and soon left to investigate a garbage can at the next tent site. Near Lost Pond, in Maine, I once was awakened by a porcupine perched on my stomach. Since I was on the ground in a sleeping bag, he probably figured I was just another log. Incredibly, that same night, a snow-shoe rabbit nibbled at my left ear and gave me a worse start than did the Minnesota bear!

I've had mink steal fish from my creel and, once when I worked for the New Hampshire Forestry Department, my wife and I encountered a wildcat on the mountain trail during the night as we were returning to my fire tower after an evening at a nearby ranger station.

However, keep in mind that these experiences occurred over a period of some twenty-five years and during none of these incidents was anyone in any danger. Trying to pick a campsite where you'll be completely free from intrusion by wild animals is difficult, unless you camp on a small is-land. You can't always count on these, either, for I once ran into a bull moose on a three-acre island! Remember that, after all, *you* are the intruder and that the wilderness is the home of the animals.

Especially you will have little or no trouble from larger species such as bear, moose, or deer. These will usually give you a wide berth, although deer are often attracted by a campfire or a bright camp lantern, but they'll keep their distance. Burn all garbage thoroughly and you'll have no trouble with bears for they are primarily scavengers once they learn about the tidbits to be had at camp-sites. Skunks, however, may be attracted if your camp is messy.

Smaller animals, like porcupines and squirrels, can be a nuisance, but you'll find them practically everywhere so that, all in all, there's little point in considering the possibility of animals when choos-ing a campsite. Learn to enjoy having them around and, after a while, you'll be plotting meth-ods to get nearer to them for observation!

Occasionally, even in the wilderness, you'll meet other camping parties and it's fun to pass the time of day with them, trading route and campsite in-formation, or fishing tips. However, they are there because they too don't like crowded campgrounds. Therefore, don't pitch your camp close to another, unless you're invited to. Incidentally, should your camp be pitched first, it is good woods etiquette to invite newcomers to share the site, especially if they are few and far between.

CAMPING ON DIAMOND LAKE, OREGON

Oregon State Highway Travel Dept.

Chapter 4

TENTING TIPS

The easiest of all tents to erect is the model with a sewed-in floor, for this requires only that the corners be staked out to square it automatically. Inserting the interior poles or framework is then easily done, or if you are using shears, these are then lifted to proper height. The eaves, parrels, or other outside guys are then staked.

For a tent without a sewed-in floor, the reverse procedure should be followed. First, insert the inside poles or framework into the tent and lift the latter into position. While someone holds the poles and tent upright for a few moments, stake out the guy lines. With factory poles, your tent will automatically be set at the correct height. With woods-cut shears, or with a rope ridge, you may have to adjust the height of these in order to stake out the beckets.

Modern exterior-framed tents, especially the Umbrella model with sewed-in floor, go up very easily. As pointed out earlier, the top sections of the frame are attached to the peak, then the corner sections are inserted one at a time, thus raising the shelter into position with minimum effort.

Good camping technique calls for slackening all guy ropes at evening time. The damp night air will tighten these, along with the tent fabric, with the result that stakes may be pulled loose. An unexpected rainstorm will cause even greater tautness of lines and fabric, possibly pulling up stakes or even tearing tent seams. Be sure, then, before retiring, that the entire shelter is slack enough to allow for shrinkage.

Tent catalogs usually show tents that have been pitched completely taut, with no sagging or slack surfaces. Very rarely, however, is such perfection possible, nor is it desirable. A tent should always be pitched with some slack in it.

Despite precautions, however, a sudden night storm may catch you with your tent too taut. You probably won't have a small camp shovel in the tent with you, but with a heavy knife or even a mixing spoon or stick, dig a small hole, three or four inches deep, next to each tent pole. Drop the butt end into each hole and this will lower the entire shelter and slacken all strain points.

This trick, of course, can't be used if your tent has a sewed-in floor. In this case, simply pull the bottom end of each tent pole to the side five or six inches. This, too, will drop your entire shelter enough to slacken the lines and the fabric.

The center-pole-type Umbrella tent is the easiest of all tents to slacken. Dropping the spreader arm sleeve on the pole eliminates tension from the eaves and allows the walls and roof to droop slightly so that they may absorb shrinkage.

If your shelter is pitched with shear poles, however, you'll have to go outside to slacken it. It will not be necessary, though, to loosen each and every line individually. Simply spread the butt ends of the shears slightly, moving them far enough apart to slacken the tent. Be sure that these shears are well anchored in earth, or against rocks, logs, or stumps, to keep them from slipping farther apart and spilling the entire outfit to the ground.

A Wall tent pitched with shears and its eaves guyed to side bars, cannot be slackened in this manner, however, without danger of ripping the tent or pulling it completely out of shape so that the door flaps will not close. If you guy the eaves to side bars, you will have to loosen the individual lines when a rain comes up.

One of the poorest suggestions I've ever seen in print calls for placing a thin log atop the lines between the eaves and the stakes or side bars, for a so-called "self-adjusting" method of guying a Wall tent. Shrinkage is supposed to lift the log instead of pulling against the stakes or fabric. This is completely impractical since it results only in additional permanent strain against the tent fabric. No matter how many times you see this stunt advised, ignore it—or be prepared to be laughed at by campers who know better.

Nearly all tents with exterior frames are suspended by means of elastic shock cord, which provides automatic tension adjustment. However, there are still tents which require guy lines. These are usually equipped with wooden or metal slides, which are moved up or down the guy line to increase or decrease tautness.

I must confess, however, that I have never used guy line tighteners. Preferring to tie the line directly to the stake with a "taut line hitch" which can be adjusted without untying and which will not slip when under tension. It's a simple knot which you can learn to tie in minutes and which you can adjust in the dark.

Look over a crowded campground sometime, and you'll discover that 99 percent of the campers drive their tent stakes in so that they lean *away* from the tent.

As a boy, watching in the predawn light of circus day, I was fascinated by the circles of Barnum & Bailey roustabouts driving giant tent stakes, swinging their huge mauls in precisionlike sequence. I was so goggle-eyed, in fact, that I failed to be impressed by the fact that the stakes which held the big top were driven vertically. As far as I know, the giant tent never collapsed because stakes failed to hold. This would seem justification enough for the camper to drive his tent stakes vertically—yet very few do.

Slanting the stake *away* from the tent, so that the guy line leaves the stake at a right angle, subjects that stake to a side pull which will enlarge the hole, especially if the stake is short. The latter then sets loosely in the ground so that a gust of wind, buffeting the tent, can easily lift the stake from the ground.

Some authorities even insist that stakes be driven so that they slant *toward* the tent. In this way, the pull from a guy rope is more in line with

WOODEN GUY TIGHTENER

TAUT LINE HITCH

the length of the stake itself. This method holds far better than might be supposed.

Actually, the angle at which the stake is set is not as important as the depth to which it is driven. Drive them so that they are anchored in 12 to 18 inches of soil, and you will have no trouble with their pulling up. Even with these longer stakes, however, driving them vertically or slanting slightly toward the tent, will guarantee that they will stay in place.

For an overnight stop almost any kind of wood will do for stakes, but if you're planning a longer stay, hardwood shoots about 1½ inches in diameter are best for 9′×12′ or larger tents. These include maple, hickory, birch, elm, and ash. Certain of the softwoods, such as red spruce, are also good. In picking saplings for stakes, try to choose straight ones, as crooked or curved lengths will be difficult to drive. If you have a bucksaw with you, square the top end and, with a sharp ax, sharpen the opposite end. Incidentally, the point need not be spear-sharp. Leave the extreme tip of the point flattened slightly—it will drive better in gravel.

Among so-called camping "hints" is the suggestion that tent stakes be painted a luminous white so that they will be visible at night, cutting down the possibility of tripping over them. If you want to paint your stakes, there is certainly no harm in the idea, but only the rankest amateur needs continuous warning that his tent is held up by stakes which might trip him! I would be a long time living it down if some of the Maine guides I used to work with found me driving luminous stakes!

On rare occasions you may have to pitch your tent without stakes. Late one afternoon when a violent thunderstorm appeared to be overtaking one of my canoe trips on a northern Maine lake, we sought shelter hurriedly on the nearest island which proved to be no more than a huge slab of rock whose surface soil was only a few inches deep. There was plenty of scrub spruce and birch, although the soil was shallow and quite loose—too much so in fact to trust with tent stakes. However, we decided to camp for the night. We worked fast, with the saw and ax and we had the tent up just as the full fury of the storm descended on us.

Two logs were cut, each a few feet longer than the tent, and about six inches in diameter. We then located one rock, from six to eight inches in diameter, for each of the tent's guy ropes. While two men held the tent in position, the other two of us tied the rocks to the lines, placing these where we would normally have driven stakes. We then laid one log on each side of the tent, across the guy ropes and snug against the rocks. The tent wobbled considerably during the storm, but it remained erect while we and our duffel outwaited the wind and rain, snug and dry in the shelter.

At some wilderness campsites you may find that the soil is deep enough to accept stakes, but too loose to hold them firmly. In this case, drive the stakes as usual, then use the log trick described above, placing the log snugly against the stakes. Any pull exerted against the stakes will also be applied against the log. Such a combination will withstand a severe buffeting.

When it comes to guying the front pole or shears of almost any type of tent, you can improve upon the usual single stake rig. With such a stake and single guy rope, a campfire directly in front of the tent is impossible. In order to leave the area directly in front of the tent clear, run *two* guy ropes from the tent, each about 45 degrees to the side. Such a rigging is especially handy during rainy weather when, with a fire close to the tent door, you can cook by reaching out to the fire from the shelter of the tent.

Many small tents have parrels sewed into the sides, for attaching guy ropes which, in effect, "balloon" out the sides, creating more room inside. These tents are usually shown with parrels staked in short pegs with the result that the tent is taut *above* the parrel, but sagging sadly *underneath* it. This is because the guy rope exerts a downward pull on the parrel. Instead drive a tall stake, and attach the guy rope to this, pulling the parrel upward. The result will be a neatly pitched tent, and a roomier one.

Ditching a tent is usually a wasted effort when you're camping in the wilderness where the soil is untrampled and absorbent. Rarely will enough water accumulate on the surface to run under a tent and I can't recall having ditched a tent more than two or three times during my life!

Beyond the fact that they are rarely necessary, ditches are unsightly and expose soil which turns to gooey mud in a rain. In an organized campground, where the earth is likely to be hard-packed from frequent use and no longer absorbs water, a shallow ditch may be necessary. Ironically, most organized campgrounds don't allow you to dig!

If ditching is necessary, the secret is to dig a trench on the two uphill sides of the tent, with a runoff ditch carrying the water away from your shelter. Three to six inches is usually deep enough. One of the most ridiculous camping illustrations I ever saw showed a trench fully eighteen inches away from the tent, dug on all four sides to a depth of one foot, and of course, a corresponding foot high ridge of dirt encircling the shelter. The project looked more like a moat!

The usual advice concerning a ditch is to dig it with a vertical drop-off immediately along the tent wall. This is fine, if your tent has a sewed-in floor or a sod cloth. However, without these, tent walls rarely stay in position as nicely as they do in catalog illustrations. Half the time, you'll find that the ditch is inside the tent! Even in the most orderly camp, such items as flashlights, matchboxes, compasses, eyeglass cases, and pocket knives have a way of straying and you'll occasionally find one of these in the ditch. Also, such a ditch allows easy access for mosquitoes.

If your tent lacks a sewed-in floor or sod cloth, dig your ditch three or four inches from the tent wall, and no more than six inches deep. Deposit the earth between the ditch and the hem of the wall. This will not only keep out water, but will also prevent insects from getting in and small camp items from getting out.

A small shovel, or military entrenchment tool, is good for digging such ditches, as well as latrines and garbage disposal pits but, don't use your ax as a shovel! When you leave, refill the trench and cover the raw earth with leaves, twigs, and duff, to prevent the possible start of erosion or the spreading of mud over what might be a suitable campsite for someone else.

Very few tents which are supposedly insect-proof will keep out all bugs. Tents with netting doors usually have a zipper running vertically between the two halves of the netting but these are likely to have only snaps along the bottom. Gaps will develop between these snaps which are quickly found by insects.

You can make such a tent absolutely insect- and snakeproof by replacing the snaps with zippers. Use the type of slide fastener known as "non-separating," that is, joined permanently at one end. Sew the zipper with this end at the sides of the tent so that, in closing the netting doorway, the three zippers meet at the center of the threshold.

While protecting the fabric floor of any tent is important, a still more frequent problem is that of keeping it clean. A household broom, with the handle cut down, is suitable except that it's bulky. A child's play broom, if you can find one that is sturdily made, will do nicely, although the job will take a little longer. Better yet, is a whisk broom. Granted, you'll have to crouch to do the sweeping but once a day will be often enough, and think of the space you'll save in packing. I suppose, one of these days some clever inventor will devise a good camp broom with a telescoping aluminum handle!

Boughs from pine, spruce, or fir trees are often suggested as brooms. Actually, they are not worth the trouble of cutting since they are so soft and pliable that little dirt gets swept and they, in turn, contribute to the litter in the form of needles. It's a romantic notion, probably, and likely every camper has tried it—once.

For a semipermanent camp, where weight and space limitations are not stringent, you might carry a small cocoa mat, say about 12 to 24 inches. The stiff upright bristles will scour dirt and mud from soles and heels which might otherwise cling and get a free ride into the tent. Rubber mats are often suggested because they can be rolled compactly, but they are next to useless for this purpose. Boughs, too, have been suggested, but these do a poor job and they are likely to trigger a nasty fall. I know of nothing as effective as a cocoa mat which, incidentally, can easily be cleaned by shaking, and may even be washed in a nearby creek.

Beckets are usually the source of the first trouble you will have with a tent for they are subject to considerable abuse. Tent stakes rub them harshly; there is almost constant strain on them; and they are exposed at all times to moisture. All in all, life expectancy of most factory-make beckets is short.

At the first sign of trouble, whether it is fraying or parting stitches, remove the faulty becket and replace it with one made of a short length of heavy webbing 1 to 1¼ inches wide. This is not unlike the webbing used in belts issued to GIs which can be purchased from most large outfitters. Don't sew the webbing to the hem as was done with the original becket. Instead, attach it with copper or brass rivets. It is important that the rivet be closed tightly so that there is no play against the fabric. Do not double the webbing over so that only one rivet is necessary, for this will place too much strain against the tent fabric at one point. Use two rivets, one at each end of the becket material and space these not more than four inches apart.

Keeping track of small items which are not carried on the person is one of the irritating problems of camping. The habit of keeping certain items in a particular spot is thrown out of kilter. Whenever you want the fly dope, sunburn lotion, or sharpening stone, these are usually in the black depths of a pack—which pack being a mystery. A cloth "catch-all" is the answer to this problem.

To make such a "catch-all," fold a square piece of material—it matters little what kind, as long as it is fairly rugged—over itself, allowing an overlap of 4 to 5 inches. Stitch this vertically at intervals, the distance between the stitching depending upon the size of the compartments you want. Double stitch the outside edges and hem the top edge of the pockets. Sew the entire unit along a horizontal tent seam, either at the eave or at the ridge, or simply hang it to an inside ridgepole.

Occasionally, two families will camp out together and I can think of no better tent accommodation for each party than what I call the "ranch-type rig." Pitch two Umbrella tents facing each other so that the awnings abut. This will form a

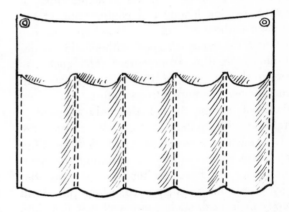

A CATCH-ALL

"breezeway," and a sort of mutual meeting ground for eating and other camp pleasures, yet each family is assured the full privacy of its own tent. If the weather is windy and cold, set up side curtains on one side of the "breezeway" to shelter the area. If the season is "buggy," insect netting can be mounted.

A similar lounging area can be rigged between almost any two tents stretching a tarpaulin or fly, lean-to style, between them. The two tents need not be the same type, so long as they are about the same height. In erecting such a rig, erect the tarpaulin on the windward side of the tents, running it from the ground to the tent peaks or ridges, then horizontally, to form a canopy.

Most campers, when purchasing a fly for a Wall

tent, will buy one that is too small and even manufacturers often suggest a fly that is inadequate for best use. For the proper size, measure the height of the tent wall and the distance from the eave to the ridge. Double the total of these two figures, and you have the correct width for a fly. Length may vary according to the length of the tent, naturally, but plan on a two foot rear and front overhang for a tent that is ten or more feet long. For smaller tents, a one-foot overhang is sufficient.

Such a fly will have to be suspended separately and it will overhang the side of the tent a distance equal to the height of the wall, much like the fly on a tropical tent. This will keep the hot sun from striking any part of the tent except the front and rear walls, thus keeping the shelter much cooler than the conventionally rigged Wall tent. It will also supply storage space alongside the side walls.

A second reason for a larger fly is that, when set up as a canopy over the area in front of a Wall tent, the sides can be dropped to match those of the tent, making in effect, a continuation of the tent itself without a front wall. Wind and rain can blow under a canopy rigged without side walls, but not under this arrangement. The cook can perform therein, out of the rain and you can lounge or eat in comparative comfort.

Rain, of course, is not the only element a camper has to contend with. Fall campers are likely to encounter cold nights, but these need not keep you at home. For this sort of outing, the open-front tent is the finest shelter there is, now that pesky insects have disappeared. A campfire built directly in front of such a tent will cast heat into the shelter, especially if a log reflector is used. However, if more than two people go on such a fall trip, take along two open-front tents and pitch them "face to face." Build your campfire between them and you'll be amazed at the comfort such a rig affords, no matter how cool the night!

Protecting a tent during transportation is something many of us overlook until it is too late and we discover worn or chafed spots. Such damage is seldom noticed until daylight or rainwater is seen coming through the roof!

If no carrying bag was supplied with your tent, it's a worthwhile off-season project to make one, preferably of some rugged material such as duck. Closed with a puckering string, such a bag will protect the tent from being damaged by rubbing against other objects. Make the bag slightly larger than might appear necessary and you'll save yourself much struggling. Also, when packing the tent

for transportation or storage, roll it rather than fold it to avoid creases.

If you don't want to bother with a bag, at least roll the tent so that your ground cloth, or sewed-in floor, acts as a wrapper. This will protect the walls and roof. A smaller carrying bag for stakes is a good idea, also. Never wrap the stakes in the tent unless they're contained in such a bag. The sharp edges might damage the fabric.

Most new tents of good quality are not likely to need rewaterproofing for four to five years. One of mine has never been treated during the 20 years that I've had it, although I must confess it's beginning to need it.

Several solutions are available for rewaterproofing tent fabrics. Note that while these are referred to in catalogs and among campers as "waterproofing," they actually make the fabric water-repellent, not waterproof, as already explained.

The method of application and the solution used depends upon the fabric's finish but, in any case, the tent should be thoroughly dry and all loose dirt brushed from it, particularly along the seams.

If you are unable to determine the finish, quite likely the dealer from whom you purchased the tent can help you. He merely has to refer to his catalogs.

In the event the tent has a dry finish, fold it loosely and spray a solution such as Rain-Chek, Secco, or Stay Put between all of the folds, with particular attention to the seams. These sprays are available in 12-, 16-, or 24-ounce aerosol spray cans from most camping equipment dealers. Once the spray has been applied thoroughly, wrap the tent loosely in a large sheet of plastic or slip into a plastic envelope, closing it as tightly as possible. Allow the tent to remain in this two or three days to permit the waterproofing to seep into every part of the fabric. The tent may then be withdrawn from the wrapping and hung in a dry place for a few more days. It will then be ready to use.

For tent fabric with a wet finish, the chore is best performed out of doors, preferably in warm sunlight. The solution required is of the paraffin or resin type, available under such brand names as Weather Master, Flex-Dri, or Canvak, and obtainable from tent dealers. This solution is best applied with a brush, a gallon covering roughly 90 to 100 square feet. If the tent is a small one, setting it up will facilitate brushing on the solution. In the case of a large tent, you will have to do one section at a time, folding the fabric as the work progresses. Once done, erect the tent and allow it to stand a day or two.

Many suggestions are made for home treatment of tents but, frankly, no homemade solution is as effective as the standard solutions available from outfitters and tent manufacturers. Despite the claims made for "easy home workshop methods" they are rarely "simple and easy."

However, the home treatments are a little less expensive and, if you don't mind the chore, they are effective. One method, which fills the pores of the cloth, involves the use of turpentine and paraffin. Heat a gallon container of turpentine in a washtub of hot water and chip a pound of paraffin into the turpentine, stirring until the paraffin has melted completely. Paint the solution on the tent, after it has been set up so that all surfaces are as taut as possible. Using a fairly stiff brush, work the solution into the fabric well. This quantity should be enough to waterproof a small tent, such as a Pup tent. For larger tents, of course, you'll need more.

One part of beeswax to three parts of paraffin will result in less stiffening of the fabric. Some prefer to melt the wax or paraffin separately over a stove, then stir it into the turpentine. Great care should be used, however, near any open flame. The suggestion has also been made to use gasoline instead of turpentine and if you use this mixture, be sure that the gas is kept away from the stove where the wax is being heated. Needless to say, it's safest to work out of doors.

The paraffin solution can be applied to any tent, no matter what type of solution has previously been applied although it will not work on nylon material. The alum and lead solution, whose description follows, should never be applied to a tent that has been treated with a paraffin or wax solution.

The lead and alum solution is best used on heavy fabrics, since it will not seal the pores of the weave. It will simply waterproof the individual threads that make up the warp and fill.

Mix one pound of alum in four gallons of *hot* water so that the former will dissolve well. Mix the same proportions, using sugar of lead. Allow the solutions to stand a few minutes, then pour the lead solution into the alum mixture. Allow the precipitation to settle thoroughly, after which the clear liquid is then poured into a large tub.

This will result in about seven gallons of clear liquid. Soak the tent in this solution, working the fabric with your hands so that every square inch becomes well saturated. The tent should then remain in the liquid six to eight hours, after which it can be wrung out lightly and hung up to dry. These proportions will treat an 8′×10′ tent amply.

Another method calls for soaking the tent in the alum solution for six hours, wringing it out, and then soaking six hours more in the sugar of lead solution. It should then be wrung out and hung up to dry. Naturally, if this method is used, don't mix the alum and the lead solutions.

A CAMPING PARTY IN MONTANA

Bill Browning

Chapter 5

THE CAMPFIRE

Even with today's modern camping stoves, the ability to build a wood fire remains well nigh indispensable, for there are certain blessings, common to wood fires, with which the best of mechanical equipment is not endowed. For example, a gas stove can't dry clothing well; it can't heat an open tent; and it's a cheerless companion when compared to the leaping flames of an evening campfire.

Building a campfire, however, is fast becoming a lost art, and this is understandable. The black iron kitchen range and the pot-bellied parlor heater are things of the past, relegated to the museum for the wonderment of people who push little buttons to broil lamb chops. It's little wonder, then, that the campfire is often the bugaboo of the camping trip, especially a prolonged rainy spell.

Actually, *it's possible to start an outdoor fire at any time of the year in any weather*—provided you know where to find the proper tinder and how to use it. Rain, snow, sleet, or wind may hinder you but they needn't stop you once you've acquired this woodsman's knack.

Natural Tinders

Woodsmen are generally agreed that the best tinder is the bark of the white birch. This bark will burn readily, even after a thorough soaking, because of its oil content. Peeling the bark will not kill the tree but it will leave an ugly permanent scar. Always try, therefore, to locate a dead birch or a fallen tree trunk or branch.

Some experts advise that you use the inner bark for tinder. This is *not* correct. The inner bark of the white birch is little more than a thin light green film, nearly impossible to peel from the trunk. Rather, use the light brown center layers and the comparatively coarse outer white bark. On a mature tree, the white bark will probably have started to peel so that it hangs in curlicues that rattle in a breeze.

U. S. Forest Service

Bark which has been lying on the ground, even for years, is still good tinder, although the wood may be rotted and punky. Often, you'll find hollow cylinders of bark from which the wood has deteriorated entirely. In these, however, the cambium layer has probably persisted, clinging to the inside of the bark cylinder. Squeeze the bark cylinder and this layer will disintegrate and fall out.

THE BARK CYLINDER

If you're caught out in a heavy downpour and the future of your fire looks dismal, try to find such a cylinder a foot or so long and six to eight inches in diameter. Using smaller pieces of birch bark and finely split kindling, build your fire *inside* the cylinder where the downpour can't get at the young flames. By the time the kindling has caught fire and starts to burn the cylinder, your fire will be well on the way toward being rainproof.

The bark of the yellow or silver birch is also an excellent tinder, although it doesn't peel as easily as that of the white birch. The bark of the gray birch, a smaller species resembling the white birch quite closely, is also good tinder.

Overlooked by many is the bark of the red and northern white cedars, both of which shred easily and burn well. To obtain this from a living tree (it does no harm if only the outer bark is taken), draw the edge of a knife or an ax up and down, applying some pressure. A few minutes' work will produce enough finely shredded bark to start a fire. Be sure that the bark is dry for, contrary to popular opinion, rain will soak cedar bark thoroughly so that it burns poorly or not at all. If you can locate a dead cedar tree, the entire bark layer makes good tinder and it can be stripped from the trunk easily in long, rope-like lengths.

Another useful bark is that of the hemlock. This tree, however, is becoming somewhat rare, since it was cut for many years solely for its bark which was used in making tannic acid. The bark will produce a very hot and fairly long-lasting fire and serves well as encouragement for poorer woods. The outer layer, obtained in much the same manner as the cedar bark, is excellent tinder. Be careful, however, with your ax or knife, as hemlock knots are closely akin to Vermont marble and will nick a sharp edge or even take a good-sized bite out of a sharp blade.

The seasoned bark from almost any softwood species that has been "stump dried" is good tinder. "Stump dried" refers to any tree which has died but still remains standing. Typical of these are lightning killed or infected trees. The one exception to this is the tamarack, whose bark is nearly fireproof.

A friend of the camper is the beaver. Although some states prohibit the disturbance of a beaver house or dam, you can often locate an abandoned structure. These are built of woods litter and small branches cut from trees felled by beaver. Invariably, sticks protrude from the house or dam, exposed to the air, where they dry quickly. Frequently these are aspen or poplar, "popple" in the North, which burns easily with a clean, almost smokeless flame. Break off dry sections for tinder or kindling.

The dead limbs from the lower part of softwood trees are usually represented as being good fire starters but these are suitable only when they have not been rained on heavily. The lower limbs of even the bushiest tree will get wet during a heavy downpour. You have only to seek shelter under such a tree during a rain to prove this to yourself.

Much better are splits from a dead "stub." You can't walk very far in a forested area without finding one of these. Usually killed by lightning, blight, high winds, or by another tree falling against it, such a stub remains standing after the top has fallen, soon to become "stump dried." Snow, rain, or sleet never penetrate more than a few inches near the top. Even stubs from which the bark has dried and fallen will be bone dry inside. This wood, however, is usually "case-hardened"—and a bucksaw is helpful. Simply make two horizontal cuts with the saw a foot or so apart, then split out the wood between these cuts with an ax. The stub of a white birch, however, is generally useless, for, when the tree dies, the bark retains the moisture within the trunk. The bark of course, remains usable.

THE CENTER OF A STUB WILL USUALLY BE DRY

Not realizing how well nature provides for us in the woods can lead to tragedy. Some years ago, while a member of a search party, I was among the group which found a hunter who had been lost for four days, after he'd gone hunting in a snowstorm.

When we found him he was dead. A small pile of wet green twigs and burned-out matches told the tragic story. Less than fifty feet away stood a huge dry pine stub, with enough kindling and good firewood in it to last a week!

"Fat" pine, spruce, and fir shouldn't be overlooked in your search for good tinder. These are among the best, especially pitch pine, long and short leaf, red or Norway, gray or jack pine, as well as red spruce. These are very resinous trees and the sap, upon the death of the tree, runs to the butt or catches in bends and knots. Long after the tree trunk has fallen and rotted, these pitch pockets remain, practically indestructible except by fire. Knock the limbs from a rotting log and you'll find chunks of resinous wood at the butt of the limb.

The dried and fallen cones of the various softwoods also make good tinder. They won't light as readily as birch bark, but once the flame has a hold on them, they'll burn briskly and long enough to ignite your kindling wood.

Dry softwood needles or fallen hardwood leaves are often used by beginners but generally they're poor tinder. Dried grass, hay, or weeds are better. Pull these up in as long lengths as possible, twist into bunches, knotting if possible, before lighting. These will smolder before blazing, but, when bunched, will burn longer than needles or leaves.

CUTTING THE PRAYER STICK   *Riviere*

This is strictly an emergency tinder which will work when all factors are favorable. In some Southern states, palmetto fans are good tinder while, in the Southwest, cactus spines and sagebrush serve well.

Another good source of kindling and tinder is the "blow-down," a tree that has been uprooted by the wind. Very rarely do softwood blow-downs fall so that the trunk rests on the ground, for the limbs usually hold it off the ground to season. In wet weather slab off chunks of this wood from the *underside* of the trunk, or break off branches that stand vertically away from the trunk.

Shavings, whittled from any seasoned softwood—pine, spruce, fir, and cedar being among the best—are most effective tinder. A hatful of these can be whittled in a few minutes with an ax or a knife. The prayer stick, feather stick, or fuzz stick is a seasoned softwood stick which has been whittled so that the shavings still hang from it, bristling in all directions. Three or four of these, eight to ten inches long, piled crisscross under dry kindling, will usually start a fire with some certainty that it will burn.

Generally speaking, kindling that can be bent or twisted without breaking is worthless, since it is probably green or so well saturated that it will not burn readily. On the other hand, if you can snap such wood so that it breaks crisply, it will probably ignite quickly.

Odds and ends of twigs and small branches, often called squaw wood, that are lying on the ground are rarely worth picking up since they have absorbed moisture from the damp earth and will not burn in a small fire.

Man-made Tinders

Paraffin seems to be the basic material used in most man-made tinders. Some soak newspaper in melted paraffin, others use cotton balls. Blocks of paraffin, wrapped in paper work well since the paper serves to ignite the former. Short stubs of candles are used by some campers though these are not as effective as paraffin blocks since the flame is small and quite likely to blow out. Solidified alcohol, in the form of "canned heat" is easy to carry and a small dab can be applied to kindling with a stick. There are, too, a number of commercially made fire starters, some of which burn for seven minutes!

Scrap paper is probably the most commonly used tinder, since most campers save wrappings from food packages for this purpose. Others carry a supply of newspapers which work well if the kindling is dry and fine enough. Campers who carry gasoline for outboard motors or lanterns are often tempted to use it as a fire starter. I once knew a guide who always piled a few sticks of wood, cabin style, poured a pint of outboard gas over these, then nonchalantly tossed a lighted match at his fire. It worked, but I used to flinch every time he did it.

Another guide and I once had to remove a boy from an island to an ambulance because he'd poured a can of gasoline onto a smoldering fire. The resulting explosion burned him severely from his chest to his knees. So, no matter how often you see this gasoline stunt performed successfully, avoid it. It's just another form of Russian roulette.

How to Build a Fire

Once you have suitable tinder and dry kindling gathered the secret to starting your fire easily is to keep the weight of the kindling from crushing the tinder to the ground. Even highly inflammable tinder needs air to burn and if it's crushed under the weight of firewood, air cannot reach it and you will have no fire! *This is the source of trouble for more than 99 per cent of campers who have fire building difficulties!*

To avoid this, lay a stick of dry firewood, two or three inches in diameter, in the fireplace. Place your tinder alongside this. Now place a dozen or so sticks of kindling over the tinder, crisscross fashion so that it rests on the larger stick. Unless it's very dry, kindling should not be much over a quarter to a half inch thick. Before lighting the tinder, make sure you have enough firewood on hand to keep the blaze going once it starts.

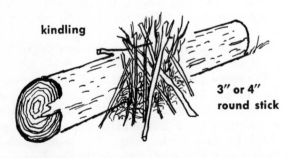

kindling

3" or 4" round stick

birch bark or other tinder

AN EASY-TO-START CAMPFIRE

Light the tinder on the *windward* side, so that the breeze will blow the infant flame *into* the kindling rather than away from it. This is a woodsman's basic trick which is overlooked too often by inex-

perienced campers. Once the kindling is aflame and burning briskly, add slightly larger wood.

Beginners are usually advised to start their fire with kindling piled in the shape of a small tepee, with the tinder in the center. The trouble with this method is that the tinder often burns out quickly and, once the kindling starts burning, it falls and scatters.

If it's raining quite hard, have your partner hold a poncho, raincoat, or small tarpaulin over the fire as you light it. Once the fire has begun to burn briskly, ordinary rain will not put it out, although a torrential downpour might.

When it is raining hard, or if a thundershower is approaching, don't gamble your entire kindling and dry wood supply on the first attempt at a fire. Sometimes it's best to wait until the brunt of the storm has passed if dry tinder and kindling are scarce. Keep your supply under cover, and when the storm has spent itself, try again.

The suggestion that a fire be built on a platform of rocks or logs in order to get a draft up through it, is sheer nonsense. Except for wind, there will be no draft until the flames start to climb and then the fire will create its own draft.

Once you have your basic fire, now is the time to develop it, enlarge it, or change its shape to suit particular purposes.

Cooking Fires

A "noonin'" fire, or one for "b'ilin' the kittle," as woodsmen call it, is simply the crisscross five we've just discussed. The noon meal in the woods, particularly if you're traveling, is likely to be sandwiches with tea or coffee if the weather is cool. For these a small quick fire is best, one that will coil flames around the bottom of the tea pail or coffeepot.

Dry soft woods, or semihardwood such as white birch, are good fuels. In the North, poplar is used a great deal because it is plentiful and gives a quick hot, almost smokeless fire. Make this fire only big enough so that flames envelop the bottom of the kettle. Don't bother with complicated forked sticks, cranes, or green log andirons.

Set the kettle on rocks or hang it from a "gin pole." This is a green stick, 5 to 8 feet long, trigged to hold the pot over the flames. It can be held at the right height by a rock, log, or a single forked stick, and its height can be adjusted easily so that the kettle sets in the flames correctly. The "gin pole" is almost as old as the North and is also called a dingle stick, tea stick, wangan stick, wambec, or as it was known to the fire as readily. For such a fire, dig your pit on a gentle slope and pile the dirt on the sides. A wire grill laid atop the pit will hold the cooking utensils.

A keyhole-shaped fireplace of stones is probably the best for most camp cooking. Build your main fire in the larger part of the fireplace, then rake coals into the narrow end for cooking as you need them. Use a wire grill across the top of the rocks at the narrow end, or two or three short lengths of pipe. One of the best wire grills available is a shelf removed from an old refrigerator. A little awkward to carry perhaps, but in a car or boat it's well worth toting along. One of the poorest grills on the market is the type that has folding legs. When weight is placed on these, one or more of the legs sinks into the earth, tilting the cooking surface.

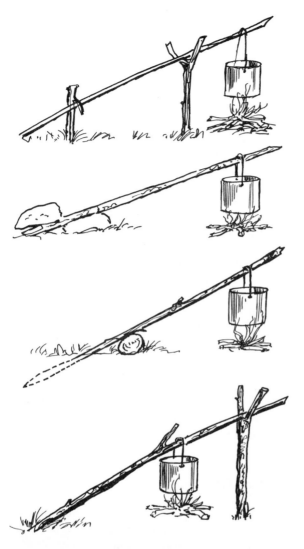

THE GIN POLE OFFERS VARIOUS WAYS OF SUSPENDING THE KETTLE OVER AN OPEN FIRE

THE KEYHOLE STOVE FIREPLACE

to Indians, the "chip-lok-waugan." Indians considered it bad luck to leave one standing over the ashes of a dead fire. It's a nice gesture, however, to leave it by your fireplace for the next fellow to use.

The romantic tripod, holding a kettle over a fire, is frequently suggested but unless you have a very heavy kettle or if you plan to simmer a stew for half a day, why cut three sticks for a tripod when a dingle stick will do the job?

A pit fire is another type often suggested and it's a practical rig, though I never could see why a fire should be built in a hole when it will do the job on the surface. There may be occasions when you'll want to make a pit fire for cooking, such as on a windy day—the theory being that the wind can't get

Another frequent suggestion is the fire built up against a log or rock. For cooking with a reflector oven, this is a sound idea and this is explained in the chapter on cooking. One trouble with building a fire up against a log is that it's a mighty job to get the log completely extinguished when you're finished with the fire.

For cooking a fully rounded meal when you may have to bake, boil, and fry all at the same time, twin andirons made of green logs used in conjunction with a crane make up the most suitable fireplace. The logs should be about five feet long and six to eight inches in diameter. If you plan to use the fireplace in a semipermanent camp, hew the top surface so that it is moderately flat. This will then hold pots and pans steady. The logs may be set parallel, but it is best to lay them butting at one end and about 16 to 18 inches apart at the other.

Two forked sticks with a green pole lying in the forks make up the crane. Don't spend any time looking for a pair of perfectly formed Y shaped forks.

They rarely grow that way and, even if you found a pair, you would probably split them trying to drive them into the ground. Instead, look for a pair of hardwood saplings with branches growing at about 45 degrees upward from the trunk. The tendency among most new campers is to cut forks that are too flimsy. Pick forks that are a couple of inches in diameter. These will stand heavy pounding from your ax when you stake them and they will hold a hefty load with safety.

Stake one fork at each end of the log andiron fireplace so that the forks are about three feet from the ground. Place a hardwood pole about two inches in diameter in the fork and your fireplace is complete. The crane, however, should be at least one foot longer than the andirons. In this type of fireplace you can build a long fire, giving you varying degrees of heat for different types of cooking. Simultaneously you can bake biscuits, broil meat, boil coffee, stew vegetables, and fry potatoes.

Cooking fires need not be built exactly as I have suggested and the same is true of fireplaces. Your imagination and the materials available at campsites are all that will limit the improvements or innovations you can rig.

Naturally, if you're camping in a state or federal park, you will have to use the fireplaces that are provided in the campsites. If the fireplaces happen to be poor ones, there is little you can do except struggle along the best you can. However, in the case of fireplaces with chimneys—which draw the heat up the chimney where it's wasted—place a flat rock atop the chimney. This will cut off excessive draft and keep the fire in the firebox where it belongs.

Night Fires

A favorite suggestion for a campfire, or all-night fire, is the "log cabin" fire. However, a true log cabin fire, four walls of logs and a center filled with assorted wood, usually burns itself out quickly in the center and leaves the outside wall logs charred, with not enough fuel left to consume them.

A better variation of the log cabin fire is the "altar fire" whereby logs are piled in layers, laid up in alternating directions. This presents an almost solid block of wood and should be built only after a deep bed of glowing coals has accumulated. For drying clothing on a wet day, for warming an open front tent, or for an evening campfire, this is a good type.

I prefer to pile the logs parallel, in pyramid form, over a deep bed of coals and a few smaller sticks of seasoned hardwood. Knots and limb stubs will keep

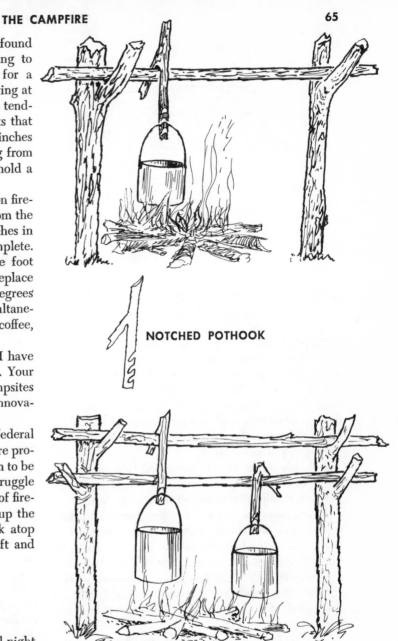

NOTCHED POTHOOK

THE COOKING CRANE

the logs far enough apart for the flames to lick through between them. The wide base makes a stable rig that isn't likely to topple during the night. It will not produce a roaring blaze but, rather, a slow, steady, and long-lasting heat.

Every now and then someone comes up with a "self-feeding" night fire which he guarantees will last all night. This suggestion usually involves inclined vertical logs from which firewood either rolls or slides into the fire. What generally happens is that the entire rig goes up in flames quickly, or else the logs fail to reach the fire and the camper

CUT GREEN WOOD TO BUILD A REFLECTOR

wakes up at two A.M. with the fire out. More frequently, the whole rig tumbles and scatters about the fire area. No woodsman will bother with such a rig.

It's practically impossible to build a night fire that will last until morning unless you build it so big that it will drive you back into the woods during the first half of the night. Instead of this, build the altar or pyramid type fire and plan to awaken sometime during the night to replenish it if necessary. Chances are, if this is your first trip, or if you are cold during the night, you will awaken.

Probably the most misrepresented type of fire is the so-called lazy man's fire which really is anything but! It's usually illustrated with three or four logs radiating from the center of a fire, much like the spokes of a wheel—the theory being that as the center burns, the logs can be shoved in for further burning. The trouble is that logs will not burn in this position unless the fire itself is constantly fed with smaller wood. You'll have to cut and split a great deal of smaller wood to burn three or four 6-inch logs.

Instead of placing the logs spoke fashion, lay them full length and *parallel* in the fire, so that they burn through in the middle. As they burn in two, which they will do with very little additional wood, pull out the unburned ends and place them atop the fire. You can burn 20-foot lengths in this manner, without using an ax or a saw.

For a reflector fire, directions call for two slanting stakes to hold up a wall of logs. Such a reflector depends upon the weight of the logs to hold them in place—and this same weight can send them tumbling down.

To avoid this, cut four stakes instead of two, each 3 to 4 feet long and drive them into the ground vertically—not slanting—so that each pair is just far enough apart to accept the thickness of the base log

beween them. A reflector, 4 feet long and 3 feet high, staked out in this manner will stay up indefinitely.

Green logs, or those which are comparatively uninflammable, make the best reflector logs. Avoid resinous softwoods, especially if seasoned, as these catch fire too easily. Have the reflector 12 to 18 inches from the fire.

Smudge Fires

I've never seen a pleasure camper use a smudge fire to keep insects at bay. It seems to be the professional woodsman's method. A 10- or 12-quart pail is best for a container, in which a small but brisk fire of hardwood should be built. The fire will burn more easily if you punch a few holes around the bottom rim of the pail. When coals start to form, throw on moss, green or wet leaves, green grass, or any material that will not burn easily. This will set up a smoke column. Then set the pail upwind ten to fifteen feet from the center of camp activities. You'll be amazed at how well a thin pall of smoke will keep down such pests as mosquitoes and black flies!

Signal Fires

Chances are you'll never need a signal fire but I've known a number of men to die because they didn't build one. You may need such a fire when someone in camp is seriously ill or injured and cannot be left while you go for help. Should you become hopelessly lost, knowing how to build such a fire could save your life.

The purpose of a smoke signal is not to transmit a

literal message but rather to attract attention and to cause someone to investigate. To a professional woodsman, a heavy column of smoke in the deep woods spells only one word: *TROUBLE.* Writers with more romanticism in their souls than a sense of the practical, often suggest that three smoke signals be sent up. This is ridiculous since forest rangers, game wardens, lumbermen, guides, or timber cruisers will immediately investigate any unusual smoke occurrence, even if it's only one column. When I worked as a forest fire lookout in New Hampshire my orders were to report *every* smoke that I could not definitely account for. Roving patrols would then check them.

Build your smoke signal in the open, if possible, such as in a clearing or on the shore of a lake so that you can easily be seen should a plane be dispatched to investigate. Before lighting the fire, gather a large supply of slow-burning materials, such as hardwood leaves, green bark (not birch!), forest duff, moss, grass, weeds, or ferns. Get the fire to burning briskly so that putting these on will not smother it. When you're ready to start signaling, pile on enough of these materials so that a heavy column of thick smoke rises. Whenever the smoke begins to thin, add more litter so that the smoke will rise in as continuous a column as possible. Remember, too, that smoke thins as it rises into the atmosphere, so keep it heavy and thick.

Once you start signaling, stay with your fire. After all, if you build a smoke signal, rescuers will be of little help if they find your fire abandoned and have to start a search for you. As silly as this may sound, I've known it to happen. Have patience and bear in mind that once your smoke column climbs up over the trees, someone will see it and rescue operations will be set into motion. Needless to say, if the woods are dry, you should take every precaution against starting a forest fire.

Fire Safety

The secret to preventing the escape of a campfire is never to build a larger one than you need and, of course, never leave it untended—not even for a few minutes.

When you clear away pine needles, leaves, twigs, and other natural forest litter from your fireplace area, carry it away some distance. Don't leave it in a circular ridge around the fire, inviting a spark or flame to jump the gap.

Never kindle a fire against a stump unless there is snow on the ground. Even after you have thoroughly extinguished the stump, its roots may continue to burn for a week before coming back above ground to burst into flame. If a strong wind is blowing, and the forests are relatively dry, try to get along without a fire. If you must have one, keep it well confined within a fireplace of rock or dirt and don't use woods that throw sparks. Keep one or two pails of water near your fire at all times. The world's worst fire could have been stopped with one pail of water when it started! When you have finished with your fire, put it out *completely.* This extinguishing process needs to be more thorough than you might think. A pail of water on a campfire *will not put it out!* Pour water on the fire until the ashes begin to float. Stir these with a stick, particularly around the edges of the fire, searching for glowing coals that may remain. Turn any unburned sticks or logs over, pouring water on them as you do. Sometimes the underside of these may still be glowing red, although the upper side may be sopping wet. Keep pouring water until the ashes are cool to the touch. You'll get your fingers black with soot but that's so much better than having a conscience black with remorse!

Before going into any forest area for any length of time, check with local forestry officials regarding the necessity for permits, and regulations which may be in force.

The danger to campers from woods fires is very small—in most camping regions, nonexistent, as long as you keep in mind the simple rules that will prevent such fires. The oft-repeated adage "Only You Can Prevent Forest Fires" is more truth than poetry!

Matches

To start your campfire, the "old-fashioned" wooden kitchen match is best. You can strike it almost anywhere—on a dry rock, axhead, tea pail, or even the seat of your britches. What's more, it can be waterproofed.

To do this, dip the match heads into shellac that has been thinned slightly with denatured alcohol, or into clear lacquer or melted paraffin. Such matches will burn even when wet.

These can be treated in package lots too. Pour melted paraffin over the matches without removing them from the box, until the sides of the latter begin to bulge a little, then squeeze it back to its normal shape and slip the cover back on. Any excess wax can be trimmed off after it hardens and individual matches can be pried out easily.

The second-best choice is the so-called "safety match," packaged in the "penny box." Apart from their smaller size and weaker flame, these have a distinct disadvantage in that they cannot be struck anywhere but on the box. Should this get wet, the matches are useless.

However, these, too, can be waterproofed. Wrap the box in aluminum foil to protect the striking surface, then wrap it a second time in common light-weight wrapping paper. Tie a string around the box and dip it in melted paraffin. Remember, though, that when the box is opened, the matches are as vulnerable as ever.

Paper matches should be carried in some quantity and these should be distributed among as many packs and packages as possible. Use them for such things as lighting cigarettes (pipe smokers don't usually like them!), lanterns, and even the camp-fire when conditions are good. Save the water-proofed matches for a wet day when you need a husky flame to get a fire started.

Each adult in a camping party should carry a waterproof match safe. Be sure that it's full when you start and keep this supply sacred unto the day when a true emergency arises. Only a fool lights a cigarette or pipe with matches from his match safe!

Glossary of Firewoods

In an organized campground or supervised area, chances are, firewood will be supplied and you will have little choice regarding what you will use for firewood. However, in wilderness areas, you will have to scramble for your own wood and, naturally, you won't always find the best of firewoods at all campsites. It is well then to learn which make good substitutes.

I'm describing the following trees only with regard to their burning qualities—or lack of them—and the ease or difficulty with which they can be cut. If you learn to recognize a dozen or so trees, fire building problems will be pretty much solved for you. Since you can hardly do without this knowledge, take along a tree guide on your camping trips until you learn to recognize most of the trees. It's an interesting hobby in itself that will pay dividends at the campfire.

Alder: I have as yet to hear anyone say anything good about the alder but it burns so hot that it will curl a stove lid! It is practically smokeless and burns to a clean white ash. However, it is inclined to spit sparks and is noisy. It will not leave a bed of coals. Suitable primarily for a quick, hot fire.

Ash: The white ash is one of the finest firewoods for the camper. It burns readily, green or seasoned, it's comparatively light, cuts and splits easily, and burns with a clear, clean flame giving off little smoke. The heartwood is relatively dry even in a growing tree.

Basswood: Also known as linden, it is very soft wood that cuts and splits easily, burns poorly when green. Suitable for backlogs or andirons. When seasoned it burns itself out quickly but is suitable for kindling.

Beech: The American beech is a delight to split when it is green, but difficult when seasoned. The heartwood is naturally quite dry so that the wood burns well, dry or seasoned. It throws sparks when it first starts to burn, then simmers down to quiet burning, forming a good bed of coals.

Birch: Except for its tendency to smoke pots and pans badly, white birch is an excellent camper's wood. Moderately easy to chop and very easy to split when green, it produces fairly long-lasting coals. Seasoned birch is somewhat harder to split but it smokes less.

Yellow birch is a very hard and heavy wood, difficult for amateurs to chop and not easy to split, even when green. When seasoned it is very tough and resists splitting. However, it's an excellent camp fuel; among the best, in fact. Green or seasoned it throws great heat and builds long-lasting coals.

Black Haw: Also called stag bush, the black haw produces one of our hardest woods and is not easily "manufactured" with an ax. Green, it burns only with coaxing. Seasoned, it is fine cooking firewood, burning hot and leaving a fair bed of coals.

Box Elder: Difficult to burn when green, the box elder is hard to chop and split, green or seasoned. When dry it burns rapidly and spits sparks in all directions.

Buckeye: Green, this is practically fireproof and therefore makes good backlogs. Very hard to split.

Butternut: The nuts are delicious and practically the tree's only contribution to the camper. The wood is very hard and difficult to burn when green. When seasoned, it burns well with considerable heat, but leaves few coals.

Catalpa: Can be burned green but quickly consumes itself. Seasoned, it burns very fast.

Cedar: Northern white cedar is the woodsman's delight. It's a most efficient tinder wood, although it will shoot sparks. The wood is soft, light, and usually fairly straight grained and requires only a tap of the ax to split it. A dry cedar stump is easy to find in the Northland.

Cherry: Black cherry requires much coaxing to make it burn green and it's hard to split. When seasoned it burns with great heat and leaves a fair bed of short-lived coals.

Chestnut: Burns very slowly when green but produces a quick hot fire when seasoned. It showers sparks, leaving no coals. It chops and splits easily.

Cottonwood: The wood is soft and light, burns slowly when green, with much sizzling and hissing. Frequently it is the only firewood available and, fortunately, when seasoned, it burns quite hot with little smoke, leaving almost no coals.

Cypress: A tree of the Southern swamps, usually growing directly out of the water. Except for backlogs or andirons, the wood has little value when green. Seasoned, it burns hot and quickly, leaving no coals.

Elm: The only elm of any value to the camper as firewood is the slippery elm and even this is only mediocre. It splits easily and is difficult to burn green. Seasoned, it burns only fairly well. All of the other elms come close to being fireproof.

Fir: The balsam fir can be a headache or a lifesaver. Green, it is difficult to burn. Seasoned, it burns rapidly and will shoot sparks in all directions. However, the fir is the most common blowdown in the Northern woods and offers easy kindling, even in wet weather.

Hemlock: Except for its bark, which will produce a good bed of coals, it burns very badly when green, is noisy and shoots sparks when dry. Hemlock knots, unlike those of pine and spruce, are practically fireproof. Also they're hard enough to chip an ax blade.

Hickory: Of all the woods used by campers, hickory is the best. There are eight or nine subspecies, most of which will burn readily, green or dry, and will produce a clean flame and an excellent bed of long-lasting coals. Heartwood is usually quite dry. Hickory splits quite well when green. Chopping it, dry or green, is tough and a saw is advisable.

Holly: American holly is excellent firewood, rating almost with hickory. It splits easily when green and burns well then. Seasoned, it burns hotly, produces good coals, but is hard to split.

Ironwood: Also called hop hornbeam, this is one of the best fuels, green or dry. It burns slowly when green but creates much heat and, when seasoned, makes a hot fire which lasts well and produces a good bed of coals. It is hard on axes and choppers! A saw is advisable.

Locust: This is one of our hardest woods. Despite this, however, it can be split easily when green. Seasoned or green, it burns with a hot blue flame, not unlike that of coal. Even the bark, quite thick on mature trees, is a good fuel. Coals are long lasting.

Maple: The sugar maple, also called rock or hard maple, is the Northern woodsman's pet wood, since it burns easily, throws a hot clean flame, builds up long-lasting coals, and splits easily when green. Even if well seasoned, it can be split with some ease if you avoid forks, knurls, and butt sections.

The red, swamp, or soft maple is the poorest of them all. Being a wetland or lowland tree, it is not easily ignited when green. When seasoned it burns quite rapidly.

Mesquite: A desert species, not large, but important to campers in the Southwest because it can be used for tinder as well as firewood. It's often the only fuel in sight!

Mulberry: The red, white, and paper mulberry are all excellent firewoods, having much the same characteristics as the locust.

Oak: Among the better oaks, as far as the camper is concerned, are the white, chestnut, overcup, post, barren, and pin oaks. These are difficult to "manufacture" whether they are green or dry. However, they burn well when green and create excellent coals. When seasoned, they burn with more rapidity. Most of the other oaks are practically fireproof.

Osage Orange: Has a naturally dry heartwood and burns well when green. It does not burn too rapidly when seasoned and leaves good coals. This is one of our hardest woods and is difficult to manufacture.

Persimmon: A very hard wood which burns poorly when green. When seasoned it is an excellent wood, burning hotly and producing a bed of fairly long-lasting coals. Difficult to chop, and splits with little ease only when green. A saw is recommended.

Pine: To most city dwellers all evergreens are "pine trees." There are, however, many varieties of pines, and their burning characteristics vary.

The white pine, also called soft pine, is a poor fuel wood. A round log, it is practically fireproof, smoldering and charring but never burning wholeheartedly. Even when split, it burns badly when green. However, when seasoned it burns with great

gusto and pops sparks all over a forty-acre lot! It is good kindling.

Red or Norway pine heartwood is relatively dry and this pine burns better than white pine when green. Seasoned it makes a quick, hot fire. It's not difficult to chop or split. It, too, tosses sparks.

Pitch pine, also called candlewood or torch pine because of pitch pockets is highly inflammable. It chops and splits easily, but also throws sparks helter-skelter.

The gray pine or famous jack pine of the North burns when green if split, and is consumed quite rapidly when seasoned. Easy to chop and split.

The short leaf and the long leaf pine are resinous species and burn well when green. When seasoned, they burn themselves out quickly, throwing numerous sparks. Dry stumps are excellent kindling. Jersey pine has much the same characteristics.

Poplar: This is the woodsman's "popple" and includes the big-toothed aspen and the trembling or quaking aspen. Green or seasoned, it's very easy to chop—a half dozen strokes of an ax will drop a five- or six-inch tree. It's light and splits with a mere tap of the ax.

Seasoned poplar burns well with a clean, almost smokeless flame that deposits little if any soot on utensils. It's a favorite in the North where hardwoods are scarce. If you're camping in beaver country, keep an eye open for beaver cuttings. These animals prefer poplar to all other species and cut down a great deal more than they use. Usually, where there are beaver, you'll find seasoned poplar.

Green poplar, however, is something else. There are those who claim it's a suitable firewood, even though it sizzles and hisses while burning—stewing is a better word for it—and I think it smells like garbage burning.

Spruce: Red spruce burns poorly when green until the fire starts to dry it out. Then it "takes off" in a roaring blaze that will drive you out of house and home. Seasoned, it's excellent kindling, although it throws sparks. Very easy to chop and split, green or seasoned.

White spruce is not a friendly tree. Known also as pasture, swamp, skunk and cat spruce, it is some-times cut for Christmas trees by newcomers to wilderness areas. Brought indoors, it soon smells as if someone had left the privy door open on a warm day! However, it's good kindling when dry and has much the same characteristics as the red variety.

Black spruce, also called bog spruce, has a liking for sphagnum bogs and is the tree found on northern Minnesota's "floating bogs." It is much like the red or white spruce except that it is an even poorer fuel when green. When dry it burns very rapidly.

Sweet Gum: Has a variety of local names the most popular of which is Liquidambar. Generally poor fuel and very hard to split. Burns quite long when seasoned.

Tamarack: Often taken for an evergreen which it is not. It is easy to "manufacture," either green or seasoned. Its bark, however, is nearly fireproof. The wood when green burns badly but when seasoned, burns too rapidly. Fair kindling when dry. Also called hackmatack, larch or "hack."

Tulip: This is another spark thrower that is nearly fireproof when green. When seasoned it burns quickly and leaves no coals. It is fairly easy to chop and split.

Tupelo: When green this is practically indestructible by fire, and splitting it is nearly impossible. A poor camper's wood.

Walnut: The value of its nuts far exceeds its value as firewood, hence it's best to leave this tree alone unless, of course, you find a dead tree. It will supply you with a fairly slow-burning wood which will leave coals. Rather hard to split or chop.

Willow: A common streamside tree, it is practically useless except for backlogs or andirons.

Dry-Ki: Don't look for this one in the tree manuals. It's nothing more than driftwood found on Northern lakes where dams have been built to raise the water level. This, in turn, killed off much growth which eventually fell and floated in the lakes for years. High winds drive it up onto shore where it dries out. For an evening campfire it is ideal and is best used in a lazy man's fire since it is usually tough to chop. Made up of mixed hard- and softwood species.

Chapter 6

AXES, SAWS, AND KNIVES

Axes

Someone once said that a Maine Guide can go into the woods with only his ax and come out driving a team and a pair of horses. Few guides will admit to such skill but they are pretty well agreed that the ax makes possible hot meals, shelter, warmth and, in an emergency, even food. It will mark a trail or clean up a blowdown from a portage. It will, in fact, not only make life in the woods possible, but pleasant.

The ax having the greatest appeal to campers is probably the little Hudson Bay ax with its 2-pound head, narrow poll, flaring blade and 26-inch handle. It's a suitable ax for light work, such as splitting slabs often supplied as firewood at public campgrounds. Unfortunately the usefulness of the Hudson Bay ax has been overstressed, along with that of various hatchets, belt axes, tomahawks, and even the double-bitted hatchet, probably the worst camp tool ever devised. As is usually pointed out, these small axes are handy to carry. I'll concede that point—but whatever energy is saved in toting them must be redoubled at the woodpile. All of those, including the Hudson Bay ax, are too light for efficient chopping or splitting.

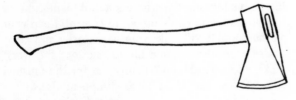

THE HUDSON BAY AX

Watch a professional woodsman chopping and you'll understand why. With a full-sized ax, weighing at least three pounds and having a 28- to 30-inch handle, he uses a slow, rhythmic swing that lets the falling axhead do the job. He doesn't lean into each stroke with a grunt. With this easygoing swing,

he can wade through a 10-inch log with hardly a pause while the average amateur, swinging a miniature ax, uses a "grunt and groan" technique that tires him within a minute or two.

The use of a hatchet is justified only by the hiker whose weight limitations are stringent. With the hatchet, he can cut light wood for cooking and with the output of considerable effort, he can chew through 6-inch logs for night wood. Incidentally, if you're planning a hiking trip, don't carry the ax on your belt. There is nothing more tiring than an unbalanced weight pulling at one side of your body. Instead, place the hatchet in your pack or strap it on the outside.

On a canoe trip, the saving in weight effected by a hatchet, or even the Hudson Bay ax, is not justified. Guides and other professional woodsmen, are likely to eliminate some small item of luxury to make room for a full-sized ax. All in all, this matter of traveling light has been grossly overstressed and, unless you can arrange for a pet beaver to meet you at every campsite to help with the firewood chores, it's better to carry a man-sized ax.

As for the double-bitted hatchet, I can think of nothing good to say about it. Like the single-bit hatchet, it is too light and too short, and presents the additional danger of an extra blade whizzing by your head within shaving distance. It's best to leave it strictly alone!

From a safety standpoint, the short-handled ax is a treacherous tool. Miss your mark with one of these and the possibility of driving the blade into your knee, calf, ankle, or foot is excellent. If you miss with a full-length ax, nine out of ten times, the blade will be driven into the earth. This is because the arc of your swing is much wider with a long handle.

Whether you plan to carry it in a car, truck, trailer, boat, or canoe, the best all-round camper's ax is the three-pound poleax with a 28- to 30-inch handle of second growth hickory. A handle of this length will lend the axhead great momentum with little effort on your part, and will allow you to stand away from your target.

Second-growth hickory, tough yet supple, will absorb tremendous shocks and makes the finest of ax handles. Maple and oak are satisfactory. If the wood in the handle is slightly discolored, it does no harm, but avoid handles, even hickory ones, having sharply contrasting layers of wood. Such handles are inclined to split easily.

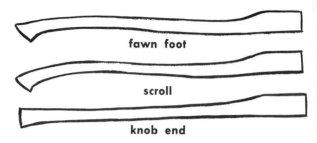

A THREE-POUND POLEAX

The "hang" of an ax is important to easy chopping and to test this when buying one, stand the ax on its bit, with the hand grip of the handle touching the counter, so that you can see the ax in profile. The bit should rest on the counter at a point slightly forward of the center of the blade.

An ax that has a warped handle will be dangerous and difficult to use. A good way to check this is to hold the blade upside down with the handle pointing away from you. Sight down the cutting edge toward the end of the handle, and if the handle is not warped, your line of sight will bisect the full length of the handle. While you're examining the handle, make sure that the grain of the wood is as near vertical as possible. Such a handle is less likely to break.

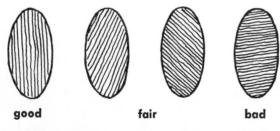

good   fair   bad

A HANDLE WITH A VERTICAL GRAIN IS LESS LIKELY TO BREAK

Of importance, too, is the shape of the handle. Most "store-bought" ax handles are of the so-called "fawn-foot" or "scroll" type, having hand grips that curve downward sharply. These are wrist breakers, even when held loosely, as woodsmen hold them. Instead, look for a moderately straight handle with

a knoblike end. These are much more comfortable to use.

Some weird notions have been advanced by those who obviously couldn't keep warm with an ax at a Fourth of July picnic. The application of lacquer to an ax handle "to protect it" is a frequent suggestion—or painting the handle with one inch alternating black and white stripes "to find it at night." Soaking a loose axhead in water overnight will tighten it, according to another expert. The weirdest advice of all, though, is the suggestion that an ax handle be buried in horse manure for sixty days to make it springy!

Painting an ax handle, or applying varnish or lacquer, is going to result in a bumper crop of blisters. If you want to protect the handle, rub it with warm boiled linseed oil. Soaking a loose ax handle in a pail of water will tighten it, by causing the wood to swell, but when it dries out it will be looser than ever and of course all the more dangerous. Instead, insert a small wooden wedge into the handle, in addition to the one already there. If the original wedge tends to work out even slightly, remove it and replace it with a larger one. This is the only safe way to tighten an ax handle. As for making your ax handle springy by burying it in horse manure, this is sheer nonsense. Hickory is naturally tough and springy enough for an ax handle.

A sharp ax is much safer than a dull one, as it will bite into a log smartly, whereas a dull blade is likely to glance off and go flying out of control. Keep your ax sharp and it will make your work easier and safer.

Use a grindstone or a file to take out the worst nicks, and a double-grit handstone for the finished edge. When the nicks have disappeared use the coarse side of the stone for further honing, and finish the job with the fine-grit side, always keeping the stone moist. Lumberjacks spit on theirs! Never use a motor-powered stone for grinding an ax as you may burn out the temper or give the bit a "rolled edge."

Once your ax is sharp, and you have picked a tree to fall, be sure that all brush and low-hanging branches are out of reach of the full swing of your ax. At least two books on camping suggest that, preliminary to cutting down a tree, the chopper swing his ax at arms' length in a circle over his head and about his feet. Any lumberjack seen doing this in a professional chopping would be pulled off the job by the "walkin' boss." Don't test the "swing zone" by this method. If there is any doubt about a limb or brush being in the way, trim it off.

To start with, pick a tree no larger than six to eight inches in diameter, preferably a softwood. There is little likelihood that you will ever have to cut a bigger tree than this while camping. Before lifting your ax, look the tree over to see which way it leans and plan to drop it in that direction. Dropping a tree "uphill" is fancy chopping for an expert. While you are examining the tree for lean, check it carefully for a "turkey."

"Turkey" is a logger's name for a dead limb, which may be hanging by a shred of wood, or balanced precariously in other branches. Striking the tree with an ax may be just enough to cause the "turkey" to fall on you. Find another tree.

Very few trees grow perfectly straight up, and nearly always a tree is a little heavier on one side than on the other. When you have decided where to fall it, be sure that it won't drop on your tent! Be sure, too, that when it drops, there is no chance that it will lodge in another tree. "Hung" trees are dangerous.

If all seems favorable, stand to one side, about an ax handle's length away, feet well apart for good balance, and start chopping on the side you intend for the tree to fall, notching slightly above the flare of the stump for easier chopping.

Beginners always make too narrow a notch so that, by the time the ax has penetrated three or four inches into the trunk, they are having to chop horizontally across the grain—tough chopping in any kind of wood. Make your notch wide enough so that the blade can be driven in at an angle of 30 to 45 degrees. Swing your ax smoothly and rhythmically, so that the weight of the axhead does the hard work without your having to bear down.

A popular fallacy is that expert axmen hit "the same spot every time." Nothing could be farther from fact. A woodsman strives to make the biggest chips possible, for this makes for less chopping. To achieve this, his blows will be inches apart, but carefully directed and gauged to take big bites.

When falling a small tree with an ax, the notch should go slightly more than halfway through the trunk. When you have reached this stage, rest for a few minutes. Then, on the opposite side, start another notch, this one slightly higher than the first— at least one inch higher. As this second notch deepens, watch closely the reaction of the trunk for the first signs of falling. You will hear wood fibers creak and this may be accompanied by crackling, as the remaining fibers start to break. Once the tree starts to fall, don't try to give it a final whack with the ax to help it along—and only a greenhorn, anxious to be maimed, will push it to hurry its fall.

Instead, step away from the tree, not hurrying, not lingering. Walk to one side, uphill if on a slope. This is the safest spot. Get as far away as possible before the tree hits the ground—but never run. You might fall and not be able to dodge, should the tree roll your way. Never, under any circumstances, go to the rear of the falling trunk. Keep away from the butt, as this has been known to "slab," or split at the stump, and kick back viciously. Sometimes, too,

not good

good

direction of fall

CUT A WIDE NOTCH WHEN FELLING A TREE. CUT THE SECOND NOTCH ABOVE THE FIRST AND OPPOSITE THE DIRECTION THE TREE IS TO FALL.

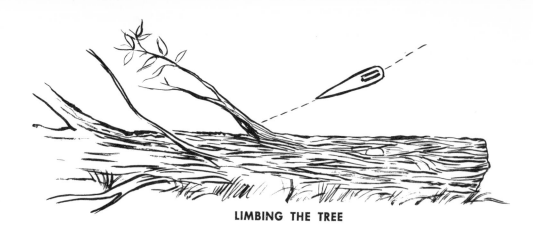

LIMBING THE TREE

THE SCHOOLMA'AM

not here   here

SPLITTING A BLOCK

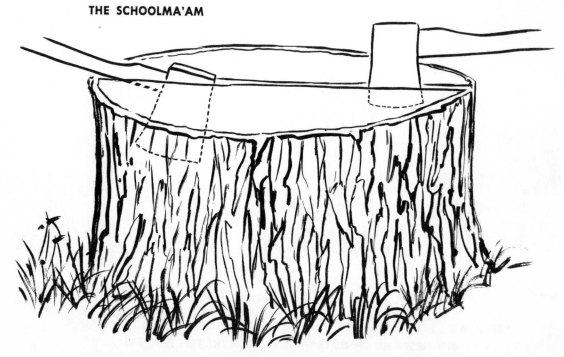

USE ONE AX AS A WEDGE ON A PARTICULARLY TOUGH BLOCK

when the springy limbs hit the ground, the butt is driven back across the stump with the speed and power of a cannon ball.

Once your tree is down, look it over to see that it will not roll. If it appears to be well anchored, start limbing the lower branches, striking them on the underside and cutting them flush with the trunk. Limbs trimmed off flush are a sign of good axmanship and the log will be much easier to handle. Stand on the opposite side of the trunk from the limbs being cut. As these drop off, take the time to cast them aside out of the way.

Unless you can call your shots accurately, don't risk nicking your ax on stones by cutting the log into lengths while it lies directly on the ground. It's better to roll it up onto another log and rest it in a shallow notch to keep it from rolling. This will not only be easier on you and the ax, but much safer. Be sure that the "cow's mouth," or notch, is plenty wide for easy chopping.

One of the disadvantages of cutting a log into short lengths with an ax is that these will not stand on end, on a chopping block, for splitting. However, there is a way around this problem. Lay the length to be split in the crotch of a "schoolma'am"—the woodsman's term for a forked log. If you can't find a schoolma'am easily, use a notched log. Splitting wood directly on the ground may result in your ax "finding" a stone under the log. One of the most dangerous practices is to lean a stick against a log and use one foot to hold it in place while swinging the ax at it. This often results in the nickname "Peg Leg."

When the blocks to be split have been sawed rather than chopped, stand them on end on a flat-topped stump, for splitting. The butt section of a log always makes a good chopping block since it's harder to split. Don't aim directly at the center of the block, unless it's a small one. Instead, aim the ax blade to strike near the edge of the block, with the toe or front corner pointing at the center of the heartwood. Almost all species split more easily this way.

Naturally you won't want to use all of the butt sections for chopping blocks. If they prove particularly tough to split, use two axes. Drive one ax into the block as directed above. This will likely start the cleft. If not, pull out the ax and strike again. Now have your partner swing his ax from the other side. The split made by his ax will loosen yours, and vice versa, so that you can keep alternating until the block gives. Lacking two axes, a splitting wedge, possibly made of hardwood, can be used by driving it into the first cleft and then driving the ax blade

into the block, close to the wedge. This may seem like a lot of work for a few sticks of wood. Naturally, if there is easier fuel available, by all means use it. However, I've seen the day—and the night—when a stubborn old butt log, found near a campsite, was a joyous discovery!

For long-lasting night wood, or a cold-weather fire, a forked log or hardwood "schoolma'am," is near-perfect fuel. However, such a log is usually too large to put on a fire whole and unless split would only smolder. To "manufacture" one, first saw off the legs about 18 inches long and squared so that the forked log will stand on a chopping block. Now, split off half of each leg, just as if they were individual logs. Next, split the fork at a 90-degree angle from the first line of splitting. You'll be surprised at how easily most forked logs will split when hit in this direction. At most, two or three blows will do it. You will now have two Y logs, each half the thickness of the original "schoolma'am." At this stage, a single blow into the crotch of each half will rend these in two so that, instead of one cumbersome forked log, you now have six pieces of long-lasting firewood.

In line with using a chopping block, some fairly good-sized poles of hard- or softwood—up to three inches in diameter—can be cut with a single blow of the ax. Lay such a stick flat on the block and hold it in position with one hand. Take a short grip on the ax handle, about halfway, and strike the pole at about a 45-degree angle to the grain. Green poles especially are easily cut in this manner. If you try to chop straight through the grain at right angles, your ax will merely bounce!

In cutting down such poles for stakes, cranes, or shears, a good "swamper" will bend the sapling, with one hand enough to create tension in the wood fibers. A single blow of the ax, a few inches above the ground, will sever such a sapling easily.

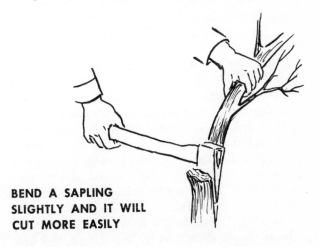

BEND A SAPLING SLIGHTLY AND IT WILL CUT MORE EASILY

When cutting tent stakes, fireplace forks, or gin poles, always sharpen them on a log or stump to keep your ax blade out of the dirt. Incidentally, such stakes or poles don't require spear-sharp points. Slightly blunted ends will drive more easily, even in hard-packed earth.

When there are two axes in camp, the temptation to use one for a hammer and the other for a wedge is great. This usually results in having no ax at all. The finest ax in the world won't stand up under such treatment, since the eye will invariably collapse after a few blows. Even if you are lucky, you will at least turn the edge of the poll, which is not only unsightly—the sign of a greenhorn in the choppings—but dangerous to use.

When your ax is not in use, keep the sheath on it for protection of the edge and for prevention of accidents. If you don't want to bother with the sheath while in camp, drive the ax into a log or stump with the handle high, so that everyone can see it. Don't lean it against a tree or stump, or someone may walk into the bit!

Even experienced woodsmen break ax handles. If you are not traveling light, a spare is a good idea. Lacking this, you can whittle a substitute from maple or oak saplings, using the old one for a pattern. Other hardwoods will do well for a temporary handle, but softwoods are not worth the trouble.

Removal of the stub left in the eye may present a problem if it is wedged tightly. One method is to bury the axhead in the ground so that only the eye and poll are showing. Build a small fire over the ax and let it burn until the handle is well charred. It is not necessary to burn the stub out completely, since the eye will expand from the heat and the wood will contract as it chars. It will then practically fall out. Burying the blade keeps the fire from drawing the temper. However, don't build too large a fire, or too hot a blaze, as the metal will transmit too much heat to the blade and possibly ruin the temper. Also, be sure the axhead is cool before you pick it up!

Clean the eye of wood fragments and insert the new handle. With a wooden billet, strike the knob of the hand grip a few blows. Some suggest that you cut off an inch or so from the "fawn foot," to give you a striking surface and to prevent the handle from splitting. This is not necessary if you use a wooden billet. You may roll or peel the edge of the knob slightly, but this is easily remedied afterward with a knife. Don't ruin an ax handle by cutting off part of the hand grip.

Striking the handle will drive it into the eye of the ax until it starts to bind. Notice, then, that tiny shavings are beginning to curl from the wood at those points in the edge of the eye where binding had started. Remove the handle and run a rasp, or a knife, over these curls, being sure to take off only the high spots. Try the handle again, until curls appear, then use the rasp or knife again. Repeat this until the handle fits snugly throughout the eye's length.

Sight along the edge of the blade to be sure the handle is properly aligned laterally. Also, stand the ax on a flat surface to see if the bit and the hand grip touch in correct relation to each other, as explained earlier. If this is not correct, use the rasp again until the handle fits perfectly. Cut off that part which protrudes from the front of the eye, cutting it flush with the axhead's surface. Insert a hardwood wedge into the vertical slot in the handle and drive it in as far as it will go. Cut the wedge off flush also and the job is done. Don't use green wood for a wedge, as it will shrink in drying and allow the handle to become loose. Hardwood wedges, as a rule, will hold better than metal ones.

THIS OUTDOORSMAN DEMONSTRATES THE PROPER STANCE FOR CUTTING WITH AN AX. NOTE THAT THE FEET ARE WELL AWAY FROM THE LOG BEING CUT

Gene Hornbeck

The Camp Saw

A saw will cut two to three times more wood in a given period of time than will an ax, and with much less effort on the part of the user. The bucksaw is the camper's best wood "manufacturer." Using one to cut logs into short lengths, and an ax to split these will make the daily chore a short one. In fact, you'll probably enjoy the work enough so that you'll cut more wood than you need with this combination.

Probably the best-known bucksaw is the old-fashioned three-piece wooden frame model with which many a farm boy of a generation or two back had more than a speaking acquaintance. There are still a few of these around. It usually has a plain V tooth blade, fairly wide and heavy—not easily broken. The entire rig weighed less than three pounds and could cut logs up to 14 inches in diameter. Supposedly more modern versions, designed for campers, have not been able to improve on this model—in fact, most present-day wooden frame bucksaws are decidedly inferior. Knocked down, the three-piece model described makes a bundle about 3" by 28" or 30", including the metal turnbuckle which holds the unit together and pulls the blade tight.

It has become increasingly difficult to find one of these and your chances are probably best in a small-town hardware store, or possibly at a country auction. The frame is made of hardwood, easily repaired or even replaced in the wilderness. Even the turnbuckle can be replaced in an emergency by tying a sturdy piece of light rope into a loop that will fit over the upper end of the frame ends. A short piece of wood, inserted into the loop, is then turned to twist the loop until proper tension is applied against the blade. Locking it so that it will not untwist is done by slipping the stick downward until it is brought up against the crossbar.

The blade is held in place by a pin at each end, often a simple iron rivet. Since these are the only parts of this saw frame which cannot be replaced easily during a camping trip, I carry them in a small cloth bag, tied to the turnbuckle. A few extra pins are good insurance.

Most of the present crop of camp bucksaws, including both the metal bow frames and the collapsible wooden models, are knuckle breakers. Two of the wooden models could be made into quite good saw frames with the addition of a slightly longer end piece to serve as a handle.

As they are, you must grasp the frame with one hand immediately above the blade and, in drawing the saw back and forth, you're bound to drive your

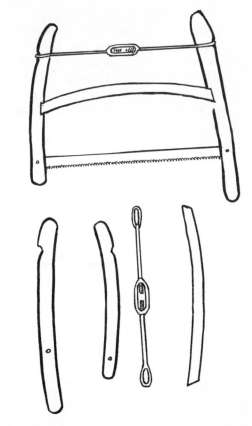

THE THREE-PIECE BUCK SAW

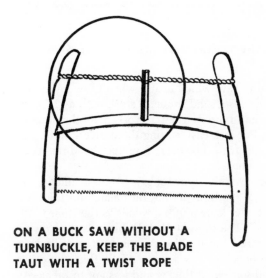

ON A BUCK SAW WITHOUT A TURNBUCKLE, KEEP THE BLADE TAUT WITH A TWIST ROPE

exposed knuckles into rough bark. If there is anything more miserable in camp than a set of raw, bleeding knuckles, it can only be a broken leg!

The basic design of most of the steel bow saws, or "Swede fiddles," is good, except that nearly all camping models lack a handle. If you wear a pair of heavy gloves when sawing, this may spare your knuckles. One type of bow saw can never be a good camp tool since one end of the frame is pitched so that it prevents a full stroke of the blade.

Metal saw frames which do not have a lower handle can be improved by the addition of one—a simple job. Whittle a piece of hardwood about six inches long, so that it is oval-shaped, and drive it into the open end of the steel saw frame. This wooden "handle" will allow you a comfortable grasp of the frame, *below the saw,* and slightly away from it, out of reach of the abrasive action of rough bark.

One of the best steel saw frame rigs is a collapsible model, held together by means of a steel sleeve which joins the two-piece frame. This type has one end of the steel frame extended below the level of the blade for a handle. This type is much easier to carry as, frankly, a full-sized steel saw frame of the solid type is difficult to pack, unless you are traveling in a truck or towing a trailer.

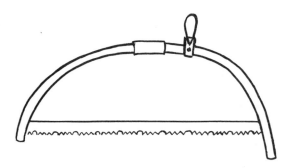

THE COLLAPSIBLE STEEL FRAME SAW

My own saw, which I carry when I tow my camping trailer, is a solid frame of steel, with a 42" pulp blade that I used when I worked in the lumber woods. For fast, easy cutting there isn't a better rig. On canoe trips, however, I prefer the three-piece wooden bucksaw.

There are three types of saw blades available, the straight V tooth blade, the Bushman, and the pulp blade, better known in the woods as the "four tooth 'n' raker." The straight V tooth blade is the slowest of the three, but it's also the toughest and the best for the beginner. It's a wider blade than the other two and somewhat thicker and less apt to break. As far as speed is concerned, it's fast enough to outdistance an ax easily.

The Bushman is a fast-cutting blade, somewhat narrower and thinner than the straight V tooth blade. Its teeth are characterized by a curving sweep of the points. It does not have the raker tooth found in the pulp blade. The raker tooth, found between every four cutting teeth, rakes the sawdust from the

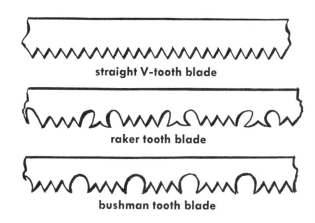

straight V-tooth blade

raker tooth blade

bushman tooth blade

saw kerf. This and the Bushman are fast blades which literally spit sawdust. It is narrow and thin and somewhat more easily broken. There is also available a Swedish import saw blade that has two teeth to each raker, but this is basically the same saw as the pulp blade.

Saw blades, to cut effectively, must be filed and "set." If you buy a simple V tooth blade, it will probably be set and filed for average work in soft- or hardwood and will be suitable for camp use. The Bushman and the pulp blade may be purchased filed and set or "flat," that is, not filed and not set, for the sawyer who prefers to do this himself.

The camper, however, need not be so fussy. Buy the blade that is set and filed for average work and it will do more than a suitable job. Such a blade will cut well for an entire camping season, and in the fall before storing, take it to a professional saw filer who will "touch it up" and set it for you. Filing and setting is a tedious job requiring great skill and is best done by a professional.

A recent development is a saw blade, available in all four patterns mentioned, which has hardened tips said to last three times longer than other blade tips.

The secret to using a bucksaw easily and efficiently is not to bear down on it while sawing. A natural inclination is to apply a downward pressure as the blade is drawn back and forth. Pressure, however, results only in the saw "running" or curving away from the original line of cut. This causes the saw to bind and eventually to stick so that it can't be moved without wedging.

In sawing, use easy, smooth strokes, pulling the saw back and forth the entire length of the blade without downward pressure. Let the weight of the saw ride the kerf and you will be amazed at the ease and speed with which you can manufacture a night's supply of wood.

For a semipermanent camp, make yourself a saw-horse. A woodsman makes this by cutting four stakes about three feet long, and some four inches in diameter. Sharpen one end of each of these and drive them into the ground at an angle so that they lean over a log, 10 to 12 inches in diameter. Drive two at each end of a log on opposite sides, so that each pair is no more than two feet apart. If they are driven into the ground solidly enough, this is all the support they will need. However, if the soil is loose or you plan to cut extra-large logs, bind each pair of stakes where they cross each other with wire or light rope. Driving a spike through each into the base log will also make the sawhorse more stable.

IMPROVISING A SAWHORSE

French-Canadian woodsmen in the Quebec woods carry a pulp blade wound around the waist and tied together to keep it from springing open. This is poor practice for obvious reasons. Instead, cut a ¼-inch deep slot or groove lengthwise in a one-inch piece of board the length of the saw blade and tie this in place with the teeth of the saw within the slot.

Camp Knives

The wise choice of a camp knife should be governed by two rules: (1) buy the best knife you can afford from a reputable dealer and, (2) buy the smallest knife you can get along with.

Unless you understand steel and what is expected of it you are better off to depend upon a well-known brand that is guaranteed, or upon a friendly dealer who will "do right" by you. This is particularly true regarding imports as well as domestic knives. Many war-surplus daggers and infighting knives brought from Europe are on the market, sold amid romantic hokum and exotic advertising appeal. The quality

of many of these is very doubtful, even if they are imported, and it's well to remember that these war-time products were made for fighting, not for slicing bacon or dressing a trout.

As to size, most new campers buy a knife that is much too big, under the impression that the more the knife looks like a bayonet hanging at the belt the more "outdoorsy" it looks. Among woodsmen a man is often judged by the size of his knife and the bigger it is the lower he rates. This doesn't mean that you should buy a tiny penknife however.

My favorite knife is a sheath model having a blade exactly 3 inches long and only ⅜ of an inch wide at the hilt. The finger grip is only 2¾ inches long which means I can wrap only three fingers around it. Over-all the knife is only 6¼ inches. However, with this I have dressed all kinds of fresh-water fish, deer, bear, and I have whittled everything from prayer sticks to pot hangers with it. The only time it failed me was when I tried to help dress a buffalo shot on a Western hunt. For this the knife was inadequate, but neither one of us is likely to have to dress many buffalo!

I use this same knife for cooking in camp—peeling potatoes and onions, slicing bacon, trimming meat, and even cutting cake. What more can be expected of a camp knife?

For general camp use, however, a knife blade up to 4½ to 5 inches is quite suitable, but don't buy one any longer than this for a personal knife. You'll find a longer one awkward to handle and dangerous to carry, even in a sheath.

Whether you buy a sheath, pocket, or combination knife is pretty much a matter of choice. I prefer the small sheath knife I've just described because it's handier to get at and I can have it out and at work in a moment. A pocket knife, however, has some advantages. The blade is always well protected when not in use and, if you tie it to a belt loop as you should, you are not likely to lose it.

The combination knife may or may not be a good choice. Some of these are mere gadget-type knives with a built-in screwdriver, awl, marlin spike, bottle and can opener, and corkscrew. Somewhere amid this jumble there is usually a knife blade too. My own tastes run to simple knives but, if you're a gadgeteer and like to tinker camp equipment, these accessories may be useful to you. If you buy one of these combination knives, spend a little more money than might seem necessary in order to get a high-quality steel. Otherwise the price of the knife may lie almost entirely within the number of gadgets attached, to the detriment of steel quality.

Among the standard shapes which are best are

the Long Clip and the Skinning blades. These are thin blades with long, tapering points which will do anything other blades will do, and then some. Their principal advantage, however, lies in the thinness of the blade which makes them easier to whittle with and much simpler to keep properly sharpened. Their points can be used for awls, and for cleaning fish they are easier to use than the more blunt type of blade.

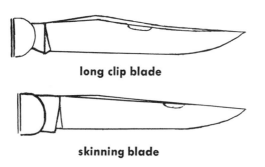

long clip blade

skinning blade

Wider blades, with sharper tapers toward the point, such as the Spear and Sheep Foot models, are likely to be thick along the "backbone," making slicing and whittling more difficult since these are more likely to bind. Any type of blade which has a ridge of extra thickness running lengthwise of its center is a very poor blade for most purposes.

Naturally, in discussing blade shapes and thicknesses, I'm referring only to knives for general personal use in camp. There are a great many specialized knives which require heavy and wide blades for ruggedness. Big-game guides, for example, are likely to use a heftier knife to cut heavy hides and sever tough tendons. Canadian Indians, who use the famous Hudson Bay "crooked knife" need a rugged tool since it is likely to be used for everything from repairing a wooden canoe to carving a sled runner.

Some authorities prefer a full-sized handle around which a man can wrap his hand for a strong grip. I can't go along with this thinking for a knife should not be used forcefully. The use of a camp knife requires skill rather than brute force. A large handle is not necessary. A large handle is going to require that the knife also have a large blade in order to attain some semblance of balance—and a large blade is an awkward one.

The material which has gone into making the handle of a knife is pretty much a matter of taste and budget, so far as the camp knife is concerned. A handle made of leather washers is a popular type despite the criticism that the washers shrink and become loose. An occasional application of a small amount of oil will prevent this. Staghorn is also well liked and much used, along with bone. Hard rubber and plastics are also used in cheap knives and these are subject to cracking. Besides, they're usually ugly things.

Wood handles are used a great deal and I like them since they acquire a high polish with use. Hardwoods of various types are used in domestic knives, while some imported cutlery is likely to sport a handle of lignum vitae, or mazer wood made in Scandinavia of maple or cherry. Except for rubber and plastic, any one of them is suitable.

Kitchen knives enter the picture, too, particularly as they concern family camping and these are discussed in the chapter on outdoor cooking.

A knife shouldn't be sharpened on a grindstone or emery wheel where it is susceptible to loss of temper. Instead, use a small handstone. Keep the stone moist, and hold the blade so that the back of the blade is about 15 degrees up from the surface of the stone. General advice is to rub the blade against the stone edge-first and this is correct, but a circular motion can also be used. Turn the knife over frequently as you hone it. A woodsman, who invariably dotes on his knife touches up the edge every day whether it needs it or not!

**TEPEE CAMP FOR TRAIL RIDERS
IN BANFF NATIONAL PARK, ALBERTA**

Canadian Government Travel Bureau

Chapter 7

COOKING IN CAMP

Camp foods and their cooking vary pretty much according to the type of camping trip. On a hiking trek, where you won't want to tote much more than 20 pounds or so of food along with your shelter and other equipment, you're likely to leave the canned goods behind in favor of dehydrated foods. On a canoe trip, where your craft will do most of the carrying, some luxuries can be included—if portages are not too long or numerous.

On a car camping trip, however, your choice of foods is limited only by your ability as a cook around a campfire or on a camp stove. Actually, preparing a list of grub for a week's camping trip is not far different from doing a week's household shopping at a nearby supermarket.

So that you won't become a slave to pots and pans, the meals should be simple and require only a short cooking time. Complicated recipes, although they can be carried out in camp, have no place there unless your purpose in camping is to enjoy outdoor cooking.

Foods should be easy to digest. Fresh fruits can be on the menu both as an aid to digestion and as excellent "snacks" that will curb between-meal appetites. Because you will be more active and use up more energy—hiking, rowing, chopping—sugar should be plentiful, preferably in the form of candy.

While you may get along with a slice of toast and coffee for breakfast at home, in camp a busy day ahead calls for more substantial foods—fruit juice, hot cereals, coffee or cocoa, possibly ham or bacon and eggs.

There is no reason why meals shouldn't be as good in camp as they are at home. The difference is that they will be prepared with an eye to simplicity, ease, and speed. You will find that food out-of-doors takes on a new flavor, at the same time

that your appetite seems to develop a gusto you never experienced before. Also, by keeping the meals simple, your chances of success are greater.

Unless you're planning a trip into a distant and remote area, it's best to renew food supplies every three or four days, instead of loading yourself down heavily for the entire trip. In this way, you can have fresh foods on the menu constantly. Keep an eye out for farmer's roadside stands where fresh produce can be bought, too.

In packing your car, arrange the equipment so that you can get at your camp refrigerator easily. This way freshly bought foods can be put into it, and ice added without having to unload most of the car or trailer.

A great number of recipes are not included for the simple reason that good cookbooks are numberless and whatever addition I might make could hardly be original. Instead, I have cited examples of simple camp cooking that can be done in the various camp utensils available today.

Once you have mastered basic outdoor cooking and you want to try more complex menus, buy yourself an outdoor cookbook, preferably one written for camping rather than backyard barbecuing. Also, start your own cookbook by clipping camp menus and recipes that appear frequently in many publications.

"Trick" cooking, such as getting a meal on a tin

can containing a miniature fire, has been pointedly omitted. This sort of thing, while it's fun upon occasion, is completely impractical for family and group camping. If you want to try some of these stunts, Boy Scout camp manuals describe the possibilities. However, I never could get excited about frying a hamburger atop an empty tomato can!

New campers often make the mistake of bringing into camp household utensils, only to find that they are not suitable, and after a couple of weeks in camp they're no longer fit for use in the kitchen. Thin aluminum gets dented, wooden handles burn off or get charred, pots are blackened beyond cleaning, glass units are broken or cracked. Camp cooking then takes on the aspects of an expensive sport. It's better to buy utensils that are designed for camp use.

The Coffeepot

Don't buy a kitchen-type percolator or pot with straight vertical sides as these are too tippy. A wide-bottom pot is much steadier on a camp stove or fire. Mine has a bottom nine inches in diameter and the top slightly more than six. Over-all height is seven inches and it has a capacity of sixteen mugs of coffee. It has a bail for lifting and hanging over a fire, and a ring brazed to the bottom rim which allows me to pour coffee with a pair of "guide's helpers" or forked sticks without having to touch the pot itself. Avoid pots with the conventional wood handle at the side since this invariably burns off.

**THE IDEAL
CAMP COFFEEPOT**

As far as camp coffee is concerned, I prefer guide's or "rolled" coffee. To make this, put one tablespoonful of coffee for each cup into a mixing bowl. Add one egg and stir this in until all of the coffee is moist. (Some guides toss in the shell, too!) When the water boils vigorously add the coffee, stirring it slowly. Move the pot away from the heat so that the coffee "rolls" gently for a minute or two, being careful that it does not boil over. Allow this until the color is about right, a rich dark brown. Set the pot aside where it will keep hot and dash in a cup of cold water. In a couple of minutes, the grounds will have settled to the bottom and the coffee will be ready to drink. The trouble with this method is that you can't make a small quantity, but you'll rarely have to throw any away!

Percolator coffee has its place in camp if you prefer it. It's more economical, certainly. Make it just as you would at home. Instant coffee, much improved in recent years, is practical and economical in camp, especially when only two or three persons make up the camping party. Drip coffee is the poorest of the lot as far as flavor is concerned.

Many campers go to a great trouble to clean the outside of sooty coffeepots, but this is hardly worth the effort. I have never cleaned the outside of my thirteen-year-old pot except to wipe off excess soot. Instead I carry it in a cloth bag so that it will not rub on other camp equipment. The inside, however, gets a thorough cleaning after each use. Otherwise, your brew will suffer if stale coffee grounds remain in the pot.

Buy coffee in half-pound vacuum-sealed tins so that the supply is always fresh. Naturally, too, you should buy a good grade.

The Tea Pail

This is the favorite small kettle of the professional woodsman, a counterpart of the famous Australian billycan. Northern woodsmen use a No. 10 can to which they add a wire bail. The pail is used for boiling potatoes, making soups and stews, and for "steepin' tea."

Although tea bags are not popular in the woods, pleasure campers will find them handy. With tea bags, any kind of kettle can be used to heat water, simplifying the tea operation. However, for real "woods tea," the tea pail is ideal. The amount of tea used, of course, determines its strength. Bring your water to a boil and toss in the equivalent of one teaspoonful of tea to each quart of water for weak tea. Woodsmen, who like their tea to "fight back a mite," make theirs somewhat stronger. Tea should not be boiled. Rather like the coffee-making procedure, set the pail aside and let the tea "steep" for a few minutes. Incidentally, if you like lemon in your tea and don't want to bother carrying whole fruit, use lemon powder, throwing in a small pinch for added flavor.

The Broiler

Many outdoor cooks think of a broiler in terms of a charcoal grill, probably the worst atrocity ever inflicted on a good cut of meat. Steaks and chops broiled over such grills in a horizontal position have the juices and fat drained out of them. These fall into the glowing charcoal which then flares up, scorching what might have been part of a good meal.

The broiler I refer to is a double, folding grill made of heavy wire, having a long handle and looking not unlike the old-fashioned bread toaster. This broils meat as it should be broiled, *in a vertical position.* In this way, steaks and chops, placed in the broiler with the fatty edge on top, are broiled while the juices and melting fats run down over the meat before dropping. These can be caught in a shallow pan or special trough attached to the broiler, and used for basting. Still another advantage of the wire broiler is the fact that glowing coals are not necessary for broiling. Leaping flames will do as well.

Before broiling beefsteak in this manner, it should be seared well on both sides by holding it over the coals or flames for a moment. Whether you salt it while broiling or after is up to you, but salt is inclined to draw out the juices. How long the steak should be kept before the fire depends upon how well done you want it. At any rate, it should be turned frequently.

Chicken should be broiled slowly and thoroughly yet scorching should be avoided. Parboiling before broiling starts the cooking process, with the result that it can be broiled much more quickly without loss of flavor or drying. If you prefer to baste chicken with a barbeuce sauce, it's permissible.

Chops, too, can be broiled in the wire broiler, also placing them with the fatty edge up and using much the same technique as for beefsteak.

Hamburg can be broiled in this manner, producing a flavor that is impossible to attain in a fry pan. Chopped onions or partially cooked chopped green peppers can be added to the hamburg. For

HOLD THE GRILL IN A VERTICAL POSITION TO RETAIN THE MEAT JUICES

full flavor, make the patties almost an inch thick and don't overcook them.

The broiling of fish is perhaps the easiest of all. Fillet or split the fish, mount it in the broiler and place it before the fire. Fish, of course, will cook more quickly than most meats. Basting it with a little drawn butter may help both the flavor and the golden tint looked for on properly cooked fish.

The proper way to split a fish is first to remove the head and tail. Then split the fish lengthwise, *down the back,* not on the belly side. Remove the innards and wash in cold fresh water. Some advocate the removal of bones before cooking but this is likely to result in a waste of meat. Cook the fish first, and the bones will come out more easily.

Even the lowly frankfurter becomes a delicacy when broiled. Cut a lengthwise slot in the frankfurter, stuff this with a bread dressing or cheese, wrap the frankfurter with a slice of bacon with toothpicks inserted to hold the bacon in place. Broil until the bacon becomes near-crisp.

The sole drawback of the wire broiler is that it cannot be used with a camp stove. Broiling over the burners will result in fat and juices running down into the burners and clogging them.

The Dutch Oven

If I were compelled to go into the woods for some length of time with only one utensil, a cast-iron

Dutch oven would be my choice because of all camp cooking equipment, this is the most versatile. It can be used for every type of cooking except broiling!

A Dutch oven, favorite of Western food wranglers, is a cast-iron—or sometimes aluminum—kettle with a rimmed cover on which hot coals can be set. They range in size from 10 to 16 inches in diameter and from 3 to 7 inches deep. Weight will run from 10 to 35 pounds in the cast-iron models, much lighter in aluminum.

A good camp Dutch oven should have short legs which keep it from direct contact with hot coals and, of course, the rim on the cover is an absolute necessity. Don't buy a household model which will probably be highly polished, without legs and with a rimless cover. One of the smaller models is completely practical.

THE DUTCH OVEN   *Riviere*

A new cast-iron Dutch oven should be "seasoned" before using. Rub the inside with an unsalted grease such as lard or vegetable oil. Rub it well, then set the oven in a warm room or low oven for two or three hours. After this, wipe off excess grease. Repeat this process two or three times for a better job. However, the oven can be used after the first greasing and each use will improve it. The greasing process will make the iron practically rustproof and it will cook better too.

While the Dutch oven is an excellent kettle, its primary field is baking. Anything you can bake at home in a kitchen range, you can bake in a Dutch oven. Preheat the oven, grease the interior as you would a baking tin, and you can bake biscuits, muffins, rolls, bread, without additional utensils. Set

the Dutch oven over a bed of hardwood coals so that no coals actually touch the bottom—that's the reason for the legs. Also, put coals on the cover to supply heat from above. Occasionally raise the cover to see how the baking is coming along. Lining the oven with aluminum foil makes it easy to remove the baking.

Casserole dishes and one-pot meals are at their best in Dutch ovens. For example, lowly hamburg can be converted into an excellent one-pot meal, the ideal type of food preparation for camp. Mix 1½ pounds of ground beef with a handful of rolled crackers, plus one chopped onion and one green pepper (stuffed olives will do in place of pepper). Add seasonings to suit and mold into one large patty and place this in the center of the Dutch oven. Add a little catsup and one-half cup of water. Lay two or three strips of bacon atop the meat. Cut a few potatoes into pieces about 1½ inches in diameter and place these on the bottom of the oven around the meat. Bake 25 or 30 minutes. The catsup can be omitted if you prefer to leave out the tomato taste.

Other one-pot meals which can be cooked with the Dutch oven are almost numberless. Don't overlook such simple, yet delicious dishes as Spanish rice, American chop suey, and chili con carne.

Probably the dish which attracts the most attention in current literature is the ever popular bean-hole beans. The Dutch oven is ideal for making these. It wasn't my intention to describe any camp dishes which take more than one hour to cook but bean-hole beans are worth the breaking of any rule. Wash and pick over enough pea or red kidney beans to half fill your Dutch oven and soak them overnight. In the morning, drain these and cover with fresh cold water, adding a teaspoon of baking soda. (Many omit the soda.) Simmer the beans until the skins crack and a "bean" smell begins to escape. Pour the beans into another container for the moment, and put a layer of sliced salt pork on the bottom of the Dutch oven. Pour in 1½ inches of beans, then another layer of salt pork, and more beans. Keep a few slices of pork to lay on top. As you lay in the salt pork, also lay in a slice of onion for each layer. (These, too, may be omitted, but what are baked beans without onions?) Add half a cup of molasses, or a little more if the oven is large, a teaspoonful of salt, a little pepper. A cup of catsup will add a strong tomato flavor for those who like beans in tomato sauce. Place in the bean hole and allow to bake for six hours or more.

In making the bean hole, dig it large enough so that you can line it with rocks. Once these are in, build a hardwood fire and allow this to burn until you have four or five inches of hot coals. Remove any unburned sticks and a few of the coals. Place the Dutch oven in the hole, preferably so that it doesn't rest directly on the coals. Put a layer of the coals on the Dutch oven cover. Now cover the Dutch oven with aluminum foil so that this hangs down over the edges of the cover, to help keep dirt out of the beans. Fill in the bean hole.

You may have noted that I did not give exact proportions for the ingredients. This is simply because they are not critical, unless of course, you overdo any one of them. The approximate proportions which I've given you will produce bean-hole beans that will qualify you as a top "food wrangler." "A little of this 'n' that" is typical of woods cooking. I doubt if any professional campfire cook can tell you the exact proportions he uses, even in complicated recipes. I know some fine outdoor cooks who don't own a measuring cup!

The Reflector Oven

The reflector oven is almost as versatile as the Dutch oven, and is easier to use by virtue of the fact that it does not require coals, but rather a flaming fire. The food being cooked is always in sight and heat can be controlled simply by moving the oven. Heat radiating from the fire strikes the sloping walls and is reflected upward—and downward—to the food, and don't think for a moment that it's inefficient. The heat within such an oven can be quite intense.

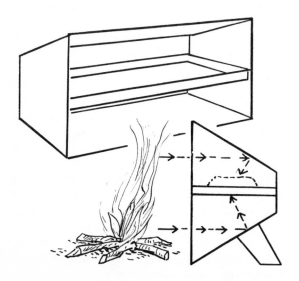

THE REFLECTOR OVEN

It's often advised that the interior be kept highly polished for greater efficiency, and this is true to some degree, but not enough to warrant a great deal of work polishing it. Keep it clean, wipe out grease and soot which may accumulate, and your oven will work well.

The solid, nonfolding type of oven with removable shelf is sturdier and what's more can be used for a dishpan! Lay the oven on its back, to use it as such. However, the solid type is a little more cumbersome to tote and pack. Of the folding models, the one with side walls is more efficient for, without these, a breeze or wind will have a cooling effect on the reflected heat.

A small hardwood fire is best for a reflector oven with the flames reaching about to the top of the oven. Keep the flames at this level, avoiding softwood which will shoot sparks and bits of ashes into the food. While food is cooking, turn the pan around occasionally to avoid overcooking one side. An asbestos glove makes an excellent pot lifter.

Because of the tremendous variety of prepared baking mixes that are available, the reflector oven makes possible a delightfully varied menu and affords much fun for the camp cook. There is no need to struggle with ingredients to obtain excellent pastries. If grandmother had had access to today's mixes, she would have used her flour barrel for a trash bin.

Freshly picked blueberries added to a standard muffin mix will be joyously received at the table when presented as blueberry muffins, or bake corn bread with bits of crisp bacon added before baking. Biscuits with maple syrup, chocolate cake, gingerbread, or even a fancy two-layer cake on the occasion of someone's birthday in camp, will all bring welcome relief from store bread and pastries. If you want to hear real howls of glee, roll out a pie crust, place it in a greased pie plate, fill with freshly picked blueberries, raspberries, or even wild apples, add sugar according to the collective sweet tooth, lay on the upper crust, and bake in your reflector! Turn the pie frequently so it will cook evenly on all sides.

Rolling a pie crust in camp is easy if you use a clean dish towel, well sprinkled with flour, for a dough board. An empty ginger ale or vinegar bottle is a good rolling pin. Use the towel on the picnic table, on a food box or even on the hood of your car! The flour will wash off easily.

Simple meat loaves and baked casseroles are easy in the reflector using a rectangular cake tin for a container. Baked eggs for breakfast some morning will please everyone. Break as many eggs as your rectangular tin will hold without blending them, first buttering the tin. Sprinkle salt and pepper to suit and add small dabs of butter. Bake until the eggs are of the consistency wanted. These are usually best when the whites of the eggs are done as with fried eggs.

Reflector ovens are generally available in 12- and 16-inch widths. Since the cost differential is so small, the larger model is best. If you want a larger model than this, you'll probably have to get it made to order.

This fine oven can't be used with a gasoline or propane gas stove, for obvious reasons. However, it can be used in an indoor fireplace and by setting it close to a sheet-metal box stove such as is used for heating tents.

Griddles

For the frying of various foods, especially if there are three or four persons in the camping party, a large griddle is a boon. You can, for example, fry bacon or ham and eggs all at the same time, or you can make six to twelve flapjacks at once.

Griddles come made of cast magnesium, aluminum, or iron. Some claims are made for the first two but none I've ever tried were satisfactory because they warped. You will find most professional or experienced outdoor cooks using cast iron. Griddles vary in size from 8 to 14 inches wide and from 16 to 30 inches long, while weight will run from 10 to 25 pounds. If you can handle the weight in your outfit, they're very worthwhile.

Griddles work especially well on camp stoves, whether you burn gasoline or propane gas, because the heat can be controlled more easily than with a campfire. Griddles can, of course, be used effectively over an open fire once you've acquired the knack of keeping the correct amount of fire under them.

Incidentally, the taken-for-granted flapjack can be embellished easily in camp for greater variety at the breakfast table. Add one egg to your batter, along with a can of whole kernel corn. Fry on both sides until a golden brown. For greater variety, use blueberries, or for increased heartiness, add a cup or two of cold boiled rice. The rice will mix more easily if it is first stirred into the milk being used for the batter.

French toast is another camp favorite which the griddle handles well. Blend eggs with milk, adding a bit of sugar, according to the amount of toast the group will eat, dip the bread slices in this, and fry on a greased griddle until light brown. Butter and maple syrup, possibly a light sprinkling of powdered sugar can be used as topping. Don't use lard or cooking oil for greasing the griddle. Use a piece of bacon or salt pork, rubbed with a fork or spatula.

For using a griddle on a camp stove, set it directly on the stove grill. Over an open fire, place a rock under each corner, leveling it as well as possible, or if the fireplace has a wire or pipe grill, set the griddle on this.

Stove Ovens

The boxlike camp stove ovens are not quite as romantic as the reflector or the Dutch oven, but they will perform the same jobs. In fact, they are easier to use since they have a heat indicator. Some of these are folding models, which help in the packing and carrying department. The better types have baffles in the bottom which tend to diffuse the heat and distribute it evenly throughout the oven.

For baking with a camp stove this type of oven is perfect. It will do anything with food that can be done in the oven of a kitchen range.

The Pressure Cooker

Very rarely is the pressure cooker included on the camp list of utensils. Yet it cuts cooking time and preserves the flavor of foods. Traveling car campers who keep an eye out for fresh vegetables from farmers' roadside stands can make good use of a pressure cooker. After all, it's no bulkier than an eight-quart camp kettle and probably will weigh under three pounds. It can be used on a camp stove or over an open fire. A two-quart model will be about 10 inches in diameter and 9 inches high. If it's to be used over a fire, buy the type without wooden handles, as these will scorch or even catch fire.

Because cooking time is cut greatly with a pressure cooker, you can enjoy any of the vegetable dishes possible at home, as well as meat and mixed vegetable-meat casseroles. Another advantage of the pressure cooker is the savings in fuel, whether gas or wood.

For a hot day luncheon, when cooking a full meal has little appeal, asparagus on toast is easy and quick. Place the asparagus in the pressure cooker so that it is piled helter-skelter, rather than stacked parallel. Add a little water, a heavy pinch of salt. Once full pressure is reached, it will cook in less than three minutes. While the asparagus is on, make

CAMPING IN WYOMING

your toast on the other camp stove burner, using the "tepee toaster," described a little later in this chapter. A cream sauce can be added to the asparagus, if you like. This entire meal, plus a cooling drink can be prepared in ten minutes.

Other fresh vegetables which can be obtained from neighboring farmers often include string beans, which take only two minutes or so in the pressure cooker. Carrots take no longer. Fresh peas are a delight, cooking in about one minute. For these add a dozen or so pods for improving the flavor. Corn on the cob, a long hot job when roasted, is quick,

easy, and more flavorsome in the pressure cooker, requiring only about five minutes at full pressure. White or sweet potatoes can be done in about ten minutes.

The secret to preserving flavor in a pressure cooker is to use as little water as possible. Manufacturer's directions will vary somewhat with different cookers but generally a half to three-quarters of a cup of water and a large pinch of salt are all that is needed besides the vegetables themselves. Regarding the operation of the pressure cooker follow manufacturers' directions, for these vary somewhat.

The French Fryer

Like the pressure cooker, the French fryer is seldom thought of as a camp cooking utensil. However, Maine Guides, working from boats on daily fishing or picnic trips, use them often. Not the usual flimsy aluminum pot with a handle, but rather a cast-iron kettle with bail and, of course, the fryer basket.

The lard is kept in the fryer at all times and it keeps well since the guides store their cooking gear aboard their boats where it is comparatively cool. How long lard lasts, depends upon how often it is used and the temperature in which it is stored.

Besides the usual French fried potatoes and deep-fried fish, the French fryer makes possible some food luxuries such as onion rings. Dip the rings in pancake batter, then deep fry them. The fat or lard should be "smoking" hot. A piece of fairly heavy wire bent into a hook, is handier than a fork for lifting the rings from the hot fat. Such onion rings, fried until the batter casing is a golden brown, will keep you busy supplying the demand.

For a different fish recipe mix a can of Alaska red salmon—or any other kind of cold, boiled fish—with ½ cup of milk, fresh or evaporated, one or two beaten eggs, one small chopped onion. Add salt and pepper to suit. Form the mixture into patties and deep fry until they are the shade of highly polished yellow birch.

The French fryer, especially the cast-iron type, is easy to use. It will work well over a gasoline or gas stove and it can be used hung from a crane over an open fire. It isn't necessary, however, that you use the heavy iron type. Over a camp stove, the household model of aluminum works well, except that the handle projecting from the side is a hazard.

Frying Pans

The best of these is the cast-iron skillet, with cast aluminum, the thicker the better—next in order of choice. Pressed aluminum pans, and covers of cook kits that may be converted to fry pans by inserting a handle, are poor rigs, as food sticks to them.

Not to be overlooked, however, is the light steel frying pan or spider. I use one that is 16 inches in diameter, and in it entire meals for four persons can be cooked. By way of comparison, the average 9- to 10-inch camp fry pan is a frustrating utensil to use.

Some camp models have removable handles, or folding hand grips of various sorts, while still others have round sockets for the insertion of a handle cut at the campsite.

Everyone, of course, is familiar enough with the fry pan to know that bacon, chops, canned meats, and potatoes are easily fried, but few campers are aware that the fry pan can be a good one-pot meal utensil. One of my favorite fry pan meals—especially in cool weather or when the trail is long and hard—is made by frying a half pound of bacon until crisp. Pour out some of the fat and fry one or two small onions. Just before these are well bronzed, add a pound of frankfurters (fresh or canned), sliced or chopped into half-inch pieces. Brown these, timing them to finish with the onions. Add two cans of cream style corn and heat through. Just before serving, stir in bits of bacon and serve on crackers.

Most frying pan meals are hearty ones, as for example the recipe which calls for rolling out biscuit dough about ⅜ inch thick. Spread a can of corned or roast beef hash on the dough and roll into a cylinder. Cut slices from this roll about a half-inch thick and brown well in the fry pan. For the dough, use a mix.

The Spit

There are on the market small metal spits which may be taken into camp and which work well, but you can devise a good one with two small forked sticks and a single green skewer.

Camp cooking possibilities with a spit are limited, of course, and most cooking of this type requires more time than most campers want to devote to a meal preparation, but if you like to putter around the cook fire, the spit is a good means of making that puttering pay off.

The simplest spit recipe, of course, is the time-honored "kabob," a cube of beef, a slice of onion, then more beef and more onion, with the entire unit wrapped in bacon. Or you can go the limit and spit a full roast of beef or fowl if you want to spend the time. Whatever you cook, place a shallow pan under the spit to catch drippings for basting. Don't cook food on a spit directly over a fire, but slightly to one side.

The Cooking Kit

Cooking kits usually include not only pots and pans, but also cups, dishes, and sometimes knives, forks, and spoons, all designed to fit within the largest kettle in the set. Aluminum kits are the most popular, with a few outfitters supplying stainless steel. Kits vary from one man units to outfits made to serve as many as 12 to 16 persons.

Generally speaking, aluminum kits have three basic faults in their design. First, kettle covers are often designed to be used as frying pans, but these are not suitable, since most pressed aluminum is too thin. Foods stick to it easily.

The second fault lies with the cups which will burn your lips when drinking hot liquids. Plates, on the other hand, cool too quickly so that while you are eating warm foods any fat or grease which may be in the food jells into gobs of unappetizing goo.

These are not serious drawbacks however and most aluminum cooking kits form a basis of suitable units to build around. As you improve your kit, discard the aluminum drinking cups, replacing them with enamelware cups having open handles which will allow nesting. The aluminum plates may be used for kitchen work, but for eating purposes, these, too, should be replaced with enamelware. As for the pot covers, use them for just that, and acquire a couple of suitable frying pans.

Drinking cups in camp are a problem. Everyone uses them for drinking during the day so that the cook or table setter has to wash them before a meal is served. Invest, then, in collapsible cups and have each member of the camp group carry one for personal use during the day. These are handy on hikes too, for drinking from springs or streams.

If there are children in the party, show them how to make birchbark cups. Cut a round piece of bark,

AN OUTFITTERS' CAMP IN MONTANA

Bill Browning

about eight inches in diameter. Crease this so that it buckles inward and fold it over, forming a cone. Now, insert a partially split green stick so that the split end binds the cone and forms a handle. If the stick has a fork at the other end, the cup can be hung up near the water supply. The children will refuse to drink from a "white man's cup" once they have made these!

The uses that cooking kit kettles can be put to are almost numberless. Soups are not a popular camp dish usually but on a cold or rainy day they're excellent fare, providing you stick to simple recipes. A delicious onion soup is made by cooking onions in butter until they begin to brown. Add these to a can or two of canned consommé, or dissolved bouillon cubes and season with salt and pepper to suit. Grated Parmesan cheese sprinkled on the soup as you serve it will mark you as a camp cook who knows his way around a kettle!

A corn chowder, properly made, is another kettle meal that sets well if the weather is cool. Peel, cube, and boil potatoes until done. Fry small pieces of salt pork or bacon until crisp, along with an onion or two, then combine with milk and one can of cream style corn and one can of whole kernel corn and allow to simmer only a few moments. The cream style corn adds more flavor than does the whole kernel type. Proportion the ingredients to match your opinions on whether a chowder should be thick or thin. I like mine thick enough to serve on crackers! Adding a gob of butter to float on top of the chowder enhances it. Also, one thing to remember: Drain the potatoes before adding them to chowder. Don't use the water.

An excellent trout chowder can be made by boiling trout until the meat flakes off the bones and adding it to the above mixture, omitting the cream style corn. Canned vegetable soups can be improved greatly by adding canned consommé, or meat broth left over from a previous meal.

One of the common omissions of cooking kits is the double boiler. Rice and oatmeal cereals, which are prone to sticking, should be cooked in this type of utensil. Creamed sauces, too. However, a suitable double boiler can be made for such foods by placing one smaller kettle within another with three or four small pebbles, all of a size, in the bottom of the larger kettle. The inside kettle should be small enough so that ample water will separate the two.

Another important camp cooking utensil is a large aluminum salad bowl type of utensil which northern Minnesota guides call a "dishup." You will find good use for such a bowl at almost every meal. Aluminum is the best material, rather than the wooden or glass types, which can be broken too easily. This can be used for mixing foods prior to cooking, for serving, and it's ideal for a tossed salad.

A set of small enamelware nesting bowls is excellent for mixing small amounts of food—such as guides' coffee—and they can also double for soup bowls.

For many years, toasting bread on a green stick over a campfire was traditional. Then came the "teepee" toaster, still in wide use over a gasoline or propane stove. However, an even better camp toaster has been devised—the Camp-A-Toaster,

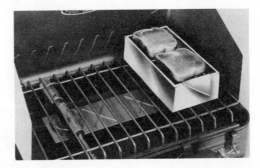

CAMP-A-TOASTER   *Thermos*

patterned much after the Girl Scout coffee can toaster. The updated version holds only two slices at a time but is so efficient that it is actually faster than the teepee style, and it makes better toast to boot! Most outfitters now carry the new model.

Salt and pepper shakers of the household type are a nuisance on a camping trip, continually leaking their contents into one of the packs. Inserting waxed paper or foil under the covers rarely works well for more than a day or so. Leave these home and buy camp-type shakers with caps which can be closed.

For hanging pots over a cooking fire, pot chains are just about the perfect rig. Nothing more than a length of light chain, 18 to 36 inches long, with an S hook at each end, these can be adjusted for length to lift or lower a kettle. Most of the larger outfitters have these, or they can be made easily. Similar pot hooks can also be made of heavy wire, bent into an S shape, but these cannot adjust the height of a utensil above the fire.

A natural fork, cut from a small sapling about 1½ inches in diameter, is more picturesque and equally effective as the pot chain. It must be hardwood, both for strength and for correct shape of the

OASTLER RIVER, ONTARIO

Canadian Government Travel Bureau

POT CHAINS

fork. The fork itself is hung over the crane or dingle stick, while notches are whittled into the shaft which hangs down. It is in these that the kettle bail fits and by moving this from one notch to another, a kettle can be raised or lowered.

Although not a cooking utensil, one of the most used containers around a camp kitchen is the water pail. This can be a 10- or 12-quart galvanized bucket, or a folding canvas pail. The latter is popular because it will fold for storage en route. However, it can't be used for heating water.

For this purpose, there is a 5-gallon square tin, offered by at least one Western outfitter. The can has been retinned and a bail added to it for easy handling. A bucket this size is not too heavy to tote when full and saves extra trips to the water supply. Also space can be saved by packing other utensils in it when traveling.

Smaller utensils which you will need include a mixing spoon. Get the solid type rather than the perforated one, so that it can be used for basting.

A long-handled fork is a necessity, but don't buy one of those extension-handle type that open to nearly three feet. If your fire is so hot that you need such a fork, the fire is too big! A shorter, sturdier fork is easier to use.

A spatula or cake turner is handy but don't make the mistake of buying a large one. A small one will flip a flapjack just as well, and will be easier to maneuver in a fry pan or on a griddle.

The can opener should be a rugged one and of simple design. Gadgets have no place in camp and,

while a can may be opened with an ax, it's hardly a safe procedure nor good campcraft.

For a kitchen knife, a long thin, somewhat flexible blade is most versatile. With this type you can slice bread or meat, fillet fish, or cut vegetables. Keep the knife's edge sharp with a small handstone and keep it sheathed when not in use.

Regarding table "silver," don't bring it from home, even if it's not sterling. You can buy a complete set of stainless-steel tableware quite reasonably and if any pieces are lost replacement is cheaper.

There are three piece sets on the market, consisting of a knife, fork, and teaspoon, which fit together in a small plastic sheath. These are ideal, even if you don't bother much with the sheath. However, these sets usually lack a soup spoon.

A camp kettle or pan should not have a wooden handle if it's to be used over an open fire. Since you will have to pick these up by metal handles an asbestos glove or a pot holder is handy for this. Another well-suited gadget is a pot and pan grip, made of aluminum, which looks not unlike a pair of pliers designed to grip the edge of utensils for lifting.

A dishpan should round out the list of utensils. Some campers wash pots and dishes in one of the larger kit kettles and even, as suggested earlier, in a reflector oven. However, a regular dishpan is better campkeeping, with some of the plastic rectangular dishpans well adapted for the job.

A frequent problem in camp is the keeping of the soap-powder box from falling to pieces, especially after a wetting or two. To avoid this, take along a metal kitchen soapbox, or one of the aluminum models which some outfitters offer. These take a standard soapbox without having to transfer the contents.

Dishcloths or a dish mop and soap pads will complete the necessities for after-cooking chores. Dish towels can be washed quickly after each meal and hung out to dry, so that a fresh, clean one is always available.

A tablecloth is a good idea when camping in parks, where picnic tables are not always clean. Oilcloth is sturdiest and easily cleaned. Plastic tablecloths are popular too, but not as long-lasting.

For packing food and the cook-kit, a chuck box, not unlike a seaman's chest, is ideal. Rig handles on it, and if you're going on a canoe trip, add a carrying harness for the portages. When packing it, include matches, fire starters, and wire grill. Make the box so that, when it is set on one end or on its side, the cover acts as a work space and the box itself as a cupboard. You can keep it from becoming soiled with soot, by storing cooking utensils in cloth bags. With a properly packed outfit such as this, the cook can set to work getting a meal within a few minutes after a stop is made.

Rubbing soap on the outside of a utensil will make the soot much easier to remove when washing but this is a tedious chore. A better stunt is to make a thick paste with soap powder and a small amount of water. This paste can be made up in quantity and carried in a friction-top can. Rub the paste on the pot or kettle before using over an open fire and when you wash the utensil, the soot will almost float away.

Aluminum-Foil Cooking

Most professional outdoor cooks look upon aluminum-foil cooking as a stunt and I'm inclined to go along with this thinking to some degree. I prefer to think of foil as another aid to cooking rather than a practical form of outdoor food preparation in itself.

The making of foil utensils to replace cooking pans and pots is fun upon occasion, but hardly a practical method of cooking as a steady diet. Nevertheless, foil has its place at the cooking fire. For example, potatoes baked in foil within the embers of a fire, come out clean, with no burned skin or scorched flakes to litter the dining table.

A complete meal can be cooked in foil by wrapping ground beef with chopped onions or peppers and fresh vegetables, possibly adding tomato sauce or paste. Wrap the ingredients well in foil and bake these in a Dutch oven, reflector, or in live coals.

Corn on the cob that has been husked, spread with butter and wrapped in foil will cook quickly either in an oven or near glowing coals. It will retain the full flavor and sweetness that would be lost by boiling or direct roasting.

Foil cooking recipes can be devised by adapting those used for cooking in pots, pans, and kettles, keeping in mind that liquids are likely to leak. Stick to solid or semisolid types of foods.

The suggestion is often made that cooking utensils be lined with aluminum foil prior to cooking so as to save washing them. Cleaning a fry pan or pot is part of camp life, just as building a fire and pitching a tent are and I would hate to see such little chores disappear. After all, we go camping because we seek a simpler life, and the constant encroachment of our gadget-ridden civilization upon this search for a slower pace will destroy the goal long before we reach it.

However, foil is a decided advantage, mechanically, at least, and instead of buying the lightweight type sold in grocery stores, buy the heavy-duty type which is sold by camping outfitters. It is slightly more expensive but much stronger and you are less likely to spill food through puncturing the foil.

An excellent oven can be improvised with foil. Build a hardwood fire in a shallow pit and keep it going until a substantial bed of coals has accumulated. Lay two green sticks across the top of the hole (after the fire has burned down), place the tin containing a cake, pie, biscuits, or rolls on the sticks. Now cover the entire rig with aluminum foil, forming a sort of hollow mound over the pit. You'll have to lift the foil once or twice to see how the cooking is coming along but this oven will produce as good a cake or pie as will a Dutch oven!

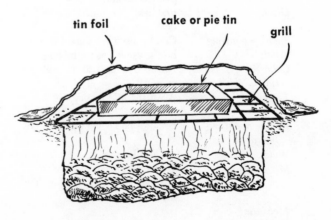

A FOIL OVEN

Check List of Cooking and Eating Utensils

The following check list is not a blanket recommendation for all of the items suggested but it is meant to serve as a reminder of certain pieces of equipment which may be overlooked.

Coffeepot	Guide's model without basket, or percolator. If instant coffee will be used, this item may be omitted.
Tea pail	One of the smaller nesting kettles can be substituted.
Broiler, wire	Size according to number of persons in camping party. 8 × 10 inches for two persons, 10×16, for four persons.
Dutch oven	Can be omitted if reflector oven is being taken along. 10- to 12-inch diameter usually large enough for four to six persons.
Reflector oven	Not necessary if Dutch oven is carried.
Griddle	Can be omitted if two or more frying pans included in outfit.
Pressure cooker	A luxury—but worthwhile. Two-quart size for four persons.
Saucepan	5- to 8-inch diameter for many purposes, reheating leftover vegetables, melting butter, etc.
French fryer	A luxury.
Kettles	Carry three (9, 7, and 2½ quarts) with lids and bails.
Frying pans	Two sizes, 9- and 14-inch (or larger) diameter. One should be equipped with lid. In buying extra lids, get the flat type with folding ring lifter rather than knob. These pack better.
Double boiler	Not a necessity. Can be made with two sizes of kettles as explained earlier.
Dishup	Practically a must. Aluminum best.
Small set mixing bowls	Can be used for cereal or soup bowls, as well as for mixing.
Cake tin, pie plates, tin, muffin tray	Necessary for use in reflector oven.
Toaster, folding tee-pee	A worthwhile luxury.
Bread or cutting board	Use dropped cover of chuck box.
Water bucket	An absolute must.
Mixing spoon	Unperforated for serving or basting, as well as mixing. Two may be carried.
Measuring cup	
Cooking fork	14″ is long enough.
Spatula or cake turner	Small one will work as well as large model.
Can opener	Buy a good one so that you won't have to use the ax!
Kitchen knife	9- to 10-inch blade, narrow, flexible.
Pot grip or pump pliers	
Keys for opening cans	Pick up a few extras in case key with can works loose and is lost.
Chuck box	
Grease can, tight fitting top	For saving grease from bacon, meats, for further cooking, gravies, etc.
Dishpan	Metal or plastic. Rectangular type easier to pack.
Dish strainer	Optional.
Dish mop or cloth	
Dish towels	Cloth flour bags excellent. Take at least three.
Scouring soap pads, or metal sponges	For pots and pans.
Soap powder or liquid	
Bottle opener	
Corn popper, wire type	For evening campfire parties. Skillet with cover may be used.
Rubber plate scraper	A big help to the dishwasher.
Food bags, moistureproof	
Icepick	Sheath knife may be used instead.
Pot holders or asbestos glove	
Tablecloth	A nicety.
Egg beater	
Pot hooks or chains	
Salt and pepper shakers	Pepper shaker may be omitted if you use store container with perforated top and sliding closure.
Dishes	One enamelware plate for each member of camping party.
Cups	One enamelware cup with open handle for each person. Paper cups or rustic birch bark cup will save frequent washing.
Table "silver"	Stainless-steel knife, fork, teaspoon, and one dessert or soup spoon for each person. Plastic handles are poor.
Aluminum foil	As aid to cooking, wrapping leftovers.
Paper napkins	
Paper towels	
Paper plates	For quick luncheons when dishwashing time can be spent for more interesting camp activities
Water bag	For desert country. Hang outside car to cool.
Vacuum bottle	For hot or cold drink en route.
Folding camp table and chairs	Worthwhile luxuries.

Food

Most camping manuals contain menus, devised for periods ranging from one week to a month. The trouble with these is that I rarely agree with the suggestions, and I'm sure that any menu which I might outline will be equally disagreeable to others.

The easiest and simplest way to plan your own menu is to work from a master food list. You know best what you and your family like, for it makes little sense to take along foods which you won't enjoy simply because they have been recommended as good camp fare.

Plan the menu well in advance of the camping trip and take into consideration the fact that you will probably eat more heartily away from home. Include meals which you enjoy most at home, eliminating those which require more than an hour to prepare. Supplement these by searching camp cookbooks for other interesting or novel camp fare.

Write the menu out for each day and, opposite, note the ingredients needed for preparing that meal. Here, especially, the experience of the mother in the home will come in handy. When the entire menu has been itemized in this manner, tabulate the total amounts of each food or ingredient you will need. Check to see in what forms these ingredients are available, what sizes are most economical, which are highly perishable or which will keep well.

In this way, you will be sure that each meal will be pretty much what you will enjoy, and purchasing the supplies will be simplified. Many campers merely enter a supermarket and pick items from the shelves as they go along, only to find that they have forgotten salt or coffee.

In planning the menu, don't depend on fish or game which you may take if your trip will involve fishing or hunting. I've gone hungry a few times with this sort of planning!

It is not necessary to buy the entire food supply at once if you are planning a car camping trip and will have access to stores as you travel. By carrying only two or three days' supply, you can save on weight and space for other items which will contribute to camp fun and comfort. Car campers used to buy most of their food at a home market because costs could be kept down, but today's food distribution methods make possible supermarkets even in comparatively small towns where shopping can be economical.

Perishable foods, of course, should be carried in a camp refrigerator and these are discussed in the next chapter. Certain foods, however, are a problem, especially for a beginner at camping. Eggs, for example, are a nuisance en route because of easy breakage and messy aftermath. Carry these in aluminum compartmented boxes made especially for the purpose and available from most outfitters. Or spray two coats of clear lacquer on cardboard "form fitting" containers in which grocers sell eggs. This will stiffen the cardboard eggbox sufficiently to prevent easy crushing. Another trick is to pack eggs in flour or baking mixes.

Moistureproof food bags made of plastic are excellent for such foods as sugar, flour, mixes, salt, and others which absorb moisture.

You can even buy polyethylene tubes, not unlike toothpaste tubes, which can be filled with such foods as jellies, peanut butter, and other semisolids, thus avoiding easily broken glass jars. So far as I know, however, the largest tube available holds only six ounces. Possibly some far-seeing manufacturer may soon produce a larger tube for the needs of campers. Also available are widenecked polyethylene bottles in pint and quart sizes, which are ideal for carrying milk and juices.

While beans, bacon, and bannock are still standbys about the cook fire, modern freeze-dried foods have simplified the cook's chores in providing a greater variety of fare in camp. These are conveniently packaged in one-, two-, four-, and six-man portions, weigh mere ounces, require no refrigeration, and last up to two years without spoilage. Nor are these to be confused with early dehydrated foods which had the texture and palatability of moosehide mukluks! When the camp cook can prepare a 32-ounce beef stew from a six-ounce package in 35 minutes, and the diners ask for seconds, the word "marvelous" is not an exaggeration.

Freeze-dried foods are somewhat more expensive than conventional household ingredients, it's true; but when you consider that all waste has been eliminated and much of the preparation completed, the convenience is well worth the extra cost, especially to campers who travel light, when refrigeration is not possible.

Carrying leftovers is always a problem. Pies, cakes, rolls, and even casserole dishes which are even better warmed over, can be carried in a unit consisting of four aluminum deep dishes which fit together one over the other. A long bail holds the four snugly in place and a cover fits the top dish. The compartments are not watertight, so that liquids cannot be carried safely but the food carrier is ideal for most other foods.

Bill Browning

Chapter 8

STOVES, LIGHTS, REFRIGERATORS

Stoves

A fisherman I had been guiding once boasted good naturedly that his gasoline stove would boil water quicker than any cooking fire. As he unlimbered his stove I reached for my ax and the small spruce blaze that I built beat his stove by nearly two minutes. However, this prompted me to take a second look at camp stoves which until that day, I had held in some contempt. My conversion wasn't complete—I still keep a sharp ax—but now I also own three different types of camp stoves!

While it's true that no stove will ever replace the campfire for cheeriness and warmth, the efficiency and speed with which a pleasure camper can prepare a meal on a camp stove has an open fire beat. The modern camp stove is as efficient and almost as easy to use as a new kitchen range.

Probably more gasoline-burning camp stoves are sold than all other types put together. These compact units are available with one, two or three burners and many will burn either leaded or unleaded (white) gasoline.

Comparatively few one-burner stoves are sold, however, since they limit meals to one-pot types and are suitable only for hikers getting along on a limited menu.

For general camping the two- and three-burner models are ideal. Some of these have folding legs, or they can be placed on a picnic table, the tail gate of a station wagon, on a flat-topped stump, and there is no reason why they can't be used on the ground. The two-burner models weighing about 17 pounds have a working area of some 12 by 18 inches. Three

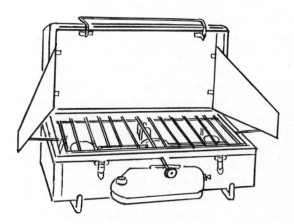

GASOLINE-BURNING CAMP STOVE

burner types weigh up to 25 pounds and their top surface is about 14 by 25 inches. When closed for carrying, they look not unlike a metal suitcase, a shape which lends itself to packing into a crowded car or trailer. When opened for use, the cover and a pair of wings fold outward to form a shield against the wind. As pointed out earlier, boxlike ovens, solid or collapsible, are available for use with these stoves and are fully as efficient as a kitchen range oven.

These stoves consume about one-half pint of gasoline per hour per burner, so that a two-gallon can of fuel may be expected to last from one to two weeks, depending, naturally, upon the use the stove gets. For economy of operation this is impossible to improve upon.

Operating the stoves is simple. Fill the gas tank and close the filler cap tightly. Remove the gas container from the immediate area for safety reasons, and pump up air pressure in the tank. Turn on the valve and light the burner with a match. Heat can be regulated just as on a home range.

Newer models cannot be overfilled and, if you use a small funnel with a fine screen for straining the gasoline, spillage is almost nil. Buy an approved gasoline container, properly marked or painted red, with a pouring spout and caps that close tightly to prevent leakage. Keep the container away from any type of open flame and never smoke while filling your stove. With this common-sense approach, your gasoline stove will give you years of danger-free service.

Carry a spare generator, according to the manufacturer's recommendations. Replacing this may be necessary once in a while and it's an easy task with a small wrench or pliers. Using clear or unleaded gasoline will lessen the frequency with which generators must be changed.

Clear gasoline, or white gas, may be difficult to obtain in a large city, but it's generally available in resort or camping areas. Apart from this, my sole criticism of the stoves is that the shields get in the way of large cooking utensils. Most models will accept only 8- to 10-inch diameter pots or pans if these are to be centered over the burners.

The stoves may be used safely inside a tent without ill effects if a window or door is kept at least partially opened. However, since burning gasoline develops monoxide gas, don't use one in a tightly closed tent. If the weather is bad and you want to cook under a canopy, take advantage of the wind shields by facing them into the wind protecting the burners from its cooling effects.

Next in popularity are stoves burning pressurized LP (liquid petroleum) or propane gas. These are actually easier to use than the gasoline-burning stoves, since no refilling is needed, no pumping or generator changing is required. Simply turn on a valve and light. Changing the fuel tank is done by unscrewing a brass collar which can often be done without pliers or wrench. Other fuel tanks have a rubber tip which fits snugly over a needlelike feed line, so that the tanks are simply pulled out and new ones pushed in. Incidentally, never throw these empties into a fire for they may explode with considerable thunder! Discard them in camp waste cans or bury them.

Their greatest disadvantage lies in the cost of operation. You will find them much more expensive to run than gasoline stoves, and in some areas replacing fuel tanks may be difficult if the dealer does not carry the particular type which fits your stove. Unfortunately, these have not been standardized. However, the luxury of this type of cooking

fuel may appeal to you enough to disregard the increased cost, in which case carry an ample supply of spare fuel tanks. These may last from two to six hours each and it's a good plan to use an entire tank at home to determine the length of its usefulness.

These little stoves come in various forms, the largest I know of having only two burners. Some are equipped with wind shields, while others have recessed burners. The wind, however, still blows between the kettle and the burner, offsetting some of the heat. A shield is preferable. A two-burner stove will weigh about six pounds while a single-burner unit will run slightly less than half of this, including the fuel tanks.

PROPANE STOVE   *Bernzomatic*

One firm supplies a small one-burner stove which operates from a household or trailer-type 20-pound tank with a 12-foot hose to connect the two. Such a tank will last about 120 hours when used with the stove, and some 200 hours when used with a lantern offered by the same manufacturer. This is the most economical way to use bottled gas.

Another outfit offers a complete two-burner "kitchen" which uses the small disposable cylinders. This unit weighs slightly more than 30 pounds and includes a cupboard and cooking kit. The entire outfit packs into the cupboard for carrying.

The two-burner units are suited to camp cooking, but the one-burner type should be regarded as supplementary units. I often carry my smaller bottled gas stove for a quick cup of coffee, or a simple noontime lunch when fire cooking would be uncomfortable during the heat of the day.

It has been pointed out by some that certain propane types cf gas will not function when the temperature drops to near freezing or below. Since many manufacturers put out fuels under their own brand names, it's difficult to tell which of these are included among those affected by low temperatures. Be sure to check before buying a stove, if you plan to use it in cold weather.

Gasoline and bottled gas are far superior to charcoal. The commercial size 20-pound propane tank will last as long as 100 pounds of charcoal, and at considerably smaller cost. Although charcoal is used a great deal on weekend trips by park campers, it's the poorest of all fuels. I have as yet to eat a "charcoal broiled" steak that didn't taste as if it had been cooked over a fire burning old barn boards! Charcoal is bulky, throws off offensive gases, and is dirty to handle.

Kerosene stoves are also available for camp cooking, but this fuel is objectionable since its smell is difficult to wash off the hands or from kettles should spilling occur. Also, most kerosene stoves require generating or priming by the burning of a small quantity of alcohol, somewhat of a nuisance.

Tiny one-burner miniature stoves which burn either gasoline or paraffin are available in this country, although I believe they are made only in Scandinavia. Recently I was sent a set of these for testing and I found them to be everything the manufacturer claimed. Especially, I liked the fact that pumping the one-burner model is unnecessary. The stoves which I tested burned lighter fluid, clear gasoline, and outboard-motor gasoline to which motor oil had been added. They boiled a quart of water in slightly over five minutes. Barely five inches square when closed the one-burner style weighs slightly more than 1½ pounds, ideal for a hiker or mountain climber.

A two-burner version of this stove worked as well, but its size is considerably smaller than the regular American two-burner gasoline stove. The imported version is too small for a family camping party, and really too large for the hiker or climber.

Tent Heaters

The heating of an enclosed tent is entirely feasible. The secret is to maintain a constant source of heat; otherwise warmth escapes through the fabric rapidly. A fluctuating wood fire in a stove, for example, will have you alternatingly shivering and perspiring.

I have never felt completely safe sleeping in a heated tent, preferring to depend on a suitable sleeping bag for nighttime warmth. Nonetheless, a heater has its place—during an evening or morning chill, on a cold, rainy day and, of course,

during the winter—but always while someone is awake.

Since they attain nearly complete combustion of fuel and thereby minimize or eliminate carbon monoxide, catalytic heaters are ideal. Once operational, they are flameless. Two types are available, one fired by white gasoline or naphtha, the other by propane gas dispensed from disposable 14-ounce cylinders or from 6- to 20-pound bulk tanks. BTU output is adjustable, up to 8,000.

The gasoline or naphtha heater has one shortcoming, however. It must be lighted out of doors since it requires priming and pre-heating, which produce a two-foot flame. This burns down in about ten minutes, whereupon the heater may safely be moved into the shelter.

The propane type, on the other hand, may be lighted indoors. Once the valve is turned on and a match applied to the burner face, a faint, blue flame appears momentarily, presenting little danger. It extinguishes itself almost immediately, and the heater is automatically at full output without delay.

Despite the "carbon monoxide-free" claims for these heaters, some ventilation should be provided, particularly during rainy weather when fabric fibers swell and decrease the passage of fresh air into the tent.

Wood-burning stoves, especially in areas where hardwood is available for a steady fire, are efficient heaters, with the added advantage that cooking can also be done on them. These range from tiny heaters, weighing under four pounds with room atop for a single kettle, to the western favorites, the Sheepherder and Sims stoves, on which you can prepare a small banquet.

Such stoves are not likely to be found in the average sporting goods store, for they are the equipment of the professional guide and woods wrangler. Practically unknown in the East, they are extremely popular in the West where they are toted on pack horses. However, there is no reason why one can't be carried in a car or boat.

The Sheepherder stove varies in width from 12 to 13 inches, and from 26 to 27 inches in length, and can be had with or without an oven. Legs may be attached to some models, as well as shelves which just about double the top working area. Some models have telescoping stovepipes. Weight will range from 20 pounds for the stripped-down type, to about 33 pounds for the deluxe model, complete with legs, shelves, and pipe. These accessories can be carried in the stove. Far from being awkward to carry, they are compact and can be stored in a car

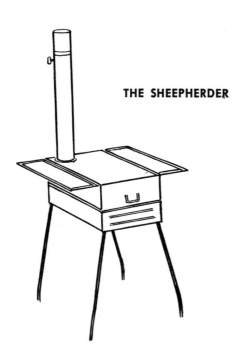

THE SHEEPHERDER

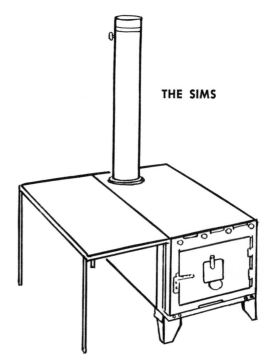

THE SIMS

or pack horse pannier with ease. A canvas carrying bag will keep soot confined.

Like the Sheepherder, the Sims stove is made of sheet steel. The latter, however, is a collapsible model 15 inches high, 13 inches wide, and 22 inches long which can be assembled in a half minute. The stovepipe is nested and is carried separate from the stove unit which is less than 4 inches thick when folded. Since this type does not have an oven within the stove itself, a reflector oven is available, as well as a side extension shelf which doubles the stove top area. There's even a six-gallon water tank which can be attached, assuring ample hot water for dishes. If you want to go deluxe, there's a faucet available! Weight of the stove and pipe alone runs 28 pounds. Another excellent stove of similar design is one known as the Kwik-Kamp.

These stoves are probably the finest type for tent heating and cooking, but there is no reason why they can't be used out of doors, even during the summer, where fireplaces are inadequate. When used in the open, only one length of stovepipe is necessary—just enough to help create a draft.

In a tent, however, the stovepipe must be run through the top or the side, preferably through the top near the ridge or peak. Wall and Cottage tents are ideal for use with such stoves. For this purpose, you can buy metal or asbestos rings which protect the fabric where the pipe runs through. Attaching such a ring requires only that you cut a hole to accommodate the pipe and bolt the two-piece ring to

the tent fabric. Exact dimensions for the hole will vary, but you should have at least three inches around the pipe free of fabric. Also, the asbestos ring is preferable to the metal type, it being a poorer conductor of heat. If you want to use the tent without a stove, a flap closes the stovepipe hole.

The stovepipe should be run at least six inches to one foot above the highest point of the tent to prevent "blow back," caused by the wind striking the sloping wall or roof of the tent and blowing downward into the top of the pipe. Be sure that the smoke stack is well guyed with wire. Rig the top with guys running in three directions and if the pipe extends upward more than six feet, rig it again about midway of its height. If the pipe wobbles or buckles, it may work the joints loose and fall.

Outfitters have a combination rain cap and spark arrester which may be used atop the pipe and this is advisable. A fine mesh wire screen can be bent into shape to form a bonnet or hood for the same purpose. If soot builds up on the screen or spark arrester, rap it sharply with a stick to knock the accumulation down. A spark arrester will not cut down the draft if it's kept clean.

One of the best tent-heating and -cooking rigs I've ever encountered consisted of a steel sheet set over a fire pit within a tent, with the stovepipe running under the tent wall and out of doors. The horizontal section of the pipe was set underground in a trench, running from the fire pit to an elbow outside the tent. From there, the pipe ran upward. While the

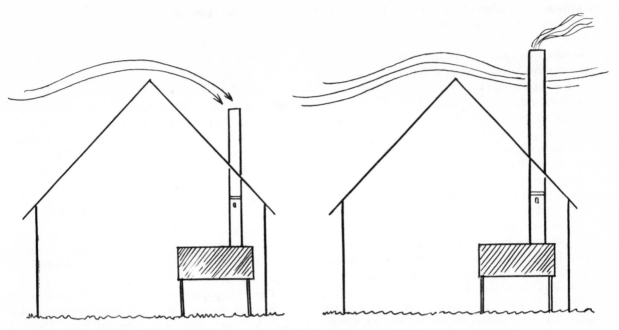

PLACE STOVE PIPE ABOVE TENT RIDGE TO PREVENT "BLOW-BACK"

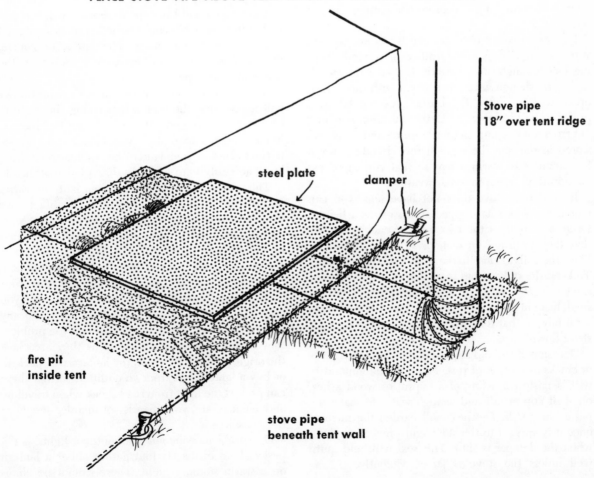

steel plate

damper

Stove pipe
18" over tent ridge

fire pit
inside tent

stove pipe
beneath tent wall

A FIRE PIT INSIDE THE TENT

steel plate was undoubtedly as heavy, if not heavier than a stove, it was less expensive. The guide who had set up the rig I saw did the cooking for four persons on the plate, and the pit fire kept the tent comfortably warm during the late November weather. The front of the pit was open and through this the guide fed the fire. He had even set a damper in the first section of pipe, the handle of which protruded upward handily.

No matter what type of tent stove you use, always place it and the stovepipe at least 18 inches away from any tent fabric, and never leave it untended while a fire is burning—not even for a few minutes.

So-called Yukon stoves or improvised heaters made of various-sized tin cans are poor rigs. Frequently a five gallon can is suggested as a "homemade" tent stove, but such improvisations are rarely successful and almost always dangerous unless you're an old hand with such jury rigs.

Always try to keep a shallow bed of ashes in your stove—for two reasons. First, the fire will burn longer, and second, the ashes will insulate the bottom, preventing the scorching of your ground cloth if you use one.

Few experienced outdoorsmen try to keep a tent warm at night, depending, rather, on a good sleeping bag for nighttime warmth. If you want an all-night fire, though, mix green wood with the dry, in order to slow down the burning of the latter. I prefer to build a new fire in the morning, reaching out from my sleeping bag for kindling and dry wood stored in the tent the night before. It takes only a few minutes to warm a tent so that you can dress comfortably, even in cold weather.

If your tent stove does not have legs, you can mount it on four flat-topped stakes of even height. Drive a 3″ nail on the two sides of each corner so that they protrude an inch or so from the stakes. Place the nails as close to the stove's sides as possible. To keep the stakes from scorching, put a handful of sand in each inside corner of the stove, or push a small heap of ashes into these. Be sure the stakes are set firmly, so that they won't wobble and bring your stove down!

Occasionally an old stove will develop small holes or cracks as a result of rust. Patch these temporarily with a paste consisting of a cupful of wood ashes, one-half cup of salt and enough water to make the paste fairly stiff. The heat will harden the mixture once it is applied to the stove and prevent smoking when the damper is shut. This seal will hold quite well unless the stove is jarred violently.

Lights and Lanterns

For the sake of fuel economy and handiness, a gasoline lantern is the best choice if you're planning to use a gasoline stove. The same is true, of course, of a propane stove and light. There is no point in carrying two types of fuel when one will do the job. However, the variety of camp lights available offers a much wider range than is offered by gasoline and propane-type gas models.

On a hiking trip where weight and bulk must be kept down, you will probably confine yourself to the tiny candle lantern which folds flat and weighs only a few ounces, or possibly to a pocket flashlight. Even on a canoe trip, where portages may be tough, there are limitations as to lights which may be carried. The car or pack-train camper, however, can enjoy luxurious lighting.

The most popular camp light is the gasoline lantern which operates on much the same principal as the stove, requiring a pressurized tank. The fuel tank will usually hold enough gasoline to burn four to eight hours and this type of lantern will throw a wide circle of white light, whether it is equipped with one or two mantles. The latter, of course, throws more light—and burns more fuel—than the single-mantle type.

Using a small funnel with a fine mesh wire strainer will assure that the fuel will not clog the lantern. Carrying a spare generator, which can be changed in minutes, is a wise plan. Also, cleaning the screen in the burner, if your lantern has such a screen, can be done easily with a child's discarded toothbrush.

The operation of various gasoline lanterns varies only slightly, but be sure to read the manufacturer's directions, and carry these with you in camp. Most makers also give tips on maintenance and repair that are worthwhile having handy.

Don't be led to believe, though, that gasoline lanterns are a constant source of trouble, for this is far from being the case. Given reasonable care, you may go an entire season without having to do any serious tinkering. Even mantles are not the problem they might appear to be, fragile as they are. Save the original carton in which the lantern was packed, or buy a lantern box from an outfitter, so that these can protect the light from road shock when traveling and, chances are, your mantle—or mantles—may last the season.

One problem, common to all outdoor lights, is the pesky cloud of insects that gather about a lantern on a warm summer night. These cannot be eliminated but they can be kept at a distance. Use a lantern with two mantles to secure greater light, and hang the unit some distance, ten to fifteen feet, from where you are working. Setting the light a few feet away will attract the bugs from you and still give you ample illumination. This is true of all types of lanterns, of course—not just the gasoline type. Amber globes which are available will prove unattractive to insects.

On a cool night when the chill in the air is slightly uncomfortable, a gasoline or propane gas lantern will do a surprisingly good job of heating a tent, but some ventilation should be provided for safety.

Propane or LP (liquid petroleum) lanterns are just coming into their own as camp lights and these are easier to operate and maintain than the gasoline counterparts. They are, however, more expensive to run. Although they require a mantle, no pumping is necessary, since they use the same type of fuel pressurized tank as do the stoves. They give an excellent light, equal to a 100-watt bulb in most cases. In buying a propane-type gas lantern seek out a model that has a wide, stable base. Some types are little more than a burner and globe set atop a fuel can and these are quite unstable.

PROPANE LANTERN   *Bernzomatic*

Another source of good camp light is the car battery. Outfitters have "trouble lights" which may be plugged into the cigarette lighter socket but care should be used not to run these too long for fear of running the battery down. There is also a fluores-

cent-type light which is reported to run for 12 to 15 hours without danger of lowering the battery's efficiency. Frankly, I haven't tried one of these and cannot personally vouch for this claim.

Another light, rarely seen nowadays, is the old-fashioned kerosene lantern. It offers a comparatively feeble but reliable light and should not be scoffed at. It requires very little fuel, is practically foolproof and it's a safe light. There are also kerosene lanterns, much like the pressurized gasoline type available, but these require priming or generating by the burning of a small amount of alcohol.

Natural torches, made of such materials as cattails or rushes, are dangerous, inefficient, and completely unreliable.

Lanterns, whether used outdoors or in a tent, are much more efficient if used with a bracket and reflector. About half the light given off is wasted as a rule, unless it is directed where it is needed most. The bracket keeps the light itself out of the way and allows you to drop the bail handle to keep it cool. A lantern that is hung by its handle will heat the latter so that it cannot be touched with bare hands.

When using a lantern in a tent to illuminate a table, do not place it directly overhead, as the base will cast a heavy shadow on the table's surface. Set it to one side, using a reflector to direct the light. One type of camp lantern has the fuel tank *over* the globe, casting light downward.

Battery-operated lights, of course, throw a brilliant and quiet light. These come with diffusing lenses for spreading the light over a wide area, and with a focus lens for concentrating light in one spot. These can be hung overhead or placed on a table or shelf as stationary lights. The variety available is slightly overwhelming, but they all have one drawback in common. When used as stationary lights and kept burning during an entire evening, the batteries don't last very long, making such lights quite expensive to operate. Most of these lights are designed to be used intermittently. Naturally, if the cost of batteries is no problem to you, they are a fine type of light.

A two- or three-cell flashlight should be carried for every two members of a camping party. Taking the camp lantern to search for a lost item can make you unpopular with those who are left in the dark. Also, they are ideal for nighttime trips to latrines. Don't buy the giant six- and seven-cell models thinking they are more efficient. Such lights are awkward to carry, expensive to refill, and a general nuisance to other campers.

Also, stay away from "trick" lights, such as self-generating models which may or may not function when wanted. Miners' lights or various types of headband lights have little real practical value in camp, unless your trip will include cave exploration. Belt lights, "leaving the hands free," also are not as practical as might appear, for the light invariably is directed in the wrong direction and must be aimed by hand.

Waterproof flashlights are well worth looking into. I have a three-cell model, now three years old, which still works well. It cost no more than the conventional type and its heavy rubber casing helps it to absorb shock which all flashlights are subject to in camp life. Spare bulbs and batteries, of course, should be carried for each light in camp.

Refrigerators

Unless you buy a well-known camp refrigerator or cooler, you'll be buying a pig in a poke. Too many manufacturers today are devising their own brand names for standard insulation material with the result that the buyer is completely at a loss as to what he is actually getting. And insulation in a cooler is far more important than its outside appearance.

Insulation in the better coolers consists of urethane foam, unquestionably the best available today. My own tests have proven this, at least to my satisfaction. In addition, the nation's two leading manufacturers, although in direct competition with each other, both insulate their chests with urethane.

Coolers come in varying sizes, but none differ greatly from two basic sizes, 9 inches wide, 12 deep, and 16 long, or the larger unit which is 12 by 16 by 22. Most have a removable or adjustable interior compartment. Be sure that the interior lining is seamless and has rounded corners for easy cleaning. Outer cases may be of light steel, aluminum, or one of the new plastics.

Even the best camp refrigerator of the portable type can't be expected to keep ice much longer than 36 hours in hot weather. However, unless you follow a few simple rules, chances are your ice supply won't last this long.

Precooling, before packing the perishables, is important. If you have a freezer at home, place the camp cooler in it for about 24 hours, leaving the cooler's cover open slightly. If you have no freezer, perhaps a locker plant, or a nearby butcher will store the box in his walk-in refrigerator for a few hours.

Otherwise, precool the box with natural ice, ice cubes, or even dry ice. Pack as large a proportion of ice in relation to food as possible. If, after packing both ice and food, there still remains room, add more ice.

If ice is difficult to obtain, fill empty milk cartons and freeze these. They will pack more compactly than one large chunk, and when the ice melts, the cartons will hold the water, instead of allowing it to flood the cooler, a common fault of all camp models. In a pinch, you can even use the wax carton for fire tinder!

Wrapping ice in newspaper within a cooler does little good, for this merely insulates the ice, and food does not get the full benefit of cooling. Replacing ice supplies en route on a camping trip is not as difficult as you might suppose, since gasoline stations in resort and camping areas often carry it, although it may be in the form of cubes packed in a plastic bag.

Some campers combine dry ice with natural ice and get a few extra hours of refrigeration. Pack the dry ice in one layer on the bottom of the box and place the natural ice over this. The latter will not melt much until the dry ice has disappeared. Dry ice, however, can give you a nasty burn if not handled properly, such as with gloves. Its temperature is said to be well under 100 degrees below zero!

When in camp, keep the cooler in the shade, but not in the midday heat of the tent interior. Placing it in a spring or running stream will help. Also, open it as infrequently as possible, for each time the cover is lifted, warm air enters.

Bucket-type coolers are not completely practical for camp use since it's difficult to fit a square chunk of ice into the round compartment. Even if you succeed, there's little room left for foodstuffs.

Natural refrigerators, such as pits in the ground covered with boughs, do not work well, although cooling foods in a cold spring or stream is fairly effective. For this use a five-gallon can which has been weighted down with rocks to keep it from floating. Sometimes the weight of the food alone will suffice. It should have a tight-fitting cover, however, otherwise you'll be at the mercy of mink and other always-hungry animals. A well can also be used, by lowering the can until it begins to float and then tying it at that level. All in all, however, natural refrigeration is, at best, a temporary improvisation and the investment in a good quality camp refrigerator will pay off in food savings and better meals.

Even if you run out of ice and have to depend

on nonperishables, use the cooler for a storage box. It will discourage squirrels, field mice, mink, and chipmunks.

Plastic insulated bags are not suitable as camp refrigerators. These are designed as picnic units. I have one of these which I use for one-day trips, cooling it with "canned ice," little more than water with a little antifreeze added. This "canned ice" which is frozen for use in a home freezer, does not keep cold long enough for use in a camp ice chest.

It had to come, of course. There is now available a portable propane-gas or electric refrigerator designed for use by campers. How well it operates I can't say, since it has been available only a few weeks at the time this is being written. It has slightly more than one cubic foot of storage space and will hold food at 36 degrees, according to the manufacturer's statement.

WELCOME LAKE, IDAHO   *U. S. Forest Service photo*

Chapter 9

SLEEPING GEAR

The Bough Bed

Every camper should sleep on an aromatic balsam bough bed at least once. You'll need a hefty armload of boughs and some 45 minutes to cut and place them.

The base of the bed should be of spruce boughs, rather than balsam, and about three-quarters to one inch thick at the butt. Spruce is stronger than balsam fir and holds its spring longer. Be sure, too, that you don't use cat or skunk spruce, for the crushed needles of this tree will emit an offensive smell. Lay the base with the butts pointing toward the head or the foot, not crosswise, so that the bed is about three feet wide and six feet long. Double the width if two campers will use the bed. Build up the spruce boughs until they're about a foot deep, being sure that all butts are stuck downward and near the bottom of the bed. On top of these, place about six inches of balsam fir boughs, about the thickness of a man's index finger. Try your bed out before turning in for the night. There may be a bough or two that will have to be adjusted to prevent its gouging you. In adjusting the boughs for comfort,

place a few extra ones around the edge of the bed, to form a sort of "nest." This will help to keep you aboard during the night. Incidentally, logs around a bough bed, so often suggested, are unnecessary.

The bough bed is for wilderness camping only, of course, since indiscriminate cutting of boughs in park campgrounds isn't allowed. Other drawbacks are the fact that a bough bed is rarely good for more than one or two nights. It then has to be "refluffed" by shifting the boughs, and by the addition of a few new ones. Also, after traveling all day, you'll have little inclination to tackle the job of building one—when five minutes work will blow up a comfortable air mattress. Heresy? I suppose so, but that's the way it works out.

The Ground Cloth

A ground cloth is a waterproofed material placed under a sleeping bag or air mattress to prevent moisture from reaching the bedding and to protect

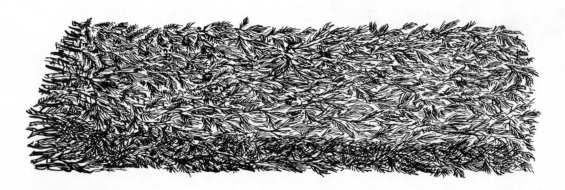

THE BOUGH BED

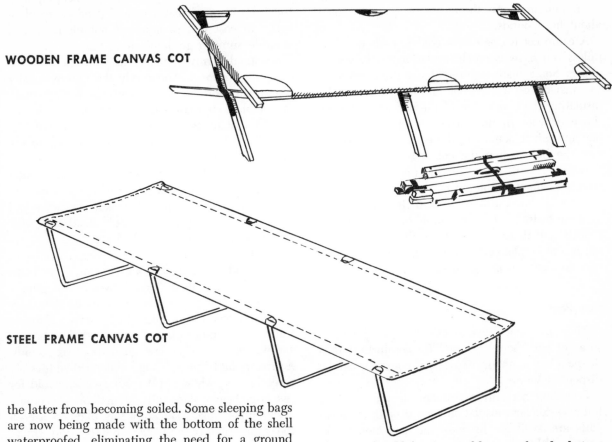

WOODEN FRAME CANVAS COT

STEEL FRAME CANVAS COT

the latter from becoming soiled. Some sleeping bags are now being made with the bottom of the shell waterproofed, eliminating the need for a ground cloth.

Materials which are suitable for a ground cloth include duck, treated nylon, rubber, and rubberized cotton fabrics. Plastics, while they may be rolled into a small bundle, make poor ground cloths, being too easily damaged.

A small duck tarpaulin, though somewhat heavy, is excellent. During winter camping trips in New Hampshire, I've used a kapok-filled sleeping bag laid between the folds of such a tarpaulin. Sleep was easy and comfortable despite temperatures well below freezing. This is not unlike the canvas shell used by cowhands, except that they use wool blankets.

A poncho made of rubber or rubberized cotton works very well and can, of course, be used as a raincoat during the day. New products, which are well suited to this use are neoprene or vinyl impregnated nylon, since these are both waterproof and tough.

The Camp Cot

It goes without saying that a camp cot should be collapsible, but don't buy a cheap one, lest it collapse when it shouldn't. A suitable one, beside being rugged, should fold into a bundle not over three feet long nor more than a few inches in diameter.

The wooden-frame canvas cots perhaps are the most compact, folding into bundles about 39″ by 4″ by 6″ and weighing about 15 pounds each. Such a cot will have a sleeping surface about 28″ wide and 78″ long. Some deluxe models, for use with wide sleeping robes, come 36″ wide and are, of course, correspondingly heavier.

In buying a cot, be sure that all joints and hinges are well reinforced with metal plates and that all rivets are tight. The cover should be of 12 ounce, or heavier, duck and the stitching should be generous. Look the legs over for straight-grained hardwood.

One of the finest cots available currently is one that has a two-piece steel rod on each side, joined in the center by a ferrule. Each side bar has four steel sockets, into which W shaped steel legs are inserted. These leg units exert a strong side thrust which keeps the cot open. The sleeping surface is about 32″ by 78″, and only nine inches above the ground, a decided advantage when the cot is used in a tent with sloping walls. When taken down it forms a bundle 2″×11″×29″ and weighs about 12 pounds. This same type of cot is available with an aluminum frame, the entire rig weighing only about five pounds.

A camp cot is one of the coldest beds possible, unless you have as much insulation under you as above. Some manufacturers have come up with the answer to the cold cot problem, however, by insulating the *under* side of the cot with Dacron, down, or wool. In most cases this adds only one to one and a half pounds to the cot's over-all weight and the bulk, when the cot is folded, is barely noticeable. With the insulation *under* the canvas cover, it cannot be matted by the sleeper's weight.

A cot is almost a luxury, but if there is room in your car or trailer, take one along for each camper, especially if there are women in the party. Camping is a more pleasant experience, if it's not necessary to sleep on the ground.

Cot Pads

There isn't much give to a tightly spread canvas, so a cot pad should be used for comfort. With a sleeping bag or an air mattress, of course, it can be dispensed with.

Providing not only a resilient sleeping surface but also excellent insulation against cold, foam cot pads are available in one- and two-inch thicknesses. Although they cannot be rolled as compactly as an air mattress, they afford far greater comfort.

Cotton comforters or quilts can be used in their place, but these are generally heavy, bulky, and prone to absorbing moisture. However, if the budget is strict, by all means use one. Never sleep on a cot without some sort of insulation under you. Incidentally, a down "puff" or quilt makes an excellent cot pad and can be used comfortably in much colder weather than kapok or cotton.

Blankets

Worn-out blankets, discarded from home use are never "good enough for camping." Sleeping out requires the best blankets you can afford, not the poorest. Blankets from which the nap has been worn and which have become threadbare have little, if any, insulation value. If you must take blankets from home, take the best you own, even at the risk of soiling them. They can always be dry cleaned.

I can see no reason, though, for using blankets on a camping trip except possibly when the budget won't allow the purchase of a sleeping bag. But keep in mind that a pair of good camp blankets will cost you as much—if not more—than a suitable summer-grade sleeping bag.

So-called Army blankets are the poorest for camping purposes. Apparently the Quartermaster Corps was more concerned with the lasting qualities of blankets than with the comfort of soldiers, as Army blankets have a close, hard weave, designed to absorb a lot of punishment. These are poor insulation against the cold.

A warm blanket must have a loose weave and a thick nap. The nap is the fuzz which you feel on the surface of a fine blanket. This loose weave and thick nap will help trap and hold dead air which prevents the escape of body heat.

The best blankets are of pure virgin wool—not reprocessed. Long famous are Hudson's Bay blankets, noted for their "point" system. Originally these were trade blankets, made in England, for which Hudson's Bay posts took beaver skins in trade. A four-point blanket was worth four beaver and was 72″ by 90″ and weighed about six pounds. A three-point blanket, being smaller, called for only three beaver, while a still smaller version sold for two large beaver skins and one small one, becoming a 2½-point blanket. Hudson's Bay blankets are all the same quality with the "points" and prices varying according to size.

There are many fine American blankets available for camping which you can buy for much less money than a Hudson's Bay blanket will cost you. Woolen mills that weave blankets usually have a "remnant store" where you can buy seconds at a considerable saving. Simply insist that the "second" be virgin wool, loosely woven and about 72″ by 90″ for single use.

As for weight, remember that two three-pound blankets will keep you warmer than a single six-pounder. Two six-pound blankets should keep you comfortable in weather down to freezing, providing you make up your blanket bed properly and have sufficient padding or insulation under you. There can be no set formula, however, for the number of blankets you will need, for these needs will vary with the time of the year, the area, and your own degree of immunity to nighttime chill.

Don't judge nighttime temperatures by daytime warmth. For example, in west Texas I have been uncomfortably warm in shirt sleeves during the day and been forced to wear a heavy hunting jacket at night! The same is true in the North, where a warm day will often be followed by a chill after the sun sets.

You have probably seen a movie hero lie down with his head on his saddle and a single saddle blanket drawn up over him, peacefully going to sleep under the Western sky. This is a cordial invitation to pneumonia, while rolling up in a single blanket is not unlike trying to sleep in a strait jacket.

Northern woodsmen who use blankets carry "hoss blanket pins" which they use to form a sort of sleeping bag with two or more blankets. To do this, lay your blanket so that one half of it, placed lengthwise, covers the cot or mattress. Lay a second blanket, from the other side, so that half the second blanket covers half of the first. Now fold the first blanket over the second, and the remaining half over both. Tuck the foot of the blankets under slightly and pin the entire rig so that it will not come apart during the night.

Slip into the bag so that there are two thicknesses under you and two over. On a warm pad, you may use only one thickness under and three over, for a comfortable and warm bed. Don't try using this bed without pins, unless you're an unusually quiet sleeper, for turning and twisting during the night will disarrange the blankets.

Don't depend upon wool blankets for protection against rain, since wool will absorb water during a downpour. You probably won't get chilled because even wet wool will keep you warm, but wool blankets take a long time to dry. Use a canvas sleeping-bag shell or sleep in a tent during rainy weather.

Some excellent wools are combined with synthetics to weave a blanket of greater durability and, these too, are excellent camp blankets, though not quite so warm as pure wool. Never take a cotton blanket on a camping trip, however, for cotton will not keep in body warmth and when the weather is wet, cotton gets clammy.

Air Mattresses

It's only been in recent years that I've succumbed to the air mattress and now I wouldn't be without one unless the trip called for unusually light travel. Sleeping on the hard ground during a car or canoe camping trip is folly.

Most mattresses consist of rubber, vulcanized to cotton sheeting, drill, or nylon, along with a large number of plastic models. The first three are all excellent materials while plastic air mattresses have little to recommend them except their low price. The best of plastic air mattresses are flimsy and generally

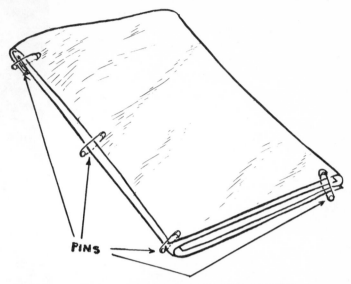

PINNING TWO BLANKETS WITH "HOSS BLANKET PINS" TO MAKE A SLEEPING BAG

unsatisfactory for extended trips. However, as a budget item they can be used if given care. When buying one, be sure the valve is metal, not plastic, and that it works properly. Check this by inflating the mattress and allowing it to remain inflated overnight. Don't take one on a camping trip without checking it.

Plastic air mattresses come in a more or less standard 24-inch width when inflated, often listed as 32" wide, which is deflated width. Lengths vary but are generally 60 to 72 inches. Short hikers' models are often about hip length or 44 to 48 inches.

Also available is a plastic station-wagon mattress which is finding popularity today. This type is usually about 60 inches wide and six feet long. Some regular-size models can be attached along one side to form a mattress for either a station wagon or a double sleeping bag.

If you use plastic, be sure that a ground cloth is used under it to avoid abrasion or puncturing. Also, use great care in packing it, so that it will not rub against a sharp object. Repair kits are available for them and it's an easy matter to make simple repairs, although patches are difficult to apply along the seams and near the valve. Buy the type with a metal valve rather than the plastic one, for accidentally stepping on the latter will put the mattress out of commission permanently.

Rubber-coated mattresses made of drill, sheeting, or nylon are much tougher and will stand considerable abuse. These, too, come in a great variety of sizes, the most popular type being 24 inches wide when inflated, for use in sleeping bags whose over-

MAKING CAMP, DONALD LAKE, ONTARIO

Ontario Travel Department

all widths are 30 to 34 inches. For saving on weight, a mattress 48 inches long is suitable but I always feel that my feet are "hanging out over the edge." The 48″ style will effect a weight saving of about two pounds over the full length type.

The 32″ wide model (inflated size), is available for use in sleeping bags of 40″ width. Air mattresses of rubberized fabric are also available for double sleeping bags whose widths are about five feet, and, there are station-wagon models too.

Since an air mattress is likely to be a long-range investment, buy the best you can afford from a reliable outfitter or sporting goods store. Bargains in air mattresses usually result in disappointment.

Air mattresses can be blown up by mouth, of course, but this is a tedious process that's hard on the lungs and cheeks. It's much easier to use a pump. The rubber-bulb type which is squeezed by hand to operate is light and compact for packing. Another type is operated by foot action, squeezing a bellows-like unit, which is also efficient, light, and compact. The piston type, not unlike a bicycle pump, is the poorest of the lot due to its weight.

Even if the opportunity presents itself, don't inflate an air mattress at a service-station air pump. No mattress has been made which will stand the sudden high pressures developed for tire use.

The suggestion that the camper hold the air-mattress valve before the exhaust pipe of an automobile while the engine idles is among the most ridiculous I've seen. Even if the exhaust pressure were great enough to fill the mattress, the thought of sleeping on a bagful of carbon monoxide gas is not a pleasant prospect.

The most common mistake made in pumping up an air mattress is to get it too hard. Most campers, inflating one for the first time, kneel on the bag to test it. Naturally, the concentrated weight goes through to rest on the ground and they assume the mattress needs more air. Test the mattress by lying on it. Your body should sink into the mattress but you shouldn't be able to feel the ground. Your shoulders and hips particularly will sink into the mattress but if they don't contact the earth, you'll be comfortable. Naturally, if you prefer a hard bed, there is no harm in inflating the mattress to greater pressure.

All air mattresses are difficult to deflate and it does no good to roll or fold them as this only traps air in pockets. Instead, when breaking camp lay the mattress out flat with the valve open, packing it last. It will deflate itself as quickly this way as any.

Sleeping Bags

Generally it's best to buy the finest you can afford when it comes to outdoors equipment, but this isn't necessarily so in the case of sleeping bags. There are three basic types of sleeping bags, the arctic robe, the hiker's bag, and the summer camper's sleeping unit. In most instances, their uses are not interchangeable, except at the risk of some discomfort.

The large arctic robe, generally considered best and most expensive, is designed for cold climates where a man's life may depend on the quality of his sleeping gear. The hiker's bag is a combination of compact lightness and warmth, for a hiker is frequently a mountain climber, too, who can't afford to tote a heavy bag yet may be exposed to semiarctic conditions. On the other hand, the summer camper's bag need not be especially light for it will probably be carried in a car and quite likely he will never sleep out when it's colder than freezing.

The arctic robe is rarely made with anything but goose down for a filler, since eider-duck down has become scarce, although some cheaper models are insulated with a mixture of down and wild-fowl feathers. Eider-duck and goose down rate at the top as prime insulating materials upon which man has not been able to improve.

Some misunderstanding constantly arises regarding the difference between a sleeping robe and a sleeping bag. A robe has a full-length slide fastener down one side and across the bottom, so that when it is opened, it literally becomes a robe. A sleeping bag, on the other hand, has only a short zipper, usually 36″, and can be opened only partially. For all practical purposes, however, the term sleeping bag is steadily superseding that of "sleeping robe."

Those designed for arctic or extreme winter use have from five to seven pounds of goose down as a filler. When closed as sleeping bags, they are usually about 40 inches wide and seven to eight feet in length. Weights range from 14 to over 20 pounds and their bulk is considerable. They are suitable for temperatures down to 40 below and, if a wool blanket liner is added to some models, these will keep a sleeper comfortable at 60 below zero. I can't argue the point because the coldest I have ever encountered was 48 below zero!

While these bags are among the world's finest—and most expensive, running from about $90 up to more than $150—it's not likely that you will ever need one for summertime camping. It is needless to spend that much money and, more important, such bags would prove uncomfortably warm, even on the coldest summer night.

There are lighter models containing three or four pounds of down but even these, which are suitable for weather down to 30 below zero, are too warm for summer camping. Those which contain only two pounds of down may be used in the summer, by leaving them partially open. As an example of the effectiveness of goose down, there is a hiker's bag that is comfortable at well below freezing, yet it contains only *one* pound of down!

If you don't mind the comparative discomfort of the body-shaped or "mummy bag," the hiker's model is suitable for summer camping, especially if your trip involves hiking or climbing side trips. Of course, if you're out primarily to hike or to climb, such a bag is almost a necessity.

Hiker's mummy bags are comparatively unknown because few sporting goods stores handle them, their sale being handled mostly through firms that sell mountain climbing and hiking equipment of a specialized nature. Rarely do they weigh more than five pounds and there is one model, reportedly suitable for winter camping, that weighs only 2¾ pounds. Between one and two pounds of down is used to fill them. In order to attain these extreme light weights, their design eliminates unnecessary material, so that they fit the contours of man's body loosely, hence the name "mummy bag." They taper from the shoulders to the feet and usually have only a short zipper opening. Turning over in one of these bags usually means rolling the bag over, too, and drawing up the knees will also draw up the foot of the bag. For warm nights, one cleverly designed model has a second zipper at the foot for additional ventilation!

There are also a few Dacron-filled bags which, although they weigh somewhat more than the down-filled models, are less expensive and excellently suited to summer hiking trips. Their tapered design is much like the down-filled bags but they are a little bulkier. Their weight averages a pound or so more than similar down bags.

Don't get the impression that, because these hiker's models are kept to a weight and bulk minimum, they are skimpy. The better ones are seven feet long, 34″ wide at the shoulders and tapering to 24″ at the feet, although some bags may not be as ample.

Generally speaking they are comfortable in temperatures ranging from slightly below freezing to about 70 degrees above. You will have to consider, however, that not all campers have the same degree of susceptibility to night chills, and what is comfort for one camper may be misery for another.

Some hiker's models, particularly war-surplus

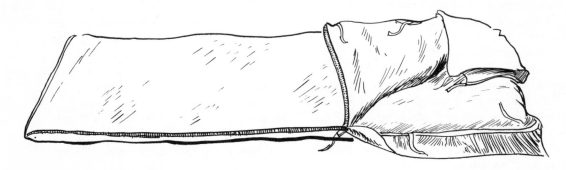

GOOSE DOWN SLEEPING BAG

THE "MUMMY" BAG

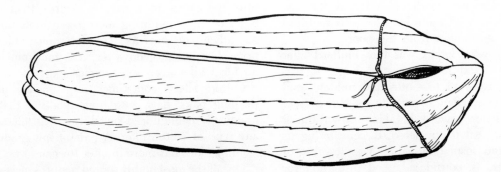

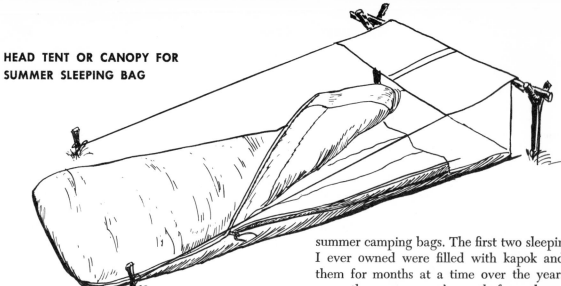

bags, do not contain all-down fillers but, rather, a combination of goose down and wild-fowl feathers. Often, too, these fillers are not virgin materials, but reprocessed. How their insulation value compares with that of new down and feathers depends on the ratio of down to feathers and their condition before being reprocessed. A half-and-half combination of *new* down and feathers will be only 15 percent less efficient than all new down. As far as the reprocessed material is concerned, there's no accurate method of testing or comparing them short of a laboratory and, therefore, it's advisable to give the reprocessed stuff a wide berth.

Since the warmth of a down sleeping bag is provided by the loft or "fluffiness" of the down, it is best to use a foam pad under this type of bag. The sleeper's weight naturally compresses the down in the lower half of the bag, allowing body warmth to seep through. Chill sets in. The foam pad, which does not compress as readily as down, substitutes as insulation.

The choice of a summer sleeping bag is not easily made unless you have some understanding of what goes into such a unit. The federal government now requires that a label be attached to all sleeping bags, specifying the type of filler and the amount. Unfortunately, that's as far as the law goes, and quite a bit more knowledge is required to pick the good bags from the poor.

For many years kapok was the standard filler used in low- and medium-priced bags. It was lightweight, resistant to moths and mildew, and almost half as efficient as pure down. However, it had a tendency toward breaking down under heavy use so that it powdered, thereby losing its resiliency and insulation value. Despite this, it was, and still is, considered good insulation for summer camping bags. The first two sleeping bags I ever owned were filled with kapok and using them for months at a time over the years I got more than my money's worth from them.

Crowding kapok out of the picture today, however, are two synthetics, notably Dacron and acetate fibers, the latter sold under various trade names. Dacron, according to laboratory tests, is about 75 percent as efficient as pure down, while acetate isn't far behind in efficiency. Sleeping bags filled with two or three pounds of Dacron or long acetate fibers are comfortable summer bags. I have one filled with four pounds of Dacron and find it too warm on a mild summer night.

These synthetics are displacing kapok because they have kapok's excellent qualities plus a few extras of their own. Moths, mildew, and rodents have no interest in them. They are lightweight, their fibers will not break down and powder, and their resiliency is considerably greater than that of kapok. Also, their cost is low.

Some claim that Dacron will not pass off body moisture as well as other fillers will but, after my family has used four of these bags during ten summers, I can find no criticism of Dacron whatsoever.

For warmth, wool rates next to kapok, although it's only about 25 percent as efficient as pure down. However, wool has disadvantages that are difficult to overlook. It's bulky, heavy, moths love it, it's inclined to shrink, and it holds body moisture and odors to a greater degree than other types of filler, requiring more time to air out. Its sole advantage, near as I can determine, is its low price. Despite this, however, it is far from being an ideal filler even for summer bags.

Cotton fillers, sometimes used in low-priced sleeping bags, have insulating qualities that are practically negligible. Don't buy a bag filled with any type of cotton filler. A pair of low-grade all-wool blankets has more to offer for comfort.

One of the most highly touted features of summer

camping bags is the "head tent" or canopy, usually shown propped up on forked sticks. This certainly makes the bag look inviting and completely safe from any wind or storm. Actually, these canopies are about as useless as one snowshoe in a blizzard!

These canopies create the impression that the sleeping bag may be used without a shelter in bad weather, which is misleading. When I first started using a sleeping bag, I once climbed to the top of New Hamphire's Mount Belknap where I rigged my canopied sleeping bag for the night. Long before morning it started to rain and there followed a hard downpour that bounced raindrops off the rocks. By daylight, both the bag and I were soaked through and I spent the following week in bed with bronchitis.

A sleeping bag should *not* have a waterproof cover, so that body moisture may escape through the weave of the material. If it were waterproofed to keep out rain, this moisture would remain within the bag, accumulating until the inner lining was wet and clammy. Since a sleeping bag cannot be waterproof, what is the sense of erecting that silly little canopy over the sleeper's head? No sleeping bag should be used without a shelter when rain is expected.

I hope that manufacturers will soon discard this type of advertising illustration and explain the design of sleeping bags more clearly for the sake of beginners. They might point out that the canopy unit should be used as a wrapper when the bag is being transported. For this purpose, the "head tent" would be put to sound use.

If there are children in your family, you can effect some savings in sleeping-bag prices by buying juvenile sizes. These are usually 30″ wide and about five feet long, while weight will run from four to seven pounds depending upon the filler and the bag material itself.

The standard-size sleeping bag is usually about 34″ wide and 78″ to 82″ long. Weights will vary with the filler and material, but will generally run between six and ten pounds.

If you're more than six feet tall, or greater in girth than the average camper, an oversized bag will be worth the extra investment. These larger bags are about 40″ wide and up to 90″ long, weighing from eight to eleven pounds, in models using four pounds of Dacron or acetate filler.

Most manufacturers now make the standard-sized bags so that two of them may be joined to form a double unit, amply large enough for two adults or three children. Sometimes, too, dealers will offer a discount when two or more bags are purchased at one time. Joining the bags is done by means of the zipper units, using one bag for the bottom and one for the top cover. This combination of sleeping bags is a good rig for use in station wagons.

Along with the canopy, the air mattress pocket, too, is practically useless. In fact, in many bags they create considerable discomfort because they are not ample enough to accommodate an inflated air mattress without crowding into the sleeping compartment. When this occurs, you will have difficulty rolling over and may even feel bound in. This is because most air-mattress pockets are simply flat envelopes designed without bellows along the sides to allow for the expanded air mattress. For this reason, I never use the pockets in my sleeping bags, preferring simply to lay the bag atop the inflated mattress. I've found that the possibility of rolling off has been grossly exaggerated and that I spend a far more comfortable night.

One firm makes a "contoured" upper cover on its sleeping bags, this upper unit being wider than the undercover so that crowding by the air mattress is not so pronounced. All in all, however, experts agree that, as it is made today, the air mattress pocket is in the same class with the head tent—a sales gimmick of little practical value.

There is still some criticism of the zipper for closing a sleeping bag, the claim being made that these occasionally stick or break. During the twenty-odd years that I have been using a sleeping bag, I've never had any serious trouble. On the other hand, I have had snaps stick and tear out of the material. Some sleeping bags have only a short zipper opening, usually 36″, so that the lower half of the bag cannot be opened for airing, unless it is turned inside out. Instead of this type, buy a sleeping bag that has a zipper running completely down one side and across the bottom. Such a bag can be aired more easily. Also, check to see that there is a padded "weather strip" just inside the zipper, to prevent cool air from entering through the slide fastener.

A few bags have a shoulder cloth or hood which can be used as a wrapper about the shoulders or, in colder weather, can be wrapped about the head, leaving only the face exposed for breathing. This hood is generally made of flannel and well worth having. Additional cost, if any, is very little.

Flannel is most often used for liners in sleeping bags, the fuzzy nap being a comfortable material to have next to the body. The nap will eventually wear off, but a good grade of flannel will last many seasons. There are also available cotton sheet liners, with tabs for tying in which can be removed easily for washing. Wool liners also can be added for additional warmth. Many campers use a wool blanket in a sleeping bag during extra cold weather.

The exterior finish or cover of a sleeping bag may be any one of many materials including drill, poplin, bengaline, Shantung, Pima or Egyptian cotton, Army duck or jean, all of which are quite long-wearing when used for this purpose. The material with which your sleeping bag is covered will depend upon the investment you want to make, and any of the above materials will prove satisfactory.

Like any other type of bedding, a sleeping bag will need to be cleaned occasionally and for this, dry cleaning is the best procedure. Most professional dry cleaners will do the job inexpensively. For home cleaning, when the bag is not soiled badly, there is a "dry-cleaning" powder available from some outfitters which will do a good job.

When camping out, sleeping bags should be aired thoroughly every day except, of course, when it's raining. On such days, simply prop them open within the tent, giving them a more complete airing during the next clear day. In storing a sleeping bag for the winter, or for long periods between trips, hang them up "by the foot," so to speak, and leave the zipper open. This will keep them "fluffier" and more comfortable for your next trip. Needless to say, they should be stored in a dry, clean room where there is little dust. If the liner or filler is made of wool, be sure to protect this against moths.

Chapter 10

PACKS AND PACKING

PACKING INTO GLACIER NATIONAL PARK, MONTANA *Bill Browning*

In the long run it takes longer to pack an outfit badly than it does to pack it well. The camper who heaves equipment into the car's trunk helter-skelter may think he is saving time and trouble but he usually ends up with a torn sleeping bag, dented cook kit, or a broken lantern. The way to save time is to pack efficiently and well.

For example, pack sleeping bags, blankets, pillows, or cot pads so that they will protect more fragile equipment. At the same time store all equipment in such a manner that it is protected from chafing and so that it is well out of reach of road dust and rain. Equipment stored in a car-top carrier that has only slats for a bottom, should be wrapped in a waterproof tarp or cover tied down so that corners and edges don't flap in the wind. This will keep rain from blowing up under the carrier and wetting the duffel.

The secret to efficient packing is to organize the equipment according to departments, so that first things come out first. For instance, pack the car trunk or box trailer so that the cook can quickly reach the things he will need, ax, refrigerator, stove, grub box, water pail, and the cook kit. He can then set to work preparing the meal while the rest of the party unloads and sets up the camp. The same type of organization should apply on a canoe trip, except that you will have fewer items to contend with in packing and unloading.

The tent should be packed with all ropes, stakes and, if feasible, poles, so that when camp is being set up someone doesn't have to search the car trunk for the stakes or a guy rope. Pack the stakes and poles so that they can't chafe the tent fabric.

Sleeping bags, pillows, blankets, and air mattresses should be bundled together in such a way that they

are easily reached once the tent is removed from the car.

For clothing take along an old suitcase—not the modern wardrobe type—but the rectangular box type with two straps for positive closing. One or two of these will take care of all extra clothing for a family of four.

Personal items which are not carried on the person and will not be needed during the day's travel, can be rolled up in each camper's sleeping bag. These can include shaving kit, flashlight, and pajamas. If there are children in the party, teach them to look after their personal gear and to keep it in one compact bundle. This will save the car from being cluttered with odds and ends and eliminate searching for strayed bits.

A family of four, on a week's camping trip, can travel in a car whose interior is completely uncluttered and uncrowded with equipment. The average car-top carrier and car trunk will hold the entire outfit if a little planning is done. A well-organized trunk load will help, too, should you have a flat tire. Only two or three bundles need to be moved to reach the spare tire, jack, and wheel wrench. Naturally, in the case of a station wagon, a part of the equipment will have to be stored within the car, but don't pile the gear so high that your rear-view mirror is useless.

Although not very often used by car campers there are three packs which are useful. These are the duffel bag, the pack basket, and the Duluth or Northwestern.

You'll find the duffel bag ideal for extra clothing. It's not unlike the sailor's sea bag, made of waterproofed duck, cylindrical in shape and closing at one end with a puckering string or along the side by means of a zipper. I don't like the side arrangement as well, because it's difficult to close if the bag is well crammed. Such bags are available in sizes ranging from 9″ in diameter and 24″ in length up to about 20″ by 40″. Some models have a built-in carrying harness which is handy for portages on a canoe trip. On a car camping excursion, however, you can get along with the single hand grip.

The Adirondack pack basket is one of my pets, despite frequent criticism that it's a nuisance when empty. There's no reason why it should ever be empty, though! The beauty of this pack is that it will carry and protect breakables such as eggs, cameras, binoculars, lantern, or other fragile gear. It's easier to pack and to unpack than any other camp-type container except the chuck box. It can even be used as a food storage cupboard in camp. In addition, it's one of the most comfortable packs to carry that I know of, topped only by the frame pack. Its weave

molds itself to the contours of the carrier's back, never gouging, as do most canvas packs.

Made of woven ash strips or willow, sizes range from 15″ high to 22″. These dimensions are for stock baskets available from outfitters. I have one that stands 24″ tall and weighs less than four pounds, made by a Maine Indian. Don't be deceived by its apparent flimsiness. I used mine guiding for eleven years and it's still in fine condition. Some outfitters supply fabric covers for them but I've found that by covering the top with a small piece of canvas, the contents will not get wet in a rain.

The Duluth pack is a large flat pocket of 12 or 13 ounce duck, with rugged shoulder straps and a tump line. Mine is 28″ square but sizes vary a little. The tump line, which is a headstrap to be worn across the top of the forehead to relieve weight from the shoulders, isn't necessary for car campers, of course, and it can be removed easily. The bag is well adapted for carrying any type of unbreakable items, including food or clothing. It's particularly well adapted to the storage of extra clothing. Empty, it weighs about three pounds and its capacity depends only on how much you can lift! On a canoe trip, I wouldn't be without a Duluth, preferring it for a long haul when I might be out for weeks, even to the pack basket, principally because of its huge

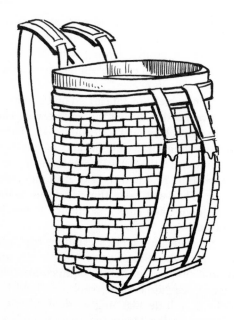

ADIRONDACK PACK BASKET

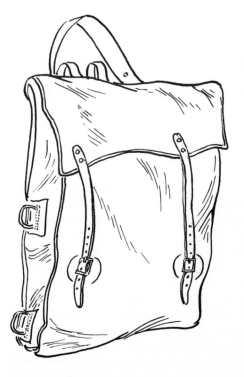

DULUTH PACK

capacity and handy tump line. Two men, out for two weeks, can carry their entire outfit in two such bags.

It should be kept in mind, though, that the duffel bag, the pack basket, and the Duluth pack are not hiker's packs, suitable for all-day carrying. They are primarily storage packs, designed to handle heavy loads during car or canoe transportation and for toting over portages. The hiker has a choice of packs of far better design for his purpose.

Hiking, unfortunately, is a phase of camp life which most car campers either overlook or avoid, in keeping with our national policy of never walking when we can ride. However, there is rare pleasure in going beyond the smell of burning gasoline occasionally. Back-country hiking is the closest thing to true pioneering that modern man can attain.

Unspoiled regions within the United States are becoming fewer every year, but there are still areas, most of them easily accessible, where you can escape the din of our daily lives in the cities. There is the Appalachian Trail in the East and, in the West, the equally adventurous Pacific Crest Trail. National forests and parks, too, as well as state-operated areas have hiking trails.

This is the kind of camping where you'll be strictly on your own—there will be no ranger to supply your firewood and you'll drink from clear mountain streams instead of pop bottles. You'll carry every need and luxury with you.

For this phase of camping a doctor's examination is part of sound planning, particularly if you tackle a long trek into remote areas. Whenever the trip is not too extended, more and more parents are taking along children, who adapt themselves surprisingly well. There is even a special frame available for toting children once they're old enough to sit up by themselves! The pack is a chairlike rig from which even the youngest child cannot fall, and is surprisingly easy to carry. It can even be hung up in camp, or set on a stump, as its design is far superior to that of the average high chair! Toting very young children on a long trek, of course, is not advisable, but there's no reason why a young couple shouldn't take a child along on a day trip to a nearby point.

Even on short trips, an adult pack should not exceed 30 pounds for men, while women shouldn't tote over 25. Five pounds less is an even more reasonable load, unless of course, you've become hardened to packing. If there are children old enough to carry small packs of their own, so much the better. They will feel more a part of the group if they are doing some of the work, but give them even lighter loads than they believe they can carry.

If the trip is only for overnight, regular camp foods can be carried, but for extended treks dehydrated foods are called for. The sleeping bag should be a hiker's model, warm yet lightweight, the cook kit simple, and clothing lightweight for daytime hiking. A rugged pair of shoes for each member is a must. Clothing and shoes are discussed in the next chapter. A small first-aid kit, flashlight or candle lantern, match safe, compass, and maps should pretty well complete the equipment and supply list. Such pleasant-to-have luxuries as binoculars, camera, nature guides, can always be crowded into a pack.

Lay out a moderate day's hike so that you can take it easy instead of having to eat up the map to stay on schedule. It's much better woodcraft to enjoy every inch of a short hike than to gobble up the miles in misery. Another point to remember is never hike alone in strange country, unless you've had experience or have left word regarding your plans. Always leave an itinerary of your trip with someone. In case you become lost, or have an accident, you will be found much more quickly for having taken this precaution.

Hiking trips need not be lengthy for you to find fun in the outdoors. One of the delights of car camping is the exploring on foot of the region surrounding a campground. There may be forest fire towers with expansive views, hidden mountain lakes, waterfalls, interesting rock formations, Indian ruins, or caves, all within a day's hike.

Don't worry about leaving your base camp unprotected for a day or two at a time, but if you're hesitant about leaving your equipment at a campground, ask a friendly neighbor to keep an eye on it.

If you plan side trips on foot, purchase your equipment so that you'll include gear that will be useful for car camping as well as for trail wandering, thereby avoiding duplication of weight, bulk, and costs.

You'll find the Norwegian frame or ski pack among the easiest to carry. This pack has a triangular frame of light steel or aluminum which holds a leather band across the small of the back, thus keeping the pack itself from bearing directly against your back. The larger models are usually 22″ high and about as wide with some eight inches of depth. A light sleeping bag can be attached on the outside of the pack, but should be wrapped in a waterproof cloth or plastic in case of rain on the trail. It's a comparatively expensive pack, however, but well worth its cost if you plan much hiking. One I bought in 1936 is still serviceable despite a tremendous amount of use over the years.

The United States Armed Forces tried to adapt

the Norwegian frame pack during World War II, but they succeeded only in producing a pack much too unwieldly for pleasure packing. However, these are available as war surplus and will serve the purpose at a much smaller cost.

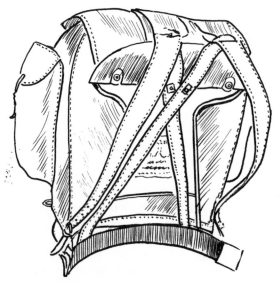

NORWEGIAN FRAME OR SKI PACK

The rucksack is a similar pack, except that it lacks the metal frame and is usually somewhat smaller than the Norwegian frame pack. It's ideal for day trips away from a base camp and, while not as comfortable to carry as the frame model, it is an excellent pack for small to moderate loads. Typical of European imports, most have leather carrying straps.

Also well suited to short trips or day-long hikes are the inexpensive Yukon pack, the Boy Scout knapsack, or the Yucca pack. These are basically "canvas boxes" with carrying straps and outside bellows pockets. They are uncomfortable packs to carry when only partially full, as they then tend to pull away from the carrier's back. To offset this tendency, take up the shoulder straps as snugly as possible. As a matter of fact, this will make carrying any pack an easier job. When using these packs, be sure that no hard objects such as cans or hatchet heads are placed so as to gouge your back.

A number of belt or shoulder bags are on the market, including surplus army field bags, which hang at the hip from a shoulder strap. These have little value as hiking packs, but will be suitable for carrying a noontime lunch. They are excellent bags for children, to hold their personal items.

The eastern half of the United States, except in a few localized areas such as the White Mountains of New Hampshire, has failed to see the value of the pack board, but in the West its popularity, already great, continues to grow.

The pack board is the professional packer's rig and he swears by it, no matter what the load, its weight, or its bulk. It has been used for toting camp stoves, game, supplies, outboard motors, and even folding boats. Injured men have been carried out on pack boards! The advantage of this rig is that, if a man can lift the load, the pack board will hold it so that he can walk with it. A well-made board will allow the load to be carried high and close to the body so that the packer can walk in an almost erect position.

The GI pack board, now war surplus, is one of the simplest and fundamentally a good type. Designed to carry mortar shells and other awkward-to-tote items, it can be converted easily to camp packing purposes. Made of plywood and canvas, it's comfortable to carry and can be bought for about $5.

The Trapper Nelson pack, invented in 1924, has been a stand-by of woodsmen for many years and still retains its popularity despite the intrusion of newer types. This pack has a wooden frame over which canvas is stretched to allow circulation of air between the carrier's back and the load. The Trapper Nelson model was a pioneer in modern design and many of the latest "up-to-date" pack boards are

YUKON PACK

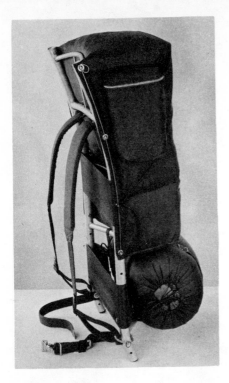

FRAME PACK *Kelty*

COMPARTMENTED PACK *Gerry*

SHOULDER HARNESSES

not too far removed from the Nelson. It is capable of tremendous loads and is sold at a moderate price.

Some of the new types merit attention, too, including a model that is "contoured" to fit a man's back. Most of these newer boards follow the concept that a heavy load should be high and close, so that models are available with high side bars, extending up above the packer's shoulders. Some of these have nylon back straps with sponge padding, a far cry from the first pack board I made many years ago from two pieces of $\frac{1}{2}'' \times 4''$ spruce and four slats of cedar!

The contoured frames can be used separately, or with a variety of canvas pouches. One such pouch has an extra long flap, ample enough to cover a rolled sleeping bag atop the bag itself. The large flap also has an outside pocket. The pouch itself, in one instance, is a pannier-type container which is loaded from the side rather than the top. These pouches limit the bulk which may be carried, but they'll handle one man's complete hiking outfit easily. Used without the pouch, the frame's load is limited only by the packer's strength.

Another type of pack frame which is gaining popularity is one which looks like a legless chair with shoulder straps. Known as the Everest, it has adopted the Norwegian frame pack's style of leather harness, including the horizontal strap which fits across the small of the back. It was designed originally for mountaineering and, with its aluminum frame, weighs only two pounds. However, it is not built so that the load is carried quite as high on the shoulders as is possible with other pack boards. It, too, has an assortment of pouches to fit the frame. This type of rig is as comfortable to carry as the Norwegian frame pack, and it can handle much heavier and bulkier loads.

All in all, for moderate to heavy toting, it's difficult to improve on the Trapper Nelson, the contoured pack frames or the Everest-type frames.

Lacking a pack board or frame, one of the handiest packer's accessories is the pack harness. Basi-

**CAMPING PARTY PREPARES FOR PACK TRIP
IN GLACIER NATIONAL PARK**

Bill Browning

cally, this is a set of shoulder straps with a built-in harness to which can be attached loose packs or bundles tied and wrapped together in a pack cloth. Some pack harnesses also have a tump line attached for additional ease in toting heavy loads.

THE TUMP LINE

The tump line is not easy for the beginner to use. Frankly, it's a brutal form of torture until you become accustomed to it, then it becomes a boon. The capacity of the tump line is even greater than that of the pack board, for its limit is set by the man who has to pick up and carry the load. It was the mainstay of the early fur brigades for toting 90-pound bales of fur over the portages of Northwest waterways. At that time the packs were carried usually without benefit of shoulder straps, the head and neck bearing the brunt of the abuse.

Modern canoemen favor the big Duluth pack with its detachable tump line, however, so that the weight can be distributed between the head, neck, and shoulders. When a load gets too burdensome, you can rest your shoulders by letting them sag a little, throwing the bulk of the weight into the tump line. When your head and neck begin to cry out, throw your shoulders back into the job. By alternating in this manner, even a beginner can tote a fair load across a lengthy portage.

A good general rule for packing is to place the bulk of the load's weight as high and as close to the shoulders as possible. This will allow you to walk erect. By all means, avoid placing great weight close to the small of the back, for this will tend to make you bend forward uncomfortably to offset the backward pull. The natural inclination is to place heavy items in the bottom of the packsack, much as a grocer packs canned goods, before placing bread and tomatoes in the bag. For back packing, this is *not* correct.

Chapter 11

CLOTHING, BOOTS, PERSONAL GEAR

Clothing

In the Northern States and in southern Canada, where summertime temperatures can range from 90 in the shade to 30 in the night, you will need a variety of clothing. For hot, dry days, wear lightweight cottons or synthetics. As the temperature drops add cotton flannel, or wool shirts and sweaters. If the wind blows, add finely woven outer clothing over the wool, such as gabardine or poplin jackets. For colder weather, woolen underwear is called for.

In the South, of course, your principal concern may be keeping cool, while at high altitudes, your problem will be one of almost constant cold. In other areas, you will have black flies or mosquitoes to contend with.

The old-time lumberjack, a man of simple means and tastes, solved variable weather problems by wearing a one-piece "hand-hammered, double-barreled" union suit of wool all year around. The long johns kept him warm in the bitter cold, insulated him against the hot summer sun, and kept pesky woods insects at bay. In the summer he wore a denim or cotton flannel shirt and he stagged his trousers a couple of inches above the ankles. If the weather turned cold or if it rained, he added a stag shirt, also of wool. He wore his clothes loosely for complete body freedom to chop, paddle, or shinny up a tree after a bear cub. For modern camping, however, the requirements of clothing comfort aren't quite as stringent.

For men's underwear, two-piece cotton units are best for summer wear, and although it's pretty much a matter of personal tastes, the snug-fitting "briefs" are popular, along with T shirts or sleeveless undershirts.

However, at high altitudes, or on large Northern lakes where the wind can be bitter even in mid-summer, long-legged and long-sleeved underwear will contribute much to comfort. Wear either wool, or cotton-lined wool two-piece suits which are much easier to change than the one-piece outfits.

Women's underwear should be the same as they wear at home for warm weather. However, the high altitude or windy lake advice applies to them also. Textile mills long ago realized that women would not tolerate the heavy, comparatively rough texture of long underwear worn by men and they have developed feminine versions that are not only comfortable but "glamorized" with color. Combinations of wool and cotton are available in most department stores, as well as more modern knitted synthetic models. Children, too, can wear the same underwear as is used at home, but they, too, should have along the long-legged variety for cold weather.

If you're going to a "country-club" type of campground where the camping area has been sprayed to kill off objectionable insects, you can wear the lightweight, ventilated-type of shirts, with short sleeves and open collar. Some of these are "drip-dry" or "wash and wear" types of synthetic fabrics, often of open mesh weave. In wearing this type of clothing be careful of overexposure to the hot sun.

Women have an even greater variety of blouses which can be worn in comparatively civilized campgrounds and most of them, including the "drip-dry" or "wash and wear" types, are suitable providing that they too keep an eye out for sunburn.

For general camp wear, lightweight denim shirts are good summer wear for men and women. These have long sleeves and collars which may be closed if insects become annoying or if it turns cool. These same shirts are available for children too.

If the weather turns noticeably cooler, cotton flannel shirts for the entire family are excellent. Flannel has considerable nap on its finished side and is much better insulation against cold than two or three unnapped cotton shirts. These are quite inexpensive and are made up in a wide selection of fun-to-pick-out patterns.

You may find occasional nights in the North, even in midsummer, when the temperature fifteen feet away from your campfire hovers not far from freezing. On these nights, swap the cotton flannel shirts for wool shirts or sweaters. My criticism of sweaters, however, is that they rarely have pockets to hold my pipe, tobacco, matches, and other minor cultch I like to tote.

Wool, however, is at its best when keeping in body warmth. It will not keep out wind, and this is where a lightweight jacket of windproof material, such as poplin or gabardine, comes in handy. Wear one of these over a wool shirt or sweater when a cold wind is blowing and you will be comfortable. Such lightweight jackets are inexpensive and are available for men, women, and children too. Don't buy light-colored ones, however, since these will soil easily, especially around a campfire. Dark browns or greens are suitable colors.

A stag shirt is also excellent, even for windy weather. Although made of wool, the yarns are heavier than those used in shirts and the weave is much tighter. A good stag shirt will turn rain for a time as well as wind. Some models are lined with nylon or sateen, and nearly all types, for men, women, or children, have ample pockets. The stag shirt, sometimes called "jack shirt" or "cruiser shirt" is characterized by the absence of tails, being cut off square at the bottom. It rates, in warmth, somewhere between a regular wool shirt and the heavy lumberman's mackinaw.

The bush jacket is one of my favorites for wear when there's a chill in the air that doesn't quite call for the stag shirt. I've thrown away the belt, preferring to hook the front with one or two buttons. Many so-called bush jackets on the market today are merely skimpy imitations and badly tailored. A properly made bush jacket should fit loosely and especially should not bind at the shoulders or across the back. There are models available for women, sometimes sold as "automobile jackets," but I don't know of any made up for children. I especially like the four large bellows pockets with the button flaps. My sole objection to bush jackets is the standard sun-tan color of the fabric, too light to be kept clean

easily. The first manufacturer who produces a dark-green bush jacket at a reasonable price is going to be swamped with orders!

Shorts are in order for the entire family on a hot day, providing mosquitoes, no-see-ums, and black flies aren't too thick. Well-tailored shorts are perfectly proper for men, women, and children in a campground. However, don't buy the extremely short, tight-fitting variety. Camping calls for a great deal of bending and sitting on such things as logs, stumps, and even on the ground, where such shorts will bind uncomfortably. The Bermuda type, if amply tailored, will serve well.

For women, so called "pedal-pushers" are badly designed for active camp wear since they are usually snug and inclined to bind. Skirts and dresses, too, are poor garb in camp and women wearing them will find modesty difficult to maintain, especially if there are biting insects about.

At any rate, eliminate any thought of wearing riding breeches, or in the case of women, jodhpurs. These are designed for riding and will bind your calves and knees. In fact, unless they're expensively tailored, they're not even fit for riding, for I've never seen a good range hand wearing a pair of them. When I was with the U. S. Border Patrol part of our uniform consisted of fancy breeches and polished field boots. I count the hours that I had to wear this rig among the most uncomfortable in my life!

For men, pants of cotton denim, blue jeans, or twill slacks are excellent. If you decide on blue jeans, don't buy the Western variety with the tight hips and narrow legs. They're uncomfortable for walking and bending over. The same applies to women's and children's models. The workman's type of blue jean is good all-round camp garb, and there are designs for women made in a variety of colors and styles. The advantage of denim is that it does not soil easily. Most men's blue jeans have extra long legs so that the cuff can be rolled up to desired height. I prefer to cut off the excess length as the cuffs are dirt catchers.

Also available for women and children are chinos, which are pants of twill having a lightweight flannel lining, and these are excellent for cool weather.

For a fall trip, wool slacks are best since these offer warmth and leg freedom. A good trick with these and other types of long pants is to spray the legs with a water-repellent solution, so that they won't soak up water when you walk through wet grass or brush. Recently I read a suggestion that camp trousers be painted in the front with enamel to make them water repellent. Such a stunt can result

**FLOAT CAMPING IN THE REMOTE
MONTANA WILDERNESS**

Montana Highway Commission

only in badly chafed legs from the stiffened material.

Few men wear suspenders today, yet they are much more comfortable than a belt, allowing more freedom about the waist. Woodsmen still wear them and in many cases a belt too. The belt is worn loosely and usually only to hold a knife sheath!

For general foot comfort, wool socks are best by far. These will pad the feet well and keep them warm even when the socks are wet. However, all-wool socks may be too warm for summer camping, in which case combinations of wool and cotton or wool and nylon, such as "athletic" or "sweat" socks, will pad the bottoms of your feet and will carry off foot moisture very well. Even if they don't appear to be soiled, they should be changed and washed daily to bring back their "fluffiness."

If your camping is going to be a leisurely type where you rarely leave the campsite except by automobile, cotton socks will do well in warm weather.

No one, not even children, should go into camp without a hat or cap of some sort. There will be times, of course, when head gear isn't necessary but if the sun is too hot or rain is falling or if deer flies are about, a hat is a blessing.

For men a felt hat with a two- to three-inch brim is best. This is the woodsman's hat and he wears it all year round for protection from sun, insects, rain, snow, cold. Many campers wear cotton caps with a broad visor and these are suitable for sun protection but a poor rig in a rain as they quickly soak through and allow water to run down the back of the wearer's neck. When wearing a felt hat in the rain forget its original design and turn down the brim, at the same time pushing up the crown so that it is dome-shaped. A good felt hat, deformed in this manner, will shed a three-hour rain, and if sprayed with water-repellent solution is better than a small roof!

Women who seek protection from rain by tying a kerchief or bandanna over their heads soon find that such protection is practically nil. The bandanna soon wets through and contributes only a cold clammy feeling. For protection of a hairdo, a feminine version of the man's felt hat is best. Tyrolean hats of felt, available in various colors and with decorations appealing to the feminine, can be purchased reasonably and will never go out of style. Similar hats are available for boys and girls, too, and are far better in rain than the usual cap worn by children.

Rainwear for satisfactory camp use must be waterproof and it should be easy to put on or remove. Although there's a great variety of raincoats, capes, shirts, and suits, not many fulfill all of these requirements.

Probably the finest rain gear is the poncho. This is simply a flat sheet with a slit in the center which fits over the head. The wearer actually has on a flat envelope of waterproof material, open at the sides and bottom. There are snaps, however, which close the sides under the arms. Ponchos are made of rubber or such practical materials as rubberized cotton or nylon, vinyl-coated nylon, or oiled cotton. The all-plastic type is not durable though it will serve the purpose if not given hard wear.

I have worked all day in a poncho, burning brush in a heavy downpour, and remained dry all of the time. When I've had to paddle a canoe in the rain, sometimes for the better part of a day, the poncho has acted as a small tent, covering even my legs and feet. The secret to buying a poncho is to buy one long enough to reach to the wearer's knees, otherwise water will drip from a shorter poncho and run down your trouser legs, quickly soaking them. Outfitters usually carry a variety of sizes in ponchos so that men, women, and children can be fitted. Boy Scout outfitters have excellent models for use by boys and girls. Some models are made with a hood.

For short exposure to rain, regular "city-type" raincoats of plastic, oiled silk, or oilskin are suitable. However, these gap open in the front and do not allow as much freedom of movement as the poncho does.

Rainshirts, looking not unlike a rubber or plastic nightgown, are excellent protection in a boat or when activity is limited. These, too, form a small tent over the body protecting everything but the face. However, ventilation is very poor and any activity will soon work up excessive perspiration which cannot escape. Also they are awkward to put on or remove.

Navy foul-weather gear, available as war surplus, was designed originally for stationary watch duty where physical activity was limited. Consisting of waterproof pants and parka they did an excellent job at sea. In camp, however, they are an uncomfortable rig, allowing little if any ventilation. What's more, it's a ten-minute struggle to get into such a suit.

Boots

New campers are prone to overdressing their feet with knee-high leather boots laced tightly about the calf. Such boots are completely unnecessary except in country infested with poisonous snakes. They bind the calves of the legs uncomfortably.

Heavy boots have so long been associated with camping that it's difficult to convince a beginner that moccasin-type loafers or "low cuts" are the best choice for summertime car camping trips, for here you will want comfort while driving as well as in camp. These are not suitable for hiking in rough country, it's true, but for use in a campground they're ideal for men, women, and children. Good leather is important to lasting quality and the soles should be of rubber-type or composition which are thick enough to protect the soles of the feet, yet flexible for easy walking. Leather soles should be avoided, as walking on softwood needles or in grass will polish these and make them dangerously slippery. Don't try to polish them for appearance's sake. Rather, rub them with Neatsfoot oil to make them waterproof and to preserve the leather. For best comfort they should be worn with medium to heavy socks described earlier. Should they cause your feet to sweat unduly use a foot talcum. Keep away from trick lacings or elastic bands across the arch. The old-fashioned shoelace still works pretty well.

For camping in somewhat rougher country where campgrounds are likely to be undeveloped and a certain amount of prowling in the woods will be required, the six-inch moccasin-type shoe fills the bill nicely for all members of the family. This is a shoe much like the low cut just described except that the uppers come to just above the ankle bone. These too should receive a Neatsfoot oil treatment occasionally. Some advocate a grease application but oil is far superior since it penetrates to all parts of the shoe for complete protection to the leather. This type of shoe is also made on a ladies' last and there are many similar types for children. They are not expensive.

New shoes should always be well broken in before leaving for camp. Some recommend that they be soaked in water overnight and worn until they dry on the feet. A better idea is to give them a thorough oiling with Neatsfoot before wearing them a little each day until the uppers have molded themselves to your feet.

Canvas shoes, sneakers, or tennis shoes are poor footwear for camp. They offer little foot support and no protection to the ankle bone if worn in rough country. In wet weather they soak up water and are miserable to wear. Children who are used to wearing them as play shoes may use them safely in most campgrounds but for hiking or camping in undeveloped areas they, too, are better off with leather shoes.

LOW CUTS ARE THE BEST CHOICE FOR SUMMER CAR CAMPING TRIPS

THE SIX-INCH MOCCASIN SHOE

A pair of lightweight moccasins or slippers is a comfort for camp for evening wear. Unless you're a postman you'll probably find your feet tired come nightfall, and for sitting around the evening campfire, soft, light shoes are a welcome relief. Such moccasins are available in ladies' styles also, as well as for children.

This type of shoe is almost a necessity on a canoe trip, for heavy boots or shoes are miserable things to wear in a canoe where much of the time is spent either sitting or kneeling. Most professionals wear soft and lightweight shoes for canoe work unless there are long and rough portages where six-inch shoes are usually worn. Some canoemen wear the light shoes in the canoe and change to heavy-duty six-inchers for the portages. When the weather was pleasant I used to kick my shoes off altogether while in a canoe, pulling them on only when I went ashore.

A hiking shoe, on the other hand, must be tough whether it is being worn by men, women, or children. Usually a six- to eight-inch shoe is worn, with a heavy, stiff composition sole and uppers of a heavy grade of leather which should be treated frequently. The main consideration in buying a hiking shoe is to get one that offers full freedom to the ball of your foot and to your toes, for it is these which do the work when you hike. A good pair of hiking shoes shouldn't weigh much more than 2 to 2½ pounds per pair. Breaking in a pair of hiking shoes is even more important than breaking in other types of camp shoes. Never start a hiking trip in a new pair of boots!

The use of calks is still recommended occasionally but these are unnecessary for average camp wear. Mountaineers, rock climbers, and sawmill workers all have specialized types of calks for their work, but these have no place in car or canoe camping.

Rubber footwear is often recommended for rainy weather, but in the summer, leather shoes that have been properly treated with Neatsfoot oil are far superior. Rubber is hot and I know of no rubber footwear that is amply ventilated, with the result that perspiration accumulates.

An excellent compromise on this point, is the rubber-bottomed leather-topped hunting boot invented by Leon L. Bean of Freeport, Maine. This type of shoe is difficult to improve upon when the going underfoot is sloppy with wet snow, slush, mud, or in swampy terrain. This boot is surprisingly comfortable to walk in. Inner soles are recommended for use in them. In recent years, manufacturers have developed such shoes for women, using a narrower last to mold the rubber bottom.

RUBBER-BOTTOMED, LEATHER-TOPPED HUNTING BOOT

Personal Gear

Towel	Two for each member, bath or medium sized.
Washcloth	Not a necessity but handy. Otherwise, corner of bath towel can be used.
Soap	One bar toilet soap for each member of family, in plastic carrying case. Single community bar of soap is always being mislaid!
Toothbrush and paste or powder	
Comb	
Mirror	Buy the polished-steel type. It's unbreakable.
Razor	There's a battery-operated electric model, too.
Shaving kit	Including cream, brush, extra blades.
Ladies' make-up kit	Facial cream, lipstick, hand lotions, talcum deodorant (for men, too!) nail clip and file.
Handkerchiefs or bandannas	Blue or red; 28″ square far better than usual pocket type.
Sun-tan lotion	Use it *before* you sunburn!
Fly dope	Small individual bottle for each member better than one or two community units.
Sunglasses	
Pocket knife or small sheath knife	For adults only, unless youngsters have been trained to use properly.
Matchbox	Waterproof type, for emergency use. Older children may carry if they've been taught value—and danger—of matches.
Head net	For use on hikes to areas where insects may be thick.
Life jacket or vest	For nonswimmers, or for entire family if boating on large water.
Collapsible drinking cup	Saves washing camp cups and handy on hikes.
Smokes	Cigarettes, cigars, pipe, tobacco, pipe cleaners, reamer, lighter, matches.
Sharpening stone	Small pocket type, to keep personal knife sharp.
Watch	If your watch is the expensive but not shock- and waterproof type, take along a "dollar watch," now available for about $2.95.
Extra shoelaces	Handy for many things besides lacing shoes.
Thermometer	Optional, but fun to prove "how cold was it last night?"

Compass — Each adult should carry one and know how to use it. Children may be supplied with inexpensive types for learning.

Maps — Carry in waterproof map case. Map mileage measure is handy gadget.

Camera — Carry in waterproof plastic bag or suitable leather case. Keep film away from abnormal dampness. Screw cap cans excellent for this.

Binoculars — Optional, but fun to have. For emergency magnifying glass, look through large end, holding eyepiece about ½ inch from the object being examined. Helpful for removing slivers or reading fine print on maps.

Notebook and pencil — You'll make new friends and want to record addresses. Also for field notes, informal diary, writing directions.

Books, magazines — Camp is good place to read that book you've "always wanted to read." If there are children, include a few books for them, not telling them in advance. When they get bored, spring the surprise.

Games — For children. Handle same as with books.

Flashlight — Yes, even if you have a camp lantern. Extra batteries, bulb.

Firearms — Fun to have on a wilderness trip for plinking, target shooting. Usually prohibited in organized campgrounds; illegal in national parks. Rifles may be taken into Canada only under special permit from Royal Canadian Mounted Police which must be obtained before arrival at border. Pistols of all types and automatic rifles prohibited in Canada. Firearms, where permitted, are suitable where adults make up camping party, but if young children are included, it's best to leave them at home.

Fishing tackle — By all means. Fun for the entire family.

Pedometer — Optional. Will record how far you've hiked. Makes it easier to follow directions involving distances.

Canteen — For hiking in dry country, or where quality of water is doubtful. One for each member of family.

Bathing suit

Sleep sox — Light wool sox worn to bed if your feet are inclined to be cold. Better than a hot-water bottle.

Chapter 12

USING MAPS AND THE COMPASS

You probably wouldn't think of going on a long automobile trip without a road map. It seems reasonable, then, that when you go into camp or on a hike to explore the surrounding country, you'll take along a map of the local area. Once you're off the main routes a road map is useless, for although it usually shows mountain peaks, streams and lakes, these are rarely denoted with any thought to accuracy. For getting along on foot, by canoe, or on horseback in a strange country, you'll need a detailed map and a good one at that.

Good maps are comparatively rare but among the best for the camper's purpose are those issued by the U. S. Geological Survey and the Canadian Department of Mines and Technical Surveys. Either offers the best bargain in maps you can get anywhere —about 25¢ per sheet!

Maps issued by the Forest Service and by the National Park Service for general public distribution are little better than road maps. Most maps issued by chambers of commerce and regional resort associations are often useless. The latter usually spend their money on fancy artwork and color, so that you'll have pictures of jumping fish and deer peeking from behind trees where there should be terrain detail. Also these maps are usually drawn by commercial artists rather than professional map makers.

Maps issued by state agencies such as forestry or conservation departments will vary in quality and usefulness. Some states issue excellent maps, others are poor, and still others issue none at all. Generally speaking those issued by Western state conservation agencies, to indicate legal hunting areas, are quite good in their general detail.

Certain commercial map makers issue folios of maps covering particular regions. One of the finest sets of canoe travel maps I have ever seen is pub-lished commercially and covers the Superior-Quetico region in northern Minnesota and southern Ontario. The features of terrain important to a canoeman such as routes, portages, campsites, and rapids are indicated clearly.

County maps are generally well detailed although some of these may run quite heavily to farm boundaries. Locally owned or operated recreation areas and camp sites will be shown with more detail than on larger regional maps. Such maps are often available from the county clerk or from commercial mappers who print them.

Timber maps, sometimes available from logging companies, will show roads and trails often not shown on other maps. These maps will also show the types of timber stands. As a rule, though, they cover a comparatively small area so that a number of contiguous maps will be necessary.

Coastal area maps are likely to take the form of salt-water charts with some landside detail included. They show detail regarding tides, channels, boat anchorages and docks, as well as public access routes. They're a great help to the amateur "beach-comber" and are issued by the Coast and Geodetic Survey, a sort of salt-water version of the Geological Survey.

River charts, covering the Mississippi, the Missouri, Ohio, and many other rivers are issued by the U. S. Army Corps of Engineers, and for camping along these big waters, the charts are nearly indispensable.

The natural and man-made features which can be shown on a map include practically everything that you can see on the actual terrain. Some maps will even indicate underground minerals, but the following list will cover pretty much the features with which the average camper is likely to concern him-

HUNTING PARTY ON THE ABITIBI RIVER IN ONTARIO

self. The more of these features your map has, the better map it is, providing, of course, they are accurately located.

Map Features

Roads, including access and private	Ranger stations
Foot trails	Overnight shelters
Riding trails	Trappers' cabins
Railroads	Wardens' camps
Airports and landing strips	Fire lookouts
Bridges	Fire-fighting tool caches
Tunnels	Mountain peaks, hills
Stream fords	Elevations (altitudes in feet above sea level)
Lakes	Benchmarks
Rivers	Cliffs
Streams	Caves
Springs	Canyons
Quicksand areas	Mines, active and abandoned
Swamps	
Pot holes	Rockslides
Waterfalls and rapids	Avalanche areas
Unsafe drinking water	Quarries
Large beaver ponds	Timbered or large open areas
Islands	
Portage trails	Burns (forest fire "remains")
Public access areas or landings	
	Phone lines
Camp sites	Power lines
Picnic grounds	Contours
Lumber camps	

Practically every one of these features could conceivably help you get a bearing or even help you find your way out of an area when lost. However, it will be a long search before you find a map which incorporates all of these, although those issued by the Geological Survey come close.

If you camp in the same general area every year as many campers do, you can improve your map by adding features as you become better acquainted with the region. In this way you will eventually have a far better map than could be made by a surveyor's crew.

Four references of importance are indicated on all good maps. These include the date of issue, the scale, the declination, and the contour interval. The last three sound technical but are basically simple and easy to understand.

The date of issue is important so that you won't be searching on your map for man-made features which were built *after* the map was drawn. In this day of marsh drainage, dam building and large-scale logging, mappers cannot keep up with the changes which should be made on many maps.

Geological Survey maps, generally considered best for hikers and campers, are sold in "quadrangles" or sheets, about 12¼″ by 17½″. Scaled at one mile to the inch, such a quadrangle will encompass about 114 square miles. However, since scales vary, the area included will too.

Scale is best explained by illustrating the one most often used on Geological Survey maps, that of 1/62,500. This means simply that one inch on the map is equal to 62,500 inches on actual terrain, or very slightly less than one mile. One mile actually equals 63,360 inches so the difference is only 71 feet, close enough for you to use the scale as one inch to one mile.

Map scales for quadrangles of the West and Southwest are usually 1/125,000 (one inch to slightly less than two miles), or 1/250,000, or one inch to slightly less than four miles. In this land of vast distances where minute detail is not important, these scales are quite suitable.

Estimating distances with any accuracy is difficult even when a scale of miles is given, because no trails, roads, or rivers always run in a straight line. Their windings can throw estimates out of kilter considerably. To overcome this problem, there's a map measurer available, selling for around a dollar. By running the instrument over the proposed route on the map, a tiny wheel activates the needle on a dial which automatically records mileage. Some of these instruments have a dial showing two or three popular scales so that they can be used on different maps.

Many camping writers dismiss "declination" too lightly. Ignoring this can put a hiker two miles off his course in a five- or six-mile walk! Declination, or the directional difference between True North and Magnetic North, is easy to understand once you visualize the location of these two points on the earth's surface. True North is the "North Pole," or top of the world. Magnetic North, to which the compass needle points, *is some 1400 miles south of the North Pole,* located on the shore of Prince of Wales Island, northwest of the Boothia Peninsula, along Canada's northern shore. For some strange reason, Magnetic North is moving slowly in a northwesterly direction but this has little bearing on compass work by campers.

However, it does mean that in the eastern United States the compass needle points *west* of true north by some 14 degrees. In the Far West the needle points to the *east* of True North by as many, and in some cases, more degrees.

For a short neighborhood hike of only a few miles, the declination can be ignored, but for traveling in vast areas, whether wooded or barren, it is necessary to orient your map properly. To "orient" your map means only to "face it in the right direction," so that location of features on actual terrain correspond to those on the map. To help you orient a map, each has a declination symbol consisting of an offset V, one leg of which points to the map's True North with the other pointing to its Magnetic North. Sometimes the difference in degrees is shown.

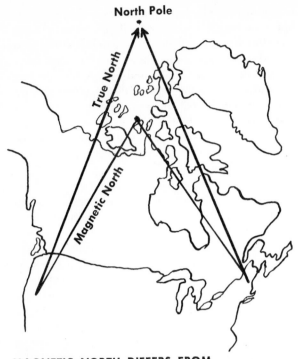

MAGNETIC NORTH DIFFERS FROM TRUE NORTH

THE DIFFERENCE BETWEEN MAGNETIC AND TRUE NORTH (DECLINATION) IS SHOWN ON THE MAP

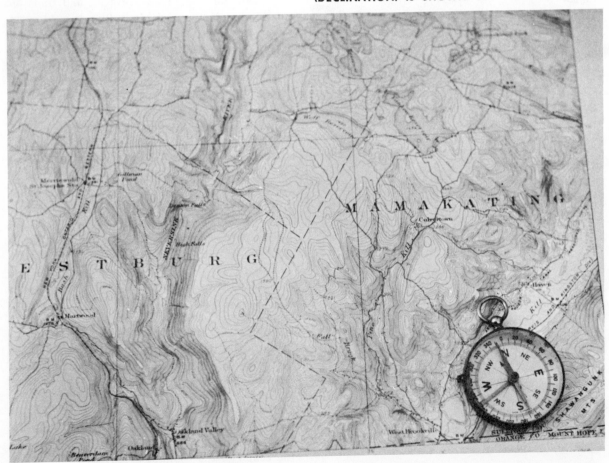

To orient the map, lay it on a flat surface with your compass atop it, setting near the declination symbol. When the compass needle stops wavering and points firmly in one direction, turn the map until the Magnetic North leg of the declination symbol is parallel to the compass needle. To do this correctly, the compass must be as close to the declination symbol as possible. Also, be sure that no metal objects such as guns or axes are near the compass to attract the needle away from its true course. Your map should now lie in correct relationship to the terrain around it, and can be considered "oriented." It's as simple as that!

Contour lines, to a beginner at mapping, may look like a plateful of fine spaghetti! However, upon closer examination, you'll see that no contour line

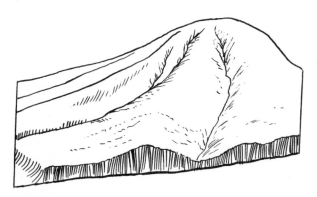

READING CONTOUR LINES

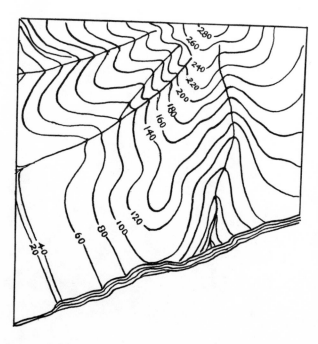

ever crosses another, the reason being that a contour line is an imaginary line (you'll find no sign of one on actual terrain) which remains always at the same altitude above sea level. They show the exact shape of hills, mountains, knolls, and valleys. The contour interval is simply the vertical distance between the lines. On Geological Survey maps that are scaled one inch to the mile, the contour interval is usually 20 feet. In other words, if you walked from one contour line to another, you would climb or descend 20 feet in altitude.

When the contour lines are close together on the map, this is an indication that the terrain is steep, while if they are far apart, the land is made up of gentle slopes. Contour lines are probably best understood by comparing them to the waterline left by receding water in a lake. The waterline is a true contour line because it remains at the same level for its entire length and it denotes exactly the shape of the lake at that particular level. On a map they have the effect of giving "depth" or relief to the area shown.

Women sometimes exclaim that the color scheme on a map is "pretty." Actually, even color fits into the pattern of symbols used. Man-made features such as houses, railroads, roads, bridges, and trails are nearly always shown in black. Blue is used exclusively for water features, including lakes, rivers, swamps, and even tiny streams are shown as a thin blue line. Brown is generally used to denote contour and a green overlay indicates timber or forests.

Most map symbols are self-explanatory, and as a rule maps have a symbol index printed on them. However, after a short period of experience with them, you will recognize features immediately and you will have reached the point where you can "read a map."

A map and a compass will be useless to you unless you check your course frequently while traveling in strange country. Forget everything you may have heard about some people having a "natural sense of direction." Contrary to popular opinion, even Indians lacked this. The Indian was trained from babyhood to observe closely, and as he traveled he noted landmarks, perhaps unconsciously, and he remembered them. The natural tendency of man is to travel in circles and this has been proven both in the field and by scientific experiments. Don't depend, therefore, on a single bearing from your compass, thinking that you can reach your goal as a result of your original compass sighting.

Getting a compass bearing requires a little care but isn't difficult. First, orient the map. Locate the point on the map where you are standing, and place the center of the compass exactly over that point.

Rotate the compass so that its North is properly lined up with True North, according to the declination scale.

A good compass will have a circular scale of degrees around the outer rim of the face, starting with zero and running clockwise 360 degrees back to North. Draw an imaginary line from the center of the compass to the point you want to reach. Where this line crosses the circular degree scale is located your "bearing," or compass course. This is known technically as the azimuth which I believe is an Arabic word meaning "the way or direction."

Assuming that the bearing you have obtained is 85 degrees from North, you certainly will not be able to walk to your goal, with compass in hand, following that 85-degree course exactly. Instead, sight along this course to the farthest landmark you can see. This may be a knoll, a particularly tall tree, or a cliff. Put your compass away and walk to that landmark. Upon arrival there pick out another landmark, still farther away, but still on the 85-degree bearing. In thick woods you may have to be content with a particular tree, no more than 50 yards away for a "station," or in open country it may be a butte or a distant windmill as much as five miles away.

Naturally, in following such a course, you'll encounter swamps, lakes, or cliffs, which you will have to go around. In skirting these obstacles you will have to compensate for deviations in your course, and if such a detour has forced you a substantial distance off your bearing, you may have to take a completely new azimuth before proceeding. This is part of the fun of compass traveling and it's an exhilarating feeling of accomplishment when you hit your goal "on the nose!"

Mapping and compass travel can be a fascinating hobby on a camping trip as well as useful knowledge, lending some purposeful intent to the trip. Even when you're hiking on well-defined trails, use the map and compass to check yourself, both as a safety measure and as training which will come in handy when you tackle the "big woods."

When buying a pocket compass be sure that it has the circular degree scale about the rim of its face. Also, it should have a locking lever to hold the needle from wiggling when the compass is not in use to prevent undue wear on the pivot. A metal ring for tying the compass to your belt with a length of rawhide will prevent loss of the instrument. A cover that closes over the glass face is a good idea too.

Never, under any conditions, doubt the accuracy of your compass. If the needle swings freely, it can point nowhere except to Magnetic North, barring of course, the close proximity of a gun, ax or large knife. Keep these objects away from the compass when you're taking a bearing and follow your compass's directions unquestioningly. There will be occasions when you'll be sure that your compass is wrong. Put such thoughts from your mind and let it bring you home! It will.

To keep your maps in good condition buy a strip of chart cloth which has a "built-in" adhesive on one side and glue the map to the cloth. To prevent wear along the folds, cut the map into convenient sections and glue these with a ¼ inch space between sections, folding the map along these cloth margins. Lacking chart cloth, use rubber cement to attach the map to muslin or sheeting. Carry your maps in a chart case, preferably one with a plastic window through which you can read without removing the map and exposing it to rain, snow, or dirt.

The mapping and compass information that I've pointed out in this chapter is, of course, elementary. You can find further compass and map data in such books as the *Boy Scout Handbook*, and particularly in the Scout's merit badge pamphlet on surveying. The latter gives numerous examples of compass problems and explains them in an easy-to-understand manner.

Since maps and camping information, especially as regards the locations of campgrounds, go hand in hand, I'm listing in a special appendix at the end of the book, the various agencies, both government and commercial, from which you may secure almost any type of map you'll want, covering practically all sections of the United States and Canada.

Chapter 13

CAMPING SAFETY

Safety isn't a popular subject. Safety publications are dull reading, because it's difficult for most of us to identify ourselves with accidents. These always happen to the other fellow. The truth is that accidents are prevented—or caused—by our own actions, or by our failure to take preventive action. And this applies to every person who walks the face of the earth. There are no exceptions!

Camping involves certain risks, just as living at home does. In the woods, however, the risks are a little greater because most campers are not familiar with them.

An old-time Maine Guide whom I knew well was once hired to paddle a New York woman along the shore of a lake each day for a week while she watched birds through her binoculars and made notes on their activities. Powder rooms are few and far between in the Maine woods. When the guide put the woman ashore during the day he stood by his canoe gazing quite properly across the lake while his guest entered the woods. A sudden screech brought him running into the woods where he found the woman in hysterical terror. He noticed a porcupine waddling away. The guide's work was clearly cut out for him, for the porcupine had slapped the lady with its tail where no lady should be slapped! The incident later had its comic aspects, especially among guides, but at the moment the situation was serious simply because the lady had not been accustomed to looking for porcupines in her bathroom. This was a risk, remote as it was, that she had not anticipated.

Most camping books devote a chapter to first-aid treatment of wounds and illnesses that arise during camping trips. Such a chapter cannot be complete and is likely to give only skimpy directions. Instead, I'm suggesting that you secure a good first-aid manual, such as the one issued by the American Red Cross for elementary training courses, along with a copy of the *Red Cross Water Safety Manual*. Study these before you go on a camping trip, and take the volumes with you for quick reference. With care and forethought accidents can be anticipated and avoided—rather than the injuries cured afterward.

This is based on the same premise that prompts explorers to have their appendix removed before going into remote areas. Before starting on an extended trip, every member of the family should receive a check-up from the family physician and dentist. This will help eliminate the possibility, for example, of a heart ailment acting up in camp or a toothache which could ruin a vacation. Tonsillitis in children can be averted and if there is eye trouble in the family, proper glasses can prevent an aggravation of the condition by the bright outdoor sky.

Give some thought to the foods which may not agree with some members of the camping party. If fried foods trouble someone at home they are certainly a poor choice for camp fare and should be substituted with baked or broiled meals.

Another point to consider is the matter of allergies. If someone in the group suffers from hay fever, it's foolish to plan a trip into an area that is littered with ragweed.

In other words, the anticipation of certain troubles may completely eliminate the possibility of spoiling the trip, or even using the first-aid kit! Take your precautions *beforehand*, rather than depend upon comparatively crude amateur first-aid treatments.

Insects

Mosquitoes, black flies, midges or "no-see-ums" are the worst bane of most camping trips. Your tent should have an insect netting, and you should choose the campsite so that the breeze will help to keep these pests down. Keep away from stagnant water holes, deep grass, or thick brushy woods.

For personal protection, spray your clothing with a "bug bomb" repellent and rub exposed skin with liquid or stick form bug dope such as ethylhexanediol or "6-12." Don't get it near your eyes. Wear shirt sleeves rolled down, and a bandanna about the neck to prevent bugs from seeking the interior of your shirt. In extreme cases, wear a head net. However, when you find conditions so bad that you must live under netting all the time and keep yourself plastered with bug dope, pack up and move on. You don't have to be miserable to enjoy camping!

Ticks, however, are another type of menace. About one in a hundred ticks carries Rocky Mountain spotted fever but the possibility of being bitten by one of these is very remote. There are three types of ticks in the United States: the Eastern dog tick, the Rocky Mountain wood tick, and the Lone Star tick. Among the three of them, they pretty well blanket the country, except parts of the Southwest and extreme Northeast.

A well-fed female may be as long as a half inch, but most are much smaller. Generally they are dark colored and have eight legs. Their bite is usually painless, so much so that persons who have been bitten often don't know it, so that it's a good plan to examine your body occasionally for them. They bite by probing their entire heads into the flesh and will remain until they have had their fill of blood.

If removed within four to six hours, there is little danger of a serious infection. The natural reaction upon finding a tick on your body is to brush it off hurriedly. *This is the wrong thing to do,* for the head will break off and remain imbedded. Instead, apply rubbing alcohol, a lighted cigarette or a match to the tick's body. It will then pull out its head and it can then be picked off with tweezers or lifted off gently. Don't squeeze the tick in removing it, for fear of releasing infected fluid. Apply a good disinfectant, such as silver nitrate, iodine, or more rubbing alcohol.

Most insect repellents will work on ticks, but none of them is absolute prevention. Oil of peppermint applied to clothing around cuffs of trousers or shirts will help keep them off. Some advocate sulphur flour applied to the skin which may be exposed to ticks, but this is not entirely effective either. The surest method is to examine yourself frequently.

Chiggers are very tiny mites which release a skin-irritating fluid. These are likely to squirm under your belt or around shoe tops, but they are not as serious a problem as ticks. Apply repellent as you would for ticks. Chiggers are very small, sometimes hardly visible, but they can be washed off with soap and water. A solution of baking soda or ammonia and water will usually relieve the itching caused by the fluid discharged by the pests.

Wild bees, hornets, or wasps are rarely a problem in camping. Keep away from wild bee trees. The honey is delicious but not worth the risk of severe bites. Hornets' nests should be left strictly alone. If

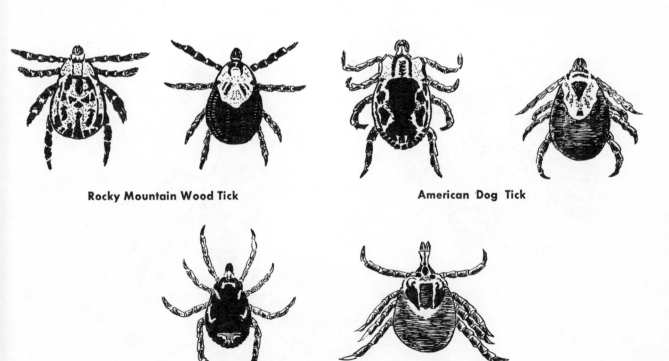

Rocky Mountain Wood Tick   **American Dog Tick**

Lone Star Tick

you notice one around an organized campground, report it to the ranger and he'll take care of it safely. They are commonly found attached to the underside of picnic tables, shelters, or on the eaves of buildings.

Poison Plants

Poison ivy is the most common of the poisonous plants, along with poison oak (which isn't an oak but simply another form of poison ivy), and poison sumac. All three have the same toxic agent, urushiol, which causes the irritation and is found in the leaves, stems, and even the roots of all three.

Some superstitions claim that eating the leaves of poison ivy will make you immune. However, urushiol is a violent irritant and this should never be attempted. "Catching" posion ivy doesn't require that you touch the plant, either. Driving your car through ivy and then changing a tire could result in a severe case. Touching a dog that has walked through it can transmit the irritation, and even smoke from burning plants has been known to infect people.

Positive identification is the best means of avoiding trouble with these plants. They are character-ized by the well-known three leaves on one stem and usually these leaves have a glossy, almost wax-like sheen on the upper sides. The undersides are lighter in color.

One of the best manuals describing the plants and the treatment of skin irritations resulting from them is Bulletin No. 1972, published by the U. S. Department of Agriculture, and available from the Superintendent of Documents, U. S. Printing Office, Washington 25, D.C. This booklet should be in your first-aid kit along with the Red Cross manuals suggested earlier.

Symptoms of poison ivy are itching which develops a few hours after contact, or as long as a week later. The itching may be followed by inflammation and possibly water blisters. Fever, enlarged glands, and abscesses may also result. Bulletin No. 1972 says "A large number of patent medicine remedies of doubtful value are commonly offered for sale." Your family physician will probably recommend a remedy that really works, or you can apply compresses saturated with a boric acid solution to relieve the itching. If the case has gone beyond the itching stage, go to a doctor. Home treatments can lead to infections worse than the original irritation.

Your doctor may also be able to give you inoculations which will immunize you against the poison,

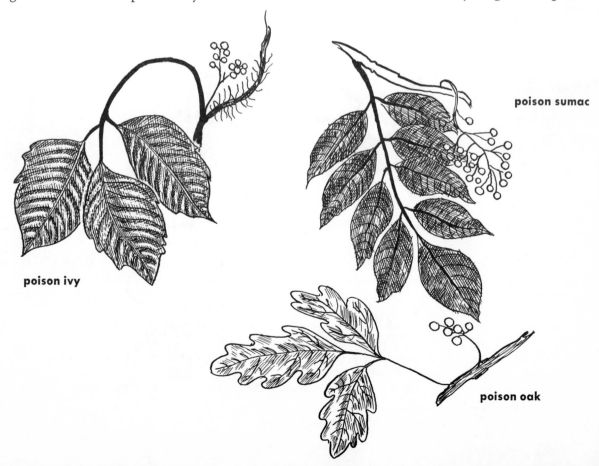

poison ivy

poison sumac

poison oak

probably using an extract of urushiol with a mild saline solution as a carrier.

Also available are tablets which may be taken internally during the winter and spring prior to your trip. These are sold commercially through drugstores and are reported to build up immunity to the poison. Experiments conducted with Coast Guardsmen cleaning brush along the banks of the Mississippi revealed that some of the men became immune to poison ivy after taking the tablets for six weeks. Check with your druggist or doctor regarding these.

Indians crushed the leaves and stems of jewelweed to obtain a liquid which, when rubbed on the irritated skin, stopped the itching. The juice obtained from hemlock needles is also said to help.

Don't be misled into believing that poison ivy grows only as a vine. It takes many forms including that of a small shrub with many stems, although it often climbs trees, completely enclosing the trunk. Fence rows, roadside ditches, open fields are common locations of the plant. Poison sumac is a small tree, ranging up to 30 feet in height.

So-called "wild" mushrooms are the only other poisonous plants which you should beware of. Unless you're an expert at identifying these, leave them strictly alone, or you may end up eating such lethal foods as fly amenita, fetid Russula, destroying angel, or deadly amenita. If you want mushrooms, take along a can or two of the commerically prepared variety. They're better, anyhow!

Water Safety

Swimming, boating, and fishing are closely allied with camping and it's in connection with these that most vacation deaths occur. Probably 99 per cent of these can be avoided by observing the simple rules of water safety.

No matter how proficient you are, *never swim alone*, and, even in a group, don't swim out into the middle of the lake. The water is just as wet and cool near shore.

Before a family group enters the water in a strange lake, have one of the good swimmers explore the bottom along the shoreline for sharp drop-offs. Make sure nonswimmers remain in shallow water and young children should wear life-preserver jackets. Never dive into strange waters without being sure that no rocks or stumps await you under water. Save wild exuberance for supervised swimming areas.

Children or adults who cannot swim well should never use inflated rubber tubes or air mattresses in water over their own depth. A sudden leak or puncture could result in tragedy.

Never stand up in a small boat when there are nonswimmers aboard, even if you're an expert. Never take a small boat out in very rough water. Those waves are often bigger than they appear to be. Also, keep an eye out for sudden squalls that accompany thunderstorms. These are particularly vicious—in fact, I'd rather face a hurricane than some summer squalls I've seen! Don't overload the boat and make sure there is a life jacket aboard for everyone, with the nonswimmers wearing theirs.

If you plan to include boating and swimming as a regular part of your camping trips, enroll in a Red Cross life-saving course and become at least a junior life saver. Not only will this assure your own camping group of safety, but you'll probably get a chance to help other campers who had less foresight than you did.

Lightning

The first man to be killed by lightning while standing under a beech tree is going to gain some degree of fame, for no such record exists. In fact, it's generally believed by many that the beech tree is lightningproof! What's more, there's quite a bit of evidence bearing this out.

"A survey made by the National Shade Tree Conference among a selected group of arborists and published in the proceedings of that body in 1946, produced some interesting data on tree species most frequently struck by lightning: Oak 317%; Poplar 117%; Tuliptree 7%; Pine 6%; Ash 5%; Maple 4%; all other species, 18%." *

I've hunted many years in beech stands because deer and bear are fond of the nuts. From habit, I've examined probably thousands of beeches, looking for broken limbs and other bear sign, and *I've never seen a beech tree that showed signs of having been struck by lightning*. Furthermore, I've never known a woodsman who has seen one!

Despite this evidence, it's a wise plan to give any tall or dominant tree wide berth during a thunderstorm. There's something terribly final about being struck by lightning! Keep away from any tree that stands out above the others in a grove, or which stands alone in a clearing, even if it's a beech. If trees are your only shelter, remain in a thick grove of young trees.

* E. W. Littlefield, "Lightning and the Beech Tree," *The New York State Conservationist*, October–November 1956.

Ignore the claim that lightning never strikes twice in the same place. A tree that has been hit once before is no safer than one which has never been hit. The forest fire lookout tower which I manned one summer in New Hampshire was struck twice, killing a man on each separate occasion. In fact, the tower was hit a few times the summer I was there, but I had long since retired to my cabin, part way down the mountain.

Incidentally, one of the safest places during a thunderstorm is your automobile. Its rubber tires insulate the entire car.

Lightning doesn't always kill. Frequently a "near miss" will render a person unconscious, or merely stun him. In that case, treat for shock. If the victim is not breathing, apply artificial respiration and continue until a doctor tells you to stop, or until breathing is restored. Be sure to send for a doctor.

Safe Drinking Water

There is little to fear from drinking water supplied at organized campgrounds. Water in other areas, however, may be another matter. Springs, streams and lakes in deep wilderness regions are generally safe, unless there is a lumber camp or other habitation upstream of your camp site. Some lumber camps are notoriously careless about polution. They usually take their water upstream of the camp, but are likely to have privies and the horse hovel near the stream below the camp. Since water for the horses is usually carried by hand, it stands to reason that the hovel won't be a great distance from the stream. One camp, in which I spent a winter, had huge piles of manure within 70 feet of an otherwise pure stream! If you're absolutely sure no such conditions exist upstream of your camp, the water is probably safe, but if you're in doubt, treat the water as if it were "civilized."

In general, the fact that water is running rapidly over rocks and gravel and appears to be clear and limpid is no guarantee that it's fit to use. If there's even the slightest doubt about its purity, use halazone—or similar tablets. These cost less than ⅛ cent apiece and one tablet will purify a pint of water in a few seconds. Most outfitters carry them.

Iodine has been recommended as a water purifier but the correct proportions are difficult to maintain in camp. Water can be boiled, of course, to purify it. This means about ten minutes of actual boiling. The water will probably taste flat but can be improved by aerating it. Simply pour it from one container to another a few times using containers which have been sterilized with boiling water.

There is available a plastic baglike water purifier. Water passing from an upper compartment, through a purifying agent, is collected, ready to use, in the bottom compartment. The purifier will handle about a quart at a time and weighs only a few ounces. Costing about three dollars, it can be used a hundred times.

Another unit is a pumplike arrangement, weighing little more than a pound, which will purify a gallon of water in five minutes, simply by pumping it from a stream or lake into your container. Its cost, however, is high, running about $25.

Heat Exhaustion and Sunstroke

Heat exhaustion and sunstroke, although affecting the victim differently, are simply the result of overexposure to the sun or overactivity on a hot day. Heat exhaustion symptoms include a weak pulse, slow shallow breathing, pale face, and sweating. The patient is usually conscious. Wrap him in a blanket, give him stimulants such as tea, coffee, or small amounts of alcoholic liquor, rub the body to stimulate circulation. Hot-water bottles or hot stones wrapped in cloth to prevent burning, will help. Keep the patient out of the sun.

Sunstroke is usually more severe than heat exhaustion and the symptoms include flushed face and body, hot and dry skin, with the pupils of the eyes often enlarged. Unconsciousness sometimes develops. Get the victim into a cool area, apply ice or ice-water packs to the face, neck, arms, and shoulders. If the patient is conscious, give him a cool drink in small quantities, but *no stimulants!* Get the victim to a doctor.

Avoiding sunstroke or heat exhaustion is simply a matter of good judgment. Take it easy on hot days. Don't sit all day in a boat without a hat, and if there is no breeze blowing, don't sit out in the sun for more than a few minutes at a time. Be careful especially about sun-bathing.

Sunburn

The advice for preventing sunstroke and heat exhaustion also applies to the prevention of sunburn. If you must be active in the sun, cover your body with a long-sleeved shirt and long trousers. Wear a hat. Be particularly careful on hazy days, when the sun seems to filter through thin cloud banks. What seems like a fairly cool day may produce a severe burn. Also, you will burn much faster in a boat than on land, for the sun's rays are reflected from the water onto your body, as well as beating down from above. Take the sun in small doses, gradually lengthening your exposure time as the tan on your skin deepens.

For a mild sunburn, any good preparation such as Unguentine will relieve some of the distress, but for a severe case, go to a doctor as soon as possible.

Burns

Probably the most common minor injury around camp is the burn, with the cook the most frequent victim. Most campfire burns can be avoided. Don't build the cooking fire any larger than absolutely necessary. Make sure that pots and pans are rigged sturdily over the fire so that they won't teeter, causing the cook to grab them quickly. Wear an asbestos glove, or use a heavy pot holder when handling pots. A removable pot grip not unlike a pair of pliers, as suggested earlier, is excellent. Be careful with hot fat. Foods that have been soaked in water, such as potatoes, will spatter fat violently when first dropped into the kettle.

Most burns which do not raise a blister can be ignored except for soaking in cold water to help dull the pain. For more serious burns, where blisters rise, puncture the latter near the outside rim with a *sterile* needle, apply ointment from the first-aid kit, and bandage loosely. For burns more serious than these, treat for shock and get the patient to a doctor.

Ax and Knife Wounds

Knife and ax wounds are quite unnecessary to camping if simple precautions are taken. Safe axmanship has been described thoroughly in Chapter VI. Knife safety will be assured when you whittle so that the blade cannot possibly strike any part of the body. Keep your fingers out of the way when slicing foods. The blade of a jackknife not being used should be closed and the camp butcher knife should be stored so that someone won't "find" the blade when searching for other items in the chuck box.

Luckily most knife wounds are minor and generally on the hands where they can be treated easily. For small cuts, allow bleeding for a short time to cleanse the wound, then apply an antiseptic and

bandage. If care against infection is maintained, that's all that's usually required.

For more serious knife or ax wounds, where the wound may be deep with the possibility of an artery being cut, a tourniquet may be necessary to stop bleeding. When this has been stopped, apply antiseptic and bandage. The patient should be taken to a doctor, but under no circumstances should he be allowed to walk.

Snakes

There are only four types of poisonous snakes in the United States and the possibility of being bitten by one of them while camping is negligible. Snakes kill so few people that statistics are not available, so far as I know.

The coral, or harlequin snake, identified by its alternating black and yellowish-red bands, is confined pretty much to the swamps of the deep coastal South and parts of the lower Mississippi Valley. A variety is also found in New Mexico and Arizona. The venom of the coral snakes affects nerves and may cause paralysis if not treated quickly.

The other three poisonous species are members of the pit-viper family and their venom is injected into the blood stream where poisoning takes place. These include the water moccasin, or cottonmouth, so called because the interior of its mouth is white. Its range, too, is limited, being confined to an area running about one hundred miles farther north than that of the coral snake.

The second member of the pit-viper family is the copperhead, recognized by the inverted Y markings on its body. The copperhead is found on dry ledges, old quarries, and generally rocky areas. Rarely growing to more than three feet, its range is from Texas and Oklahoma, northeastward through parts of Missouri and then eastward to Massachusetts. The copperhead is responsible for most of the biting done in this country by snakes, but such bites are rarely fatal.

The third pit viper is the rattler, the most famous of which is the diamondback, easily recognized because of these diamond-shaped markings.

Rattlesnakes are found in most of the United States, except northern Maine, which has no poisonous snakes. In fact that state has long claimed that no part of it harbors poisonous species, but around 1954 a rattler was reported to have been killed in the southern part of the state. A stray from New Hampshire, no doubt!

Don't place any stock in the many snake super-

GROTON STATE PARK

Vermont Development Commission

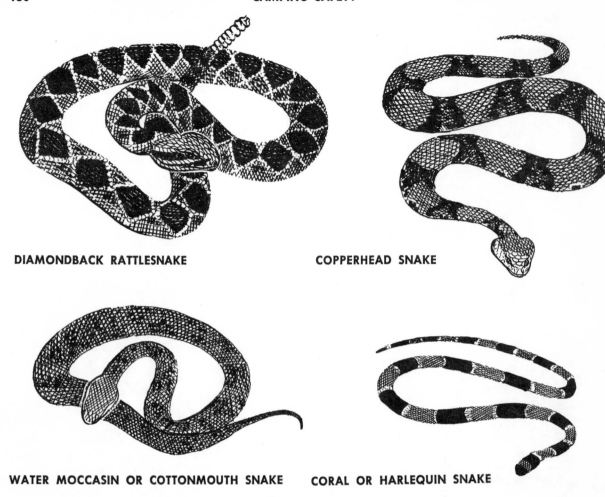

DIAMONDBACK RATTLESNAKE

COPPERHEAD SNAKE

WATER MOCCASIN OR COTTONMOUTH SNAKE

CORAL OR HARLEQUIN SNAKE

stitions such as a snake not crossing a hair rope, a water moccasin not biting underwater, or any poisonous species attacking a man on sight. All of these are false.

So few people are bitten by snakes that precautions are often taken lightly, which is exactly what brings about the few snakebite cases that do occur. Wear knee-high, *loose fitting* leather boots in snake country. Never reach into a hole, or up over your head onto a ledge, or under a bush, where you cannot see clearly, and never sit down before examining the ground. Be careful in stepping over a log—a snake may be lying close on the other side. When walking in snake country, it's best to "stroll" in a leisurely manner. If you're hurrying you may blunder into a snake, causing it to strike because it believes itself to be attacked. Don't go strolling at night, however, because that's when snakes are most active.

The treatment of snakebites is not for amateurs to take lightly and it's unfortunate that some advisers try to make treatment seem like a simple procedure. First aid for such bites cannot be properly

described in a few paragraphs. Here again, the *Red Cross First Aid Manual* is the best reference you can find on the subject. From it you should learn *beforehand* the methods of treatment.

Basically, the treatment consists of treating the patient for shock or trying to keep him from hysteria, a common reaction after being bitten by a snake. *Identify the snake* if possible. If it was a pit viper, apply a tourniquet between the wound and the heart as close to the bite as possible, providing no great time has elapsed since the bite. This should be loosened for one minute out of every ten.

Cut a tiny incision with a *sterile* razor blade or very sharp knife, making the cut longitudinally. Do not make a crisscross cut unless you are a doctor. Induce bleeding. Apply the suction cup from your snakebite kit, or lacking this, use your mouth to suck the wound. Do the latter only if there are no cuts on your lips or in your mouth.

Don't give the victim any stimulants and keep him as quiet as possible. The action of the venom can be delayed considerably by applying ice to the wound. Ethyl chloride can also be used to reduce the temperature of the flesh around the bite, thus slowing the action of the injected poison. This is nothing more than fire-extinguisher fluid. Be careful, however, not to freeze the flesh or cause frostbite.

In the case of a coral or harlequin snake, the tourniquet will not be necessary and stimulants may be given. Watch for signs of paralysis which may cause breathing to stop, in which case artificial respiration will be needed.

These steps in the treatment of snakebites may seem to be quite simple. However, remember that they are only preliminary treatment and the patient should be rushed to a doctor, but he should never be made to walk. If first aid can be given in a car while on the way to the doctor, so much the better.

Naturally, it's a good plan to kill all poisonous snakes you may encounter but very likely you may look for years before finding one. This is, of course, barring the deliberate search for them. Shooting is the safest method, or clubbing with a fairly long stick. Once the snake is killed, let it be. Many a man has been bitten by a "dead" snake and there is even a case of a rattler biting a man after its head had been severed from its body. Snake reflexes take a long time to die.

Serious Injuries

Unless you have been thoroughly trained in first aid, it's best not to attempt treatment of such injuries as broken bones, back injuries, chest wounds, stomach punctures, and other major injuries which can occur. First send for a doctor, or seek help from the nearest forest ranger, game warden, state trooper, or sheriff. Make the patient as comfortable as possible without moving him, treat for shock, and stop any profuse bleeding. Amateur first aid can result in greater injury to the victim, so that it's best to await trained help.

Camp Sanitation

Camp sanitation is rarely a problem in organized campgrounds where garbage containers are provided, toilet facilities are maintained and, in some campgrounds, spraying is done to kill flies. When camping off the beaten track, you will be on your own.

Carry a small shovel with which to dig a garbage pit. Burn the food refuse and then bury it well. Tin cans, also, should first be burned and then crushed before burial. Many wilderness campers merely throw garbage and rubbish into the nearby woods, and then wonder where all of the flies come from, or why they are bothered with such pests as skunks, raccoons, porcupines, and bear!

Important for health as well as esthetic reasons, is the camp latrine. Walking into the nearby woods with a roll of toilet paper in one hand and an innocent look on your face doesn't comply with the rules of health and decency. Dig a small pit some distance away from camp and well away from the water supply. Leave the shovel there and after using the latrine cover the waste with dirt. Toilet paper can be kept there, too, propped on a stick with a tin can inverted over the roll to keep it dry.

Somehow, no matter where you camp, flies will find you. Don't be afraid to spray about your picnic table, camp stove, or fireplace. A fly trap is often well worth carrying along on a trip. This is a jar with a conelike entrance leading to some bait. Once in, the flies can't get out.

Don't leave dishes unwashed from one meal to another, or even for a short time. These will attract flies and other camp pests. Always keep your camp looking as if you expected company at any moment. Don't throw dishwater into the woods. It's better to drain it into a pit filled with coarse gravel, if such is available. Otherwise, rocks and sand will do. If you use a camp stove, wipe off all grease that may have spattered it.

Soiled clothing should be washed frequently, rather than allowed to accumulate in a corner of the tent or in a duffel bag. A few pieces done each day make the task much easier than spending a half day cleaning up a week's accumulation! Camp bedding should be aired daily, barring rain, of course.

Personal cleanliness is just as important in the woods as it is at home. Letting slide the common-sense rules of cleanliness is not "he-mannish" one bit. If the weather is warm, use a nearby stream or lake for a bathtub. Don't overlook brushing teeth or even combing your hair daily. Shaving is not absolutely necessary and many men start out to "raise a beard." After three or four days of itching, you get the razor out. Fingernails are likely to get grimy in camp, more so than in city life, and these should get frequent attention.

The First-Aid Kit

The trouble with most ready-made first-aid kits is that they are rarely fitted to individual family needs. Also, the container is likely to be jammed tight, with little room left for additional items.

**WATERFALL ON THE DEVIL'S RIVER
MONT TREMBLANT PARK, QUEBEC**

Province of Quebec Publicity Office

The best first-aid kit is one which you can assemble yourself, possibly with the help of your family physician who may prescribe certain remedies peculiar to the needs of your family. For example, a child with a nasal allergy may need nose drops, not found in stock kits.

The best container for your kit is a small fishing-tackle box. Be sure it has a firm latch, but after making sure it is unlocked, throw away the key. Should the key be mislaid, a locked first-aid kit can be frustrating. The following items are suggestions.

Assorted Band-Aids or similar adhesive compresses	For smaller cuts and wounds
Gauze compresses, sterile and packed in sealed envelopes	The 3-inch-square size is good
Roll gauze, at least one roll of 1 inch wide and one roll of 2 inch	
Adhesive tape, 10-yard roll, ½ or 1 inch wide	
Aspirin or Anacin. Take along small bottle of 100 tablets	For headaches and reducing fever
Toothache drops	
Iodine, Mercurochrome, or Merthiolate—check with your doctor or druggist	For application on cuts to avoid infection
Unguentine or similar unguent	For burns
Laxative	A change in food or drinking water may cause constipation for a day or two
Tweezers	For removing slivers, splinters
Small magnifying glass	Also helpful in removing splinters; binoculars will serve the purpose when reversed
Fly-tying scissors	Much better than the manicure type as they have large finger holes and the blades are generally better honed
Spirits of ammonia	For shock treatment and for insect bites
Safety pins	For holding large bandage or sling
Small flashlight	Always loaded with fresh batteries before each trip. Accidents happen at night, too, and the camp lantern may not be working!
Sterile cotton	For making swabs, with toothpicks, or buy a package of ready-made swabs
Water-purifying tablets	For emergency use *only!*
Kaopectate, or similar	For diarrhea condition which may also be caused by food and water change
Thermometer, oral type	For checking for fever. Be sure it has a sturdy case
Small pair wire-cutting pliers	For removing fishhooks
Sulfa powder	For open wounds, cuts
Chap stick or similar soothing agent	Chapped lips or skin need something like this
Poison-ivy lotion	
Salt tablets	For those hot days when heat exhaustion is a possibility
Snakebite kit	Small enough to be contained within the first-aid kit
Boric acid powder	For eyewash or burns

Chapter 14

THE CANOE

The canoe is the only watercraft inherently associated with camping. True, the outboard motorboat is being used more and more but these are generally in the nature of cruises, or fishing trips, with camping a nightly incident. The canoe, however, brings to mind the North, wood smoke, deer standing ankle-deep in remote waterways, the roar of rapids, and a nostalgia for faraway places.

No piece of camping equipment has had more nonsense written about it than the canoe, with the result that the general public has come to fear what is really the safest craft afloat.

Even the American Red Cross has contributed to this fear. A Red Cross demonstration of canoeing technique which I watched some years ago was nothing more than a lesson in fear. The instructor handled the craft as if he were negotiating a tightrope, his every move deliberate and cautious, showing none of the ease and grace associated with skilled canoeing. On another occasion, at an Eastern sportsman's show, two local Red Cross "experts" demonstrated canoeing in the show's pool by paddling nervously about—with the canoe wobbling unsteadily because the demonstrators were concentrating on balancing rather than on canoeing. To make matters worse, they wore bathing suits, the implication being that, if you're going canoeing, you're also going swimming! A few minutes later a pair of Nova Scotia guides leaped nimbly into a canoe, and while one of them stood securely on the forward gunwales, challenged the Maine Guides to "come out 'n' fight"—with tilting poles.

Somewhere between these two extremes there's a happy medium. Contrary to widespread belief, the canoe is *not* a dangerous craft. In fact, when a bad wind makes up, I prefer to be in a good canoe than in the best of small outboard runabouts or so-called fishing boats. The canoe, in fact, is the safest of all small watercraft when properly handled.

The Aluminum Canoe

The aluminum canoe has captured the imagination of this generation of campers, and with good reason. It never needs painting and a dent can be pounded back into some semblance of the original shape. Underwater rocks won't hurt it and dropping one from a car doesn't mean an expensive repair job. It can be used as a reflector, close by a night fire for additional warmth and—a blessing on a long portage—many models weigh considerably less than the wood-canvas models of the same length. The aluminum canoe, with its air pockets at each end, is self-righting and it usually flips itself right side up so quickly that very little water is taken aboard.

However, it has some minor drawbacks, not likely to influence the average camper. When left in the sun it's liable to get quite hot and, when used in cold water, transmits that cold to the knees. I personally dislike the tinny "slap-slap" caused by tiny waves striking its side. I dislike it in rapids because the aluminum seems to want to cling to rocks, and the self-righting feature could be dangerous in a high wind when the canoe might be flipped out of your reach quickly. Another objection I have is that it rides too high in the water when empty and is more susceptible to wind than the wooden canoes.

However, these disadvantages are offset by the toughness of the craft, its lightness, and a minimum need for maintenance. All in all, it's a good choice for a camp canoe.

The Canvas-Covered Canoe

The fact that the canvas canoe is still pretty much a favorite is backed up by the output of five major canoe builders, three in Canada and two in this country. This is the canoe of the North and remains the favorite of the professional canoeman. True, in the hands of the inexperienced or careless, it won't last long, but neither will a good double-bitted ax!

Apart from tradition and romance associated with the canvas-covered canoe, this type of canoe has advantages. For one thing, there's a much greater variety of types and lengths available. One Canadian firm offers 19 sizes and types, while an American company has 18 models. You can buy exactly what you want—if it's canvas-covered. It's a quiet craft, made for probing silently along a wild shore, and it's much steadier than the aluminum, as well as easier to handle in a wind. It maintains better momentum against the wind, too.

The canvas canoe, contrary to some opinions, is tough. Each fall, at the end of the guiding season, my canoe usually looked as if a bear had sharpened his claws along the entire length of the bottom, with most of the paint left being above the waterline. Yet it rarely leaked.

On the negative side of the comparison, however, is the fact that if the canoe is used to any extent, it will require repainting every year, with the removal of the old paint called for to do a good job. The interior, too, will need refinishing, otherwise moisture and rot will set in.

A sharp rock may cut the canvas, or it may be a nail on the dock. Also, it must be stored carefully for the winter. I once left a sixteen-footer at Little Kennebago Lake, Maine, propping it carefully. Someone borrowed it, failed to replace the props. In the spring I found only a heap of flattened ribs, planking, and canvas, crushed by the winter's six feet of snow.

However, if you like to work around watercraft and don't mind the task of "making a new one out of an old one" each year, with paint and gentle care, you'll like a canvas-covered canoe. Otherwise, possibly the aluminum or Fiberglas canoe will be a better choice.

The Fiberglas Canoe

This is a newcomer to the field, and although indications are that it will gain some popularity, its sales lag far behind those of the aluminum and canvas-covered models.

Fiberglas is not the exclusive product of any particular canoe manufacturer, but rather, in the case of watercraft, a woven material of glass fibers available to all boat manufacturers. Canoes are usually molded, with two layers of woven glass cloth and one layer of "glass mat," bonded with a resin to which color is added for a "built-in" paint job. Contrary to the claims of some manufacturers, the color may fade.

On a pound per pound basis, the claim is made that a Fiberglas canoe "is as tough as steel" and this may be true. At any rate, a well-bonded Fiberglas canoe is about as tough as any camper would want.

Fiberglas has all of the advantages of aluminum except light weight. It can be left out of doors all year round without repainting each season. Puncturing it is practically impossible. It is quiet—much more so than aluminum and does not conduct heat and cold as well. It, too, can be used for a night fire reflector.

One type of Fiberglas canoe which you should avoid is the model that is trimmed with cast aluminum. One such canoe which I tested thoroughly some years back proved to be little more than a clumsy scow, due to the additional weight of the metal. Also, avoid the model that has floatation chambers under the seats. Since Fiberglas canoes will not float when filled with water, foam-type floatation units are installed. However, when these units are placed under seats, it's impossible to kneel directly in front of the seats. Floatation units should be placed in the peak at each end.

Except for its weight, the Fiberglas canoe has few disadvantages, providing, of course, you purchase a well-designed model, avoiding the bad features of construction which I've mentioned. Its weight is greater than that of the canvas-wood canoe but, despite this, its toughness and durability are worth considering.

Types of Canoes

Probably the best all-round canoe for cruising and camping is the 18-foot guide's model. Its low ends offer little resistance to wind, its flat bottom gives it stability and its width, carried well into both ends, makes for ample carrying capacity and buoyancy. For most canoe trips, the keel-less model is preferable for the simple reason that a canoe without a keel can be handled on a lake, whereas one with a keel makes skillful canoeing in swift water almost impossible. The guide's canoe is not a fast craft, being designed rather for heavy loads and riding out rough water.

Dimensions of guide's models made by various manufacturers will vary slightly, running 36 to 37 inches in beam with a depth amidship of 12 to 13 inches in the 18 foot models. Weights, for canvas-covered craft, will range from 82 to 90 pounds. Aluminum canoes built on these lines will weigh from 60 pounds to about 78.

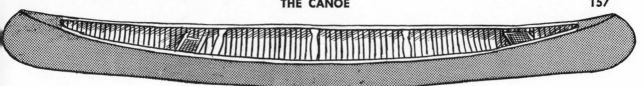

GUIDE'S MODEL

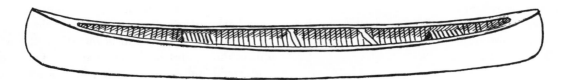

STANDARD SIXTEEN-FOOT CANOE

ALUMINUM CANOE

A canoe having these dimensions will handle a 700-pound load and will ride out tremendous blows if skillfully handled. My wife and I once crossed Maine's Mooselookmeguntic Lake, considered treacherous for canoes, in a northwest blow that rolled up waves that were 25 feet between crests. We traversed better than four miles of this sort of going, plus five more not quite as rough, without shipping an appreciable amount of water other than some spray. Our canoe was an 18-foot guide's model Kennebec, with a two-weeks' outfit aboard.

Many favor smaller canoes, such as the 16-footers that are sold for use in juvenile summer camps, under the impression that they are easier to handle. This, however, is not so. A 16-footer, with two men aboard, sets lower in the water than does a larger canoe and is, therefore, more difficult to paddle. Most standard 16-footers are 33 inches wide and about 12 inches deep. They are, of course, somewhat easier on the portages, weighing an average

of 15 pounds less than 18-foot models. However, their seaworthiness is far less than that of a larger canoe. All in all they are a poor choice for an extended cruise, except in hands of experts. For sheltered waters, however, such as rivers having no "white water," or for small lakes, they are suitable. Beyond that, I make no concessions in their favor!

There is a 16-footer, however, which does merit consideration. This is the well-known (in Canada) Prospector model. It's 36 inches wide amidship, 14 inches deep, and has a load capacity of 850 pounds. This is a canvas-covered canoe which weighs 75 pounds. For a short canoe, this is about the finest type you'll find on waterways anywhere. The Prospector is the favorite of professional woodsmen in the Far North. As you can see, its capacity is greater than that of the 18-foot American guide models.

In the chart on page 158, the *standard* 16-foot canoe is included merely for purposes of comparison, not as a recommendation.

Construction	Length	Beam	Depth	Weight	Capacity
Canvas Guide Model (standard)	16′	33″	12″	70 lbs.	600 lbs.
Fiberglas ″ ″	16′	33″	13″	80 lbs.	600 lbs.
Canvas Prospector	16′	36″	14″	75 lbs.	850 lbs.
Canvas Guide Model	18′	36″	13″	85 lbs.	700 lbs.
Aluminum Guide Model (lightweight)	18′	36½″	13″	70 lbs.	700 lbs.
Aluminum Guide Model (standard weight)	18′	36½″	13″	78 lbs.	700 lbs.

This chart will help you to grasp quickly the over-all advantages of the 18-foot guide's model and the 16-foot Prospector over the standard 16-foot canoe.

There is, of course, a tremendous variety of canoes, including 20-foot guide models which are too heavy for average cruising; freight canoes with capacities up to almost three tons; short 12- and 14-footers, ideal for toting but poor for paddling; racing canoes, sleek, narrow, and treacherous; and even sectional canoes designed to be flown into remote areas. All in all, however, those included in the chart—with the standard 16-footers recommended for sheltered waterways only—will give the best all round service.

A secondhand canoe sometimes is the answer to a struggling budget. Keep away from the round-bottom "fool killers" and choose one whose flat bottom is carried well to the sides so that it has a "good tumble home." Weigh a canvas-covered craft and compare it with the manufacturer's specifications. Overweight means layer upon layer of paint, or possible water-soaked planking which will lead to rot. Check the planking and ribs for breaks. An occasional crack does no harm, providing the member hasn't sprung outward and bulged the canvas. Look for rot in the canvas along the gunwale and in the planking up under the forward and rear decks.

If you can locate a canoe whose wood hull is sound, it may pay to buy it and replace poor canvas with Fiberglas cloth. You can get full directions for applying this from any Fiberglas dealer and you'll find the job surprisingly easy to do, and you'll have a sleek, tough craft.

Incidentally, don't buy a sponson canoe. Sponsons are simply air pockets running the length of the craft just below the outside gunwale. These canoes are heavy, difficult to paddle, and actually no safer than other types.

Seats

The American Red Cross advises that seats be removed from canoes[*] and this seems to follow its policy of teaching fear of a canoe. By all means *keep the seats in your canoe!* When you're paddling in rough water, kneel on the bottom of the canoe, with your knees a foot or more apart and lean back against the seat. This will lower your center of gravity to a safe level. When the wind quiets down, slip back onto the seat. On a long trip, you'll find it necessary to rest your knees and ankles. Northern Indians paddle all day in a position that calls for squatting on the inside of their ankle bones, but they have been conditioned to this position for numberless generations.

The Red Cross attitude toward the canoe seems inconsistent when it advises that seats be removed for safety, yet its manual on water safety gives instructions for changing places in a canoe. I first started using canoes more than 30 years ago and *never once do I recall it was necessary to change places in one of them.* To heighten the inconsistency of the Red Cross claims, the canoe shown in an illustration depicting the position-swapping technique has a stern seat!

The American Red Cross alternative to a canoe seat, a thwart, is much more dangerous than the original seat. Human nature being what it is, a canoeman is going to sit on that thwart when his knees begin to hurt. The varnished finish on the thwart will soon be polished smooth and a slight rocking of the canoe will cause him to slip to one side. This can result in a big splash and even tragedy.

Paddles

Canoe paddles are usually made of spruce, linden, maple, or ash. The first two are poor woods which are easily broken. They are popular with inexperienced canoemen because of their lightness, but experts keep their distance from them. Ash paddles are slightly heavier but tougher, while maple offers the ultimate in canoe paddles. Ash and maple paddles are springy and much less tiresome to paddle with than the stiff spruce "pud-

[*] *Life Saving and Water Safety* (Garden City, N.Y.: Doubleday & Company, Inc., 1956) p. 73.

ding sticks." Their extra weight will be hardly noticeable once you are used to them.

The bow paddler should have a paddle which will reach to his chin when he stands, while the stern paddler's blade should reach the top of his head. There are variations of this formula and I suppose I'd probably add to the confusion if I stated that my favorite paddle is six inches longer than I am tall. A paddle that is long enough will allow you to submerge the entire blade for a full stroke without reaching awkwardly.

The shape of a canoe blade has been argued around ten thousand campfires and no one has come up with a blade agreed upon by all—and I hope they never do! Actually, the shape of the blade matters little.

One of the worst crimes committed against a canoe paddle is to paint or varnish the shaft. Lacquer, paint, or varnish on a paddle shaft will blister your hands, just as these will on an ax handle. If you want to protect the paddle, rub it with boiled linseed oil. The blade, of course, may be varnished or painted if you like, but I prefer the oil treatment.

Never lay a paddle down where it can be stepped on and never leave one in the sun, where the heat will warp the blade so that you find yourself paddling with a spoon-shaped paddle! This is especially true of a thin-bladed maple paddle. In storing a paddle for the winter, hang it up in a cool room.

To do this, place a small screw eye in the top of the grip to fit over a nail on the wall or camp rafter.

Paddling

Don't paddle alone from the stern seat, even if you kneel. The frequent advice that a heavy rock be placed in the bow to hold it down is a mighty poor suggestion. Should you tip, the rock could well lodge in the peak or under a forward thwart, with the result that the canoe would be little more than a vertical buoy, offering little support to a tired swimmer. When paddling alone, kneel amidship, slightly ahead of the middle thwart if you're going upwind, and slightly back of the center when traveling downwind. Practice this a few times in quiet water, and you'll find that you can safely tip the canoe to one side slightly for greater speed and ease of paddling. You'll find this position steady, contrary to popular belief.

For paddling from the stern, as well as the bow, the Indian stroke is often suggested. In this stroke, the paddle is given a quick dip and sharp backward thrust, close to the gunwale. Then the shaft is rolled over the gunwale, driving the blade outwardly away from the canoe. This is a powerful and fast stroke, but it's hard on paddles, gunwales, and unless you're accustomed to it, still harder on the paddler.

The strokes which propel a canoe are all quite easy to learn, but only experience can teach you

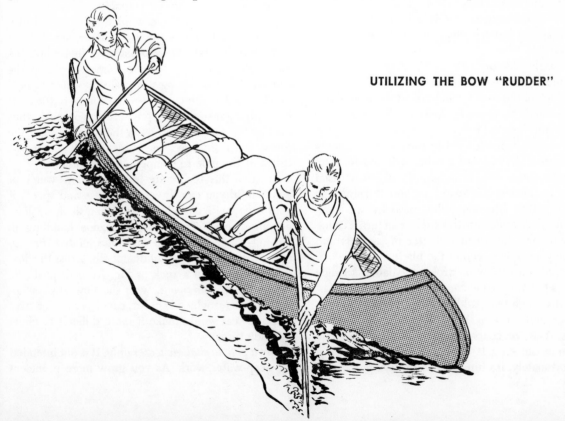

UTILIZING THE BOW "RUDDER"

which to use under a specific condition. The bowman's cruising stroke is the simplest one, consisting of reaching out and drawing the blade back *parallel to the keel*, but no farther back than your body. The stern man's corresponding stroke is the J, or Canadian, stroke. This is similar to the cruising stroke up to the point where the blade reaches your side. Then it is given a backward and outward thrust, to offset the canoe's tendency to turn away from the stern man's stroke.

For turning a canoe within its own length, the draw stroke can be used, each man reaching out at right angles to the canoe on opposite sides and drawing the flat of the blade vertically toward himself. This same maneuver can be varied by using the side sculling stroke, weaving the blade in a small semicircle as it is pulled toward the paddler. This is usually easier than the straight side draw.

For a sudden turn, when there's no time to warn the stern man, the bow rudder is effective. This consists simply of driving the blade into the water at a 30- to 45-degree angle from the line of the canoe, *but ahead of it*. This is a form of the jam stroke, in which the blade is dropped suddenly in a vertical position, close to the gunwale, so that the blade is at a right angle to the canoe. This stroke requires strong arms and good paddles but is an effective brake.

The pushover stroke is the opposite of the side draw. The blade is dropped into the water close to the gunwale and parallel to the keel, and pushed away from the canoe. This is a tricky one which takes practice, but it's effective for driving a craft sideways.

The backwater or back stroke is the reverse of the cruising stroke. The blade is dipped into the water back of the paddler and pulled forward, causing the canoe to move backwards. It can also be used to stop forward motion.

The sweep stroke is used to turn a canoe slowly and consists of sweeping the blade in a wide arc, just under the surface of the water. It can be used with a forward or backward motion, turning the canoe in either direction. When used by one man, paddling alone amidship, this stroke can turn a canoe within its own length in a matter of seconds and with only a single sweep of the blade.

With such a variety of strokes available, a canoe becomes the most maneuverable watercraft there is, especially when two paddlers have learned to work together and to use the correct combination of strokes. This, of course, cannot be taught in one chapter on canoeing. It takes practice and experience and, fortunately, it's fun to learn by trying.

However skillful you may become with the paddle, you won't become a canoeman until you learn to pole your craft. Most writers advise against this for beginners, probably because they've never tried it! First, however, you'll need a "settin' pole." Most canoemen cut their own of light but strong wood such as spruce. Such poles are generally 12 to 14 feet long and 1¼ to 1½ inches in diameter or slightly heavier, depending upon the taper. A shoe of soft metal at the bottom end will grip rocky underway surfaces. You can buy such poles, made of ash, from some canoe manufacturers and logging-equipment supply houses.

The best place to start is in the shallow water along a lake shore. *Forget all of the advice you've ever heard about not standing up in a canoe.* Stand in front of the stern seat, with your feet apart, one somewhat ahead of the other so that you're facing slightly to the side. Keeping the canoe in no more than a foot or two of water, drop the pole into the water at one side just back of your position until it strikes bottom.

Now, with both hands apply a backward and downward pressure against the lake bottom and, as the canoe starts to move forward, work your hands up the pole, hand over hand. As you reach the top of the pole, give a final surge against it, and lift it quickly out of the water. While doing this, stand loosely, in a semirelaxed position, with your knees slightly bent. This will keep you from pushing the canoe out from under yourself!

In bringing the pole forward for the next thrust, don't drag it in the water but, rather, snap it forward smartly, and take "another bite." Skillful poling, like skillful paddling, is done from one side of the canoe only. Don't swing your pole from side to side. You'll find that you can direct the course of the craft by applying a slight side pressure as you push, thus turning the canoe slightly. On the other hand, if the canoe skids sideways, or turns unduly, alter the thrust of the pole to compensate for this.

Practice this technique in the shallow water of a lake until you can direct the course and speed of your canoe with ease. Next, try it in a shallow, slow-moving stream. The secret to canoe handling in flowing water is to *keep the bow pointed directly into the current.* Never cut diagonally across the flow of water to avoid a rock or log. Instead, push the canoe directly *sideways*, with the bow always upstream. This is why a keel-less canoe is best for river work. A keel would make it more difficult to effect this side thrust.

Use a pole in shallow water only. It is not intended for deep-water work. As you grow more proficient with the "settin' pole," you can graduate to swifter, but never deeper water.

In using a canoe on a stream, whether you are poling or paddling, load the craft so that the bow is light for upstream travel, and heavy for down-river work. For lake travel, the load may be set so that the canoe rides "an even keel."

Just in case you're not convinced that poling is easy to learn, a group of eight 12- to 14-year-old Boy Scouts whom I accompanied on a canoe trip up the St. Croix River, flowing swiftly between Minnesota and Wisconsin, proved it even to my surprise. We ran into stretches of river gliding powerfully over sand bars, a foot or two below the surface, which made paddling muscles cry out and progress slow. I slipped ashore and cut a 12-foot pole and, standing in the stern of my canoe, I drove the craft upstream with comparative ease. Within ten min-

utes, all eight of the boys had slipped ashore too, and cut poles. Soon all were standing in their canoes pushing their way upriver. They were awkward and wobbly, but they made faster time with less effort during the next two days. Not a single canoe tipped over, although only one of the eight boys had had any previous canoe experience!

Travel downstream is also done with a "settin' pole," only in this instance, it is used to "snub" the canoe and to dodge around rocks. It's best not to "shoot" the rapids, smarter canoemanship calling for "lettin' 'er down easy." Once you've become an advanced canoeman, then you may run the rapids if you choose. More likely you'll decide to carry around the bad ones.

Carrying a canoe weighing up to about a hundred pounds is best done alone. Strange as it may seem, two men have more difficulty than one, because they

PORTAGING IN ALGONQUIN PROVINCIAL PARK, ONTARIO   *Canadian Government Travel Bureau*

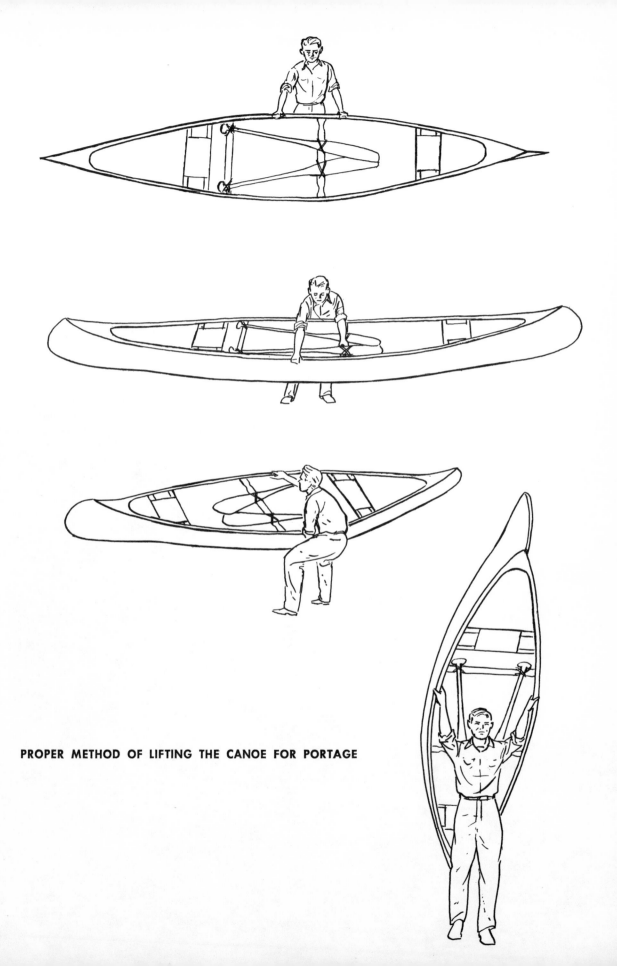

PROPER METHOD OF LIFTING THE CANOE FOR PORTAGE

cannot synchronize their footsteps, especially on a rough trail. Each man jars the upturned canoe so that it gouges the other fellow's shoulders. On a long portage this can break up the strongest friendship!

To lift a canoe for a portage, grasp it by the near gunwale amidship and stand it on its opposite side. Holding the near gunwale with one hand, reach over with the other and grasp the far end of the center thwart. Give the craft a slight shove with one knee and pull it upward in a rolling motion. Actually, this technique will "throw" a canoe to your shoulders lightly. As the canoe rises, twist your body and duck your head downward, so that one gunwale passes over it, allowing the yoke to drop on the back of your neck and shoulders.

This is much easier than it sounds, but if you find it too difficult, have your partner lift one end, while you set the canoe on your shoulders.

A carrying yoke can be made of two paddles, lashing them to the thwarts so that one blade rests on each shoulder. A sweater or heavy shirt will supply ample padding. You can also buy a factory-made yoke with built-in shoulder pads which can be attached to the canoe.

At a portage, always load or unload a canoe while it is parallel to shore, especially if it's a canvas-covered model. It should float freely while being loaded or emptied. Also, never land one by driving the bow up on to the shore and then walking the length of it. Aluminum and Fiberglas canoes will take this sort of treatment, but if you do it to a canvas canoe you'll "break its back."

Occasionally a canoe has to be towed by a power boat. If the towline is attached to one of the forward thwarts or to one gunwale, the canoe will "hog"— that is, it will travel with the bow down, resulting in its weaving back and forth across the wake of

the towing boat. To avoid this, attach a towing bridle. Tie one end of a 4-foot length cord to a forward thwart, run the line *under* the canoe, and tie the other end of the cord to the same thwart. Now, attach the towline to this cord close to the keel line. Towing the canoe with this rig will tend to lift the bow and it will allow the canoe to follow directly behind the boat on a straight course.

Sometimes a canoe has to be towed upstream against a strong current, as in the case where there is no portage trail. This can be done without even getting your feet wet. Tie a 50-foot line to a forward thwart and another to the stern thwart. Holding onto the lines, push the canoe out into the current and start walking upstream along the bank, towing the craft behind you. By pulling on the stern line, the canoe will be driven farther out into the stream and, by pulling on the forward line, it will be brought closer to your side of the river. In this manner you can steer the craft around rocks without touching it! With two men towing, it's even easier, one man handling each line, or one man riding in the canoe and helping with a paddle or settin' pole. The latter, however, is tricky, as a sudden tug by the man on shore may unseat the man in the canoe. It's for experts!

If you're going to use a small outboard motor with your canoe, buy a double-ended model and mount a side bracket for the motor. These are far easier to use than the so-called square-sterned types which are little more than a regular canoe with one point cut off. These have too little bearing surface at the stern which tends to ride too deep. Also, the motor is directly behind the operator and very tiresome to steer. With a side bracket, the outboard steering handle is conveniently at your left.

Some companies make a wide-sterned canoe and

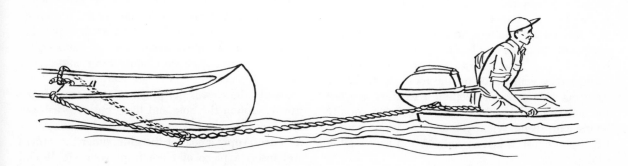

TOWING THE CANOE WITH A POWER BOAT

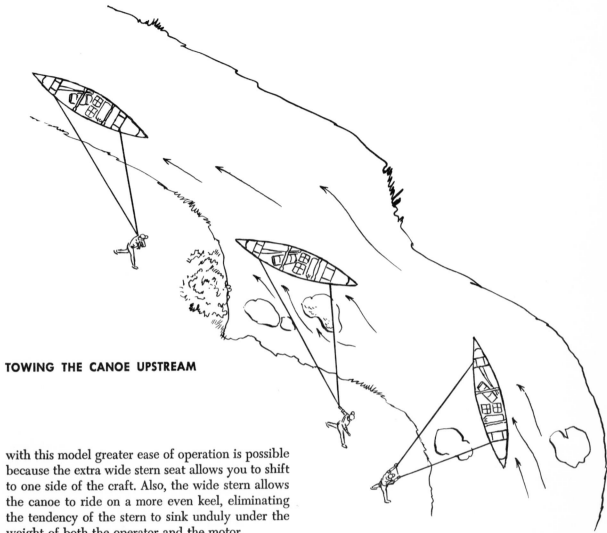

TOWING THE CANOE UPSTREAM

with this model greater ease of operation is possible because the extra wide stern seat allows you to shift to one side of the craft. Also, the wide stern allows the canoe to ride on a more even keel, eliminating the tendency of the stern to sink unduly under the weight of both the operator and the motor.

If a strong wind is blowing and the lake is rolling with whitecapped crested waves, stay ashore unless you've mastered your canoe thoroughly. If you're caught out by a sudden squall, and there's no time to run, face the bow into the wind, kneel as low as you can on the bottom, and keep paddling, not necessarily to make any headway against the storm but to keep off the windward shore where rollers could wreck your canoe on the rocks. Even better canoemanship calls for keeping a weather eye out for masses of black clouds that will bring squally winds with them. When you sight a storm coming, get to shore just as fast as you can and wait for the blow to pass.

When you start your practice sessions with a canoe, always paddle *upwind*—or into the wind. In this way, you won't find yourself bucking a wind on the return trip when you're tired. Instead, the wind will help drive you home more quickly.

You'll have little to worry about from possible damages to an aluminum or Fiberglas canoe while on a trip, but if your preference is for a canvas-covered canoe—as mine is—carry a canoe repair kit. This should include a small can of canoe glue, available from any canoe manufacturer, and one or two small pieces of lightweight canvas.

Should the canvas get punctured or torn, lift the canvas around the hole and blow out or brush out any sand or grit that may have worked in. Allow it to dry. Apply a coat of the glue under the canvas and insert a piece of cloth from your kit. Round off the corners and work under the canoe canvas with a knife until it lies flat. Now apply another coat of glue *over* the cut, and lay on another round-cornered patch *over* the hole. Press it down, wait a few minutes for it to "set," then renew your trip.

Learn to handle your canoe well, treat it as the valuable piece of equipment that it is, disregard the old wives' tales concerning it, and you'll get the full benefit of the finest small craft afloat!

Planning a canoe trip is almost as much fun as making one. First, learn the capacity of your canoe and don't forget to figure in your own weight. Even if there are no portages on your proposed route, never overload the craft. Take into consideration, if there *are* portages, that you will have to tote every item your canoe carries. Keep the number of packs to a minimum, for one large pack is much easier to portage than are a half-dozen smaller ones. A well-planned canoe outfit can be toted over a portage without a return trip for odds and ends.

This is not intended, by any means, to be a complete course in canoe camping. Rather, I have tried to point out how a beginner can learn to use this fine craft and, at the same time, I've tried to dispel some of the many fallacies that exist regarding the canoe. The best way to become an accomplished canoeman is to follow the suggestions I have made on sheltered waters, close to home. Go canoeing as often as you can and take along your camp outfit. You'll find peace, relaxation, and contentment that goes with no other outdoor activity.

166

RIDING MOUNTAIN NATIONAL PARK

Canadian Government Travel Bureau

Chapter 15

THE WEATHER

There are two methods of predicting weather. One is scientific: using a barograph, a recording thermometer, wind indicator, cloud charts, weather maps, and endless records. You'll run into such things as *alto-cumulus translucidae undulatis*. After much study and practice you'll become—if you're as accurate as the professional experts—about 80 per cent correct in your predictions.

The other method involves informal observations of such things as mare's-tails, mackerel sky, sundogs, and a series of homely but surprisingly accurate weather proverbs and backwoods beliefs. As for accuracy, neither method can justifiably criticize the other!

The longer you observe weather at firsthand, the more respect you'll have for the men of the Weather Bureau. But unless you have a scientific penchant and you're willing to devote much time and some expense, you'll find their methods too complicated and technical. The immediate natural signs, properly interpreted, will do the job, at least for camping purposes—and they're more fun to read besides.

To the average person, especially the city dweller, clouds mean rain and a clear sky indicates good weather. The countryman knows this isn't necessarily so. Predicting weather is not *that* simple! Sometimes a clear sky isn't to be trusted, and quite often clouds are the advance sign of good picnic weather.

Misreading weather signs can lead to misery on a camping trip. I once ran across a group of girls on a canoe trip whose island camp had been hit by a night storm. Two of their three tents were down, the fire was a sad smolder, and five teen-age girls were huddled in wet blankets when my canoe hove into sight. I put ashore to lend a hand and was met by the counselor, who out of range of the girls' hearing, sobbed, "I can't understand it . . . the stars were out last night . . . the wind was so nice and warm . . ."

As we worked to get the outfit back on its feet and its collective stomach filled, their good spirits returned and we had a short lesson in basic weather predicting. The bright stars against a black sky, I pointed out, portend bad weather, as a rule. More certain of bringing rain was the "nice, warm wind," for this had been a southerly one which had grown during the night until the trees had had their pleas for mercy drowned out by the roar of the storm. Had the counselor realized what the south wind was bringing her way, she would have camped on the north side of the island in the lee. Very shortly the group was laughingly repeating:

> *When the wind is in the South*
> *The rain is in its mouth.*

Wind is one of the most reliable of the natural weather signs. A wind from the northeast, ranging through east, southeast, and south, will bring rain, generally within twelve hours or less. A northeaster, however, will often blow for three to five days, whereas a storm from the southeast or south seldom lasts more than twenty-four hours. I once camped out on a hunting trip near Moosehead Lake for five days, almost every minute of which was cursed by a steady fall of rain or sleet borne on the wings of a northeast wind!

A wind from the north, though, and ranging through west, to southwest, is a clearing wind. The nearer the north quarter it blows from, the colder it will be. Also, a west wind will usually drop with the sun, something not true of winds from an easterly quarter. One of the oldest of weather rhymes will help you to remember which winds are favorable to outdoor activity:

> *When the smoke goes West, gude weather is past*
> *When the smoke goes East, gude weather is neist*

Even when there's a complete absence of wind, the action of smoke helps predict weather. When

**CANOE CAMPING ON THE ATHABASCA RIVER,
JASPER NATIONAL PARK**

Canadian Government Travel Bureau

your campfire smoke rises fairly straight into the sky in a long thin vertical trail, you'll have good weather for the next twelve to twenty-four hours. However, let that smoke rise a short distance, then drift slowly away to form in "pockets," or settle in low places, and you'll soon have rain.

Another helpful sign on a windless day is sound. When you hear distant sounds, such as voices on the opposite shore of a lake, so that they are clear and distinct, the lowering canopy of clouds usually present under these conditions will open up on you shortly. Hence the rhyme:

> *A stormy day will betide.*
> *Sound traveling far and wide*

On a quiet, windless day, watch the leaves of trees too, particularly those of the maple and oak. When these turn their undersides upward, rain will be along soon, usually within a few hours. The sign generally appears late in the day and often gives advance notice of a thunderstorm, long before the rumble of thunder is heard.

An extended period without wind, with the sky blue, the temperature comfortably high, and the lakes a flat calm that invites canoeing, is known as a "weather breeder." I once had a woods partner who never thoroughly enjoyed this kind of weather; he spent most of the time worrying about what was coming. "It's nice," he'd agree, "but we'll pay for it in a couple of days." Usually he was right, for a change is bound to follow such weather, and since you can't very well improve on perfection, any change is likely to be for the worse.

A colorful sky is likely to set a color photographer agog, but the outdoorsman is more apt to start evaluating these colors and their location in the sky, with regard to weather. To his mind will come another weather rhyme:

> *Red sky at night, sailors' delight,*
> *Red sky at morning, sailors take warning.*

Note that the colors referred to apply to the sky, not to the sun itself. Nevertheless, a brilliantly red sun, seen at sunrise through a grayish haze, will produce a storm before the day is over. I recall driving one winter morning to the lumber camp where I worked. During the drive, the sun poked its head over the forested mountains, a glowing ball of orange-red. By midafternoon, we had the bulldozers out, clearing the heavy snow which was falling. The warning is good for summer and winter.

On the other hand, a brilliantly red sunset is an assurance of a clear day coming tomorrow. In the summertime such a sunset is common during a heat wave and is an indication that the heat will continue. If the sunset features a graying mass of thin clouds, with sky streaked with green or yellow tinges, foul weather is on the way, possibly accompanied by high winds.

A sundog, or halo, around the sun is another indication of stormy weather on the way. This sundog is caused by sunlight shining through high cirrostratus clouds which contain ice particles. Occasionally there may be two sundogs, one within the other, but the prophecy is the same. In the winter, the sign is not reliable.

A ring around the moon, also more reliable in the summer than during winter, indicates a storm coming. There is a belief that the number of stars seen within the ring are an indication of the number of days still to come before the storm, but this is a fallacy. Also, the saying "the bigger the ring, the nearer the wet" is unreliable. Such rings, around either the sun or the moon, portend a storm within twenty-four to forty-eight hours in the summer.

Still another belief is that the horns of a partial moon pointing downward make a "wet moon" with rain to follow, while on the other hand, when the horns point upward, it will not rain. This would be helpful, but the theory is not correct. However, the clarity with which the moon's horns can be seen is a reliable weather sign. If the points stand out sharply against the night sky, high winds will follow. If they are "fuzzy," calm weather will follow.

The color of the moon bears watching also. If the moon is yellow or orange when overhead, a storm will often arrive within a day or so. A brilliantly white moon means that clear weather will continue. Don't judge the moon until it's well up in its zenith, since a rising moon is often orange as it peers over the horizon. Also, forest-fire smoke may cause the moon to look a reddish yellow, without any bearing on the weather. Such a haze can be quite widespread and I have smelled smoke in Maine from a fire burning in northern Quebec. Wind storms in the Great Plains region, carrying great quantities of dust to high altitudes, will "discolor" the moon.

Generally speaking, high-flying clouds will not bring immediate rain, whereas low clouds almost invariably do. Nevertheless, clouds do help to predict weather. A good example of this is the old-time sailor's ditty:

> *Mackerel sky and mare's-tails*
> *Make tall ships carry low sails.*

The mackerel skies are simply cirro-cumulus clouds arrayed in a mottled pattern to form a mackerel-scale effect. Some prefer to think of them as "sand waves" such as seen on the seashore. The mare's-tails, flying at extremely high altitudes, are cirrus clouds, thin wispy curls that speed across the sky, often at more than two hundred miles per hour! When these mare's-tails form a filmy overcast with substantial mackerel formations underneath, you'll get rain within a day or so. Isolated instances of either of these formations mean nothing.

The most frequently seen clouds in the summer are white cumulus formations, shaped not unlike giant balls of cotton. When the weather is going to be fair, these are spaced quite evenly and their edges are rounded. Also, they appear smaller than most storm clouds.

When cumulus clouds begin to bunch up, and their edges become ragged, with towers or "parapets" forming on their topsides, they form themselves into rolling layers called strato-cumulus. These will lower rapidly, turn dark, and rain will soon wet down the countryside. Cumulus clouds can, then, portend either good or bad weather. It becomes a case of learning to recognize the characteristics of both types of cumuli.

Thunderstorm clouds, of course, are most easily recognized, with their billowing thunderheads reaching well into the 20,000-foot level. Invariably, those which will bring a storm your way will come from the west or northwest. Those to the south or east will bypass you, or else already have. Towering even above the thunderheads are the anvilheads, a sort of flattening of the top of the uppermost thunderheads, with an overhang in the direction the storm is traveling.

Don't underestimate the speed with which a thunderstorm can approach, and only a fool remains in his boat when one of these develops to the West or Northwest, for running under the thunderheads are low-hanging, gray-black cloud formations that scud close to the earth, bringing drenching rains and vicious winds. I once spent a summer on an island in a large northern lake, and when I saw a thunderstorm making up in the distance, I put extra one-inch lines on the 30-foot boat which we used.

A nighttime thunderstorm is even more easily identified and here, too, its direction from you indicates whether or not it will strike. Only a few days before I wrote this, my family and I watched the approach of a thunderstorm in Wisconsin's Chequamegon National Forest where we had pitched our tent for the weekend. The lightning was at first so distant that we couldn't hear the accompanying thunder, but less than a half hour after we made out the first rumbles in the northwest, our camp was hit by rain that sounded like birdshot bouncing off our tent and by winds that made even the most rugged trees sway. Fortunately, we'd taken advantage of the warning to snug our camp and we rode out the storm without harm.

Estimating the distance to a thunderstorm is easy. Count the seconds between the time you see a flash of lightning and the time you hear the thunder. Since the sound of thunder travels at 1100 feet per second, it will take about five seconds for the thunder's rumble to travel one mile. Divide your count by five, and you will have the number of miles to the storm.

Don't rely on the prevailing winds to keep a thunderstorm away. The surface wind may be blowing in a completely different direction than the path of the storm. Before the Chequamegon storm, the wind had been blowing from the south all day, yet the storm bore down on us from the northwest. The south wind continued to blow until only a few moments before the storm struck. Then there was a dead calm, followed by a series of wicked blasts out of the northwest.

Completely unlike thunderclouds are those which form a thin gray film across the sky at sunrise and different, too, is their effect, for they will usually disperse and bring a fair day. However, if dark gray clouds scud along under a higher film of light clouds, foul weather is on the way. This condition will rarely clear without a rainstorm preceding the clearing.

Fog is a reliable natural sign, well explained in the rhyme:

> *Evening fog will not burn soon*
> *Morning fog will burn 'fore noon.*

I've known morning fogs to last until almost 11 A.M., but the rest of the day was usually cloudless and pleasantly warm. On the other hand, a fog which lays in during the late afternoon or evening will not clear before the next morning. However, it doesn't necessarily mean rain is coming, as night fogs are frequently followed by good days.

One of the most reliable weather signs is dew—or lack of it. When dew is on the grass in the morning—or during the night before—you can bank on a rainless day. Dry grass during the night, however, means rain before morning and a lack of dew in the morning indicates rain before the next night. Hence the weather proverbs:

> *When the grass is dry at morning light*
> *Look for rain before the night;*

When the grass is dry at night
Look for rain before the light.
When the dew is on the grass
Rain will never come to pass.

Even rainbows do their part in warning campers about the weather. A rainbow seen in the morning usually indicates rain, whereas one seen in the evening promises a fair day to follow. During the day, however, a rainbow seen upwind is likely to portend rain, while one seen in the lee means clearing weather. Hence one of the favorite rhymes of deep-water sailors:

Rainbow to windward, foul fall the day;
Rainbow to leeward, damp runs away.

Some say they can smell a storm coming, and strangely, this is often true. Storms are borne by low-pressure areas in which smells become more perceptible, smells such as swamps, bog holes, and even cooking odors. The musky smell of a skunk is much more pronounced just before a rain and hunting dogs do a better job of running game during low-pressure days. It's not the storm itself that you will smell but rather you will know one is coming because natural odors are sharper, indicating a low-pressure area moving in, sure to bring rain!

The next time someone says "It's going to rain. My corns hurt," don't laugh at him. Arthritis, old wounds, corns, bunions, all react to low pressures, thus "predicting" rain.

Animals and birds predict weather in their own peculiar fashions. Sea gulls, for example, feel the approach of a storm and are likely to remain close to shore, or even perched on land. You'll rarely find one flying very far from land when a storm is in the making.

Swallows will fly over water when it's about to rain, flying so low, in fact, that they often touch the water. But they are not long-range predictors, for they take to these antics only a few minutes before the rain starts. Also they are deceitful, for they will do the same thing on a warm summer evening when no rain is in the offing. Then, they are usually feeding on an evening hatch.

The rain crow, which is really the yellow- or black-billed cuckoo, with its throaty croaking cry, is said to predict rain when it calls. I can't vouch for this claim, but many woodsmen and farmers swear by it.

When you see the common crow flying crazily, darting downward, sideways, or suddenly zooming upward, chances are a strong wind is in the making. Be sure the crow isn't flying crazily because it's trying to escape from the tiny kingbird, however!

Deer will leave high ground at the approach of a storm and head for thick cover at lower elevations. One fall, while hunting just below the subarctic level high in Maine's Caribou Valley, we noticed one day that all fresh deer tracks were headed downhill and slightly easterly toward a boggy area at the foot of the valley. We took the hint and got out quickly. That night it snowed enough to close the valley for the winter!

Even the cricket helps—not to predict, but to record temperatures. Crickets are much more sensitive to changes in temperature than are most thermometers, which actually are slow to react to a change. Count the chirps of a cricket during a measured fifteen-second period, add forty to the total, and you'll have an amazingly accurate temperature recording. The warmer it is, the faster a cricket will chirp. When the mercury drops to about fifty, the cricket is rarely heard. Probably shivering interferes with his chirping, or else he'd rather be silent than wrong.

Appendix

NATIONAL AND REGIONAL AGENCIES

Appalachian Mountain Club, 5 Joy Street, Boston, Mass. 02108. Hiking, climbing, canoeing information; guidebooks.

Appalachian Trail Conference, 1718 N Street, N.W., Washington, D.C. 20036. Information on Appalachian Trail, Maine to Georgia.

Army Corps of Engineers, U. S. Department of Defense, Washington, D.C. 20315. Maintains 11 regional offices (list available from Washington office). Each publishes descriptions of recreational facilities, including camping, within its district.

Bureau of Indian Affairs, U. S. Department of the Interior, Washington, D.C. 20242. Information for camping on Indian lands.

Bureau of Land Management, U. S. Department of the Interior, Washington, D.C. 20240. Information for camping on public lands.

Bureau of Outdoor Recreation, U. S. Department of the Interior, Washington, D.C. 20240. National clearinghouse for information on outdoor recreation, including camping.

Bureau of Reclamation, U. S. Department of the Interior, Washington, D.C. 20240. Administers multiple-use projects in 17 western states, which include outdoor recreation and camping.

Family Camping Federation, American Camping Association, Bradford Woods, Martinsville, Indiana 46151. Family camping information.

Fish and Wildlife Service, U. S. Department of the Interior, Washington, D.C. 20240. Bureau of Sport Fisheries and Wildlife within this department administers National Wildlife Refuges, some of which permit camping.

Forest Service, U. S. Department of Agriculture, Washington, D.C. 20205. Information on camping in national forests. List of regional offices available.

Geological Survey, GSA Building, U. S. Department of the Interior, Washington, D.C. 20242. Publishes topographical maps of entire United States. Free index map available for each state.

National Campers and Hikers Association, 7172 Transit Road, Buffalo, N.Y. 14221. Family camping information, publications.

National Park Service, U. S. Department of the Interior, Washington, D.C. 20240. Information on camping in national parks. List of regional and park offices available.

North American Family Campers Association, P. O. Box 308, Newburyport, Mass. 01950. Family camping information, publications.

Sierra Club, 1050 Mills Tower, San Francisco, Calif. 94104. Hiking, climbing, camping information. Publications.

Superintendent of Documents, U. S. Government Printing Office, Washington, D.C. 20402. Issues numerous camping-related publications described in free periodical bulletins.

Tennessee Valley Authority, New Sprankle Building, Knoxville, Tenn. 37902. Issues maps and information on camping in TVA lake areas.

STATE AGENCIES

ALABAMA

Bureau of Publicity & Information, 304 Dexter Avenue, Montgomery 36104. Camping information.

Department of Conservation, Division of State Parks, Administrative Building, Montgomery 36104. Camping information.

ALASKA

Department of Economic Development, Alaska Travel Division, Pouch E, Juneau 99801.

State Division of Highways, P. O. Box 1841, Juneau 99801. Information on Alaskan section of Alaska Highway.

ARIZONA

Development Board, 3443 North Central Avenue, Suite 310, Phoenix 85012. Camping information.

ARKANSAS

Publicity and Parks Commission, 412 State Capitol Building, Little Rock 72201. Camping information.

CALIFORNIA

Department of Parks and Recreation, Box 2390, Sacramento 95811. Camping information.

COLORADO

Game, Fish, and Parks Department, 6060 Broadway, Denver 80216. Camping information.

CONNECTICUT

State Park and Forest Commission, Hartford 06115. Camping information.

Connecticut Campground Owners' Association, Route 2, Danielson 06239. Information on camping in privately operated campgrounds.

DELAWARE

State Development Department, Dover 19901. Camping information.

DISTRICT OF COLUMBIA

National Capital Region, National Park Service, 1100 Ohio Drive, S.W., Washington, D.C. 20242. Camping information.

FLORIDA

Development Commission, 107 West Gaines Street, Tallahassee 32304. Camping information.

Florida Private Campground Owners' Association, Box 15452, Sarasota 33579. Information on camping in privately operated campgrounds.

GEORGIA

Department of State Parks, 7 Hunter Street, S.W., Atlanta 30334. Camping information.

Southeastern Campground Owners' Association, Cherokee Campground, Jekyll Island 31520. Information on camping in privately operated campgrounds.

HAWAII

Visitors Bureau, Waikiki Business Plaza, Honolulu 96815. Camping information.

IDAHO

Department of Commerce and Development, Capitol Building, Boise 83701. Camping information.

ILLINOIS

Department of Conservation, Division of Parks and Memorials, 100 State Office Building, Springfield 62706. Camping information.

Department of Conservation, Boating Section, State Office Building, Springfield 62706. Information on canoe trails.

Association of Illinois Rural Recreation Enterprises, Morris 60450. Camping information.

INDIANA

Tourist Division, Department of Commerce, Room 334, State House, Indianapolis 46204. Camping information.

Department of Natural Resources, Division of Water, 609 State Office Building, Indianapolis 46204. Information on canoe trails.

IOWA

Conservation Commission, East 7th and Court Avenue, Des Moines 50309. Camping and canoe trail information.

Iowa Association of Private Campground Owners, Postville 56162. Information on camping in privately operated campgrounds.

KANSAS

Park and Resources Authority, 801 Harrison Street, Topeka 66612. Camping information.

Forestry, Fish and Game Commission, Box 1028, Pratt 67124. Information on camping in state lakeside areas.

KENTUCKY

Department of Public Information, Division of Tourist and Travel, Capitol Annex Building, Frankfort 40601. Camping information.

LOUISIANA

Parks and Recreation Commission, Old State Capitol, P. O. Drawer 1111, Baton Rouge 70801. Camping information.

MAINE

Forestry Department, Augusta 04330. Information for camping on wild lands.

Department of Economic Development, State House, Augusta 04330. Information on canoe trips; camping in state parks.

Park and Recreation Commission, State House, Augusta 04330. Information on Allagash Wilderness Waterway and Baxter State Park (special regulations).

Prentiss and Carlisle Company, 107 Court Street, Bangor 04401. County maps published commercially.

MARYLAND

Department of Forests and Parks, State Office Building, Annapolis 21404. Camping information.

MASSACHUSETTS

Department of Natural Resources, Division of Parks and Forests, 100 Cambridge Street, Boston 02202. Camping information.

Department of Natural Resources, Division of Fisheries and Game, Information and Education Section, Room 1902, State Office Building, 100 Cambridge Street, Boston 02202. Information on camping in certain wildlife management areas.

Massachusetts Association of Campground Owners, 10 Kenwood Road, Holden 01520. Information on camping in privately operated campgrounds.

MICHIGAN

Michigan Tourist Council, Stevens T. Mason Building, Lansing 48926. Information on travel trailer camping.

Department of Conservation, Stevens T. Mason Building, Lansing 48926. Information on camping in state parks; canoe trails.

Clarkson Map Company, 725 Desnoyer Street, Kaukauna, Wis. 54130. Maps and campsite information for Michigan, published commercially.

MINNESOTA

Division of State Parks, Centennial Building, St. Paul 55101. Camping information.

Minnesota Vacations, 57 West 7th Street, St. Paul 55102. Camping information.

Clarkson Map Company, 725 Desnoyer Street, Kaukauna, Wis. 54130. Maps and guidebooks published commercially.

W. A. Fisher Company, Virginia. Maps of Minnesota canoe country published commercially.

Department of Business Development, State Capitol, St. Paul 55101. Information on canoe trips.

Minnesota Association of Campground Owners, Route 3, Elk River 55330. Information on camping in privately operated campgrounds.

MISSISSIPPI

Travel Department, Agricultural and Industrial Board, 1504 State Office Building, Jackson 39201. Camping information.

Park System, 1104 Woolfolk State Office Building, Jackson 39201. Camping information.

MISSOURI

Division of Commerce and Industrial Development, 803 Jefferson Building, Jefferson City 65101. Camping information.

State Conservation Commission, Farm Bureau Building, Highway 50 West, Jefferson City 65101. Map of state recreation areas.

Department of Conservation, P. O. Box 180, Jefferson City 65101. Information on Ozark canoe streams.

MONTANA

Advertising Department, State Highway Commission, Helena 59601. Camping information.

NEBRASKA

Game, Forestation and Parks Commission, State Capitol, Lincoln 68509. Camping information

NEVADA

Department of Economic Development, Carson City 89701. Camping information.

NEW HAMPSHIRE

Department of Economic Development, Concord 03301. Camping information, covering public and privately operated camping areas.

New Hampshire Campground Owners' Association, Route 3, Winchester 03470. Information on camping in privately operated campgrounds.

NEW JERSEY

Department of Conservation and Economic Development, 520 East State Street, Trenton 08609. Information on camping in state forests and parks.

New Jersey Campground Owners' Association, P. O. Box 208, Andover 07821. Information on camping in privately operated camping areas.

New York-New Jersey Trail Conference, GPO Box 2250, New York, N.Y. 10001. Information on Appalachian Trail in New Jersey and New York.

NEW MEXICO

Park and Recreation Commission, P. O. Box 1147, Santa Fe 87501. Camping information.

NEW YORK

State Conservation Department, State Campus, Albany 12226. Information on canoe trips.

Department of Commerce, 112 State Street, Albany 12207. Camping information.

Division of State Parks, State Campus, Albany 12200. Camping information; map of parks.

New York-New Jersey Trail Conference, GPO Box 2250, New York, N.Y. 10001. Information on Appalachian Trail and other hiking paths.

Campground Owners of New York, Route 3, Kraft Road, Ithaca 14850. Information on camping in privately operated campgrounds.

NORTH CAROLINA

Blue Ridge Parkway Association, c/o Miller Printing Company, P. O. Box 1880, Asheville 28802. Information on Blue Ridge Parkway.

Department of Conservation and Development, Division of State Parks, Raleigh 27602. Camping information.

NORTH DAKOTA

Park Service, Vogel Building, Bismarck 58501. Camping information.

Travel Department, State Capitol Building, Bismarck 58501. Camping information.

OHIO

Department of Natural Resources, Division of Parks and Recreation, 913 Ohio Departments Building, Columbus 43215. Camping information.

Department of Natural Resources, 1500 Dublin Road, Columbus 43212. Information on canoe trails.

Ohio Turnpike Commission, 682 Prospect Street, Berea 44017. Information on travel trailer parks.

Ohio Campground Owners Association, Box 376, Worthington 43085. Information on camping in privately operated campgrounds.

OKLAHOMA

Industrial Development and Park Department, 500 Will Rogers Memorial Building, Oklahoma City 73105. Camping information.

Department of Wildlife Conservation, 1801 N. Lincoln Boulevard, Oklahoma City 73105. Map of recreation areas.

OREGON

State Highway Department, Travel Information Division, Salem 97310. Camping information.

PENNSYLVANIA

Department of Forests and Waters, State Capitol Building, Harrisburg 17101. Information on camping in state parks.

Campground Association of Pennsylvania, R.D. ＃ 1, Tamaqua 18252. Information on camping in privately operated campgrounds.

RHODE ISLAND

Development Council, Roger Williams Building, Hayes Street, Providence 02908. Information on camping in state parks and privately operated campgrounds; recreation map; canoe routes.

SOUTH CAROLINA

Department of Parks, Recreation and Tourism, P. O. Box 1358, Columbia 29902. Camping information.

SOUTH DAKOTA

Department of Game, Fish and Parks, Pierre 57501. Camping information.

South Dakota Campground Owners Association, Box 1327, Rapid City 57701. Information on camping in privately operated campgrounds.

TENNESSEE

Department of Conservation, Division of State Parks, 2611 West End Avenue, Nashville 37203. Camping information.

TEXAS

Parks and Wildlife Department, John H. Reagan Building, Austin 78701. Camping information.

UTAH

Department of Natural Resources, Division of Parks and Recreation, 132 South 2nd Street West, Salt Lake City 84101. Camping information.

VERMONT

State Board of Recreation, Montpelier 05601. Connecticut River canoe trip information.

Department of Forests and Parks, Montpelier 05602. Camping information.

The Green Mountain Club, 108 Merchants Row, Rutland 05701. Information on Long Trail.

Vermont Association of Private Campground Owners and Operators, Box 25, Pittsford 05763. Information on camping in privately operated campgrounds.

VIRGINIA

Department of Conservation and Economic Development, 911 East Broad Street, Richmond 23219. Camping information.

Commission of Game and Inland Fisheries, P. O. Box 1642, Richmond 23213. Camping information.

Virginia Campground Owners' Association, The Cove, Gore 22637. Information on camping in privately operated campgrounds.

WASHINGTON

State Parks and Recreation Commission, 522 South Franklin, Olympia 98501. Camping information.

WEST VIRGINIA

Department of Commerce, State Capitol, Charleston 25305. Camping information.

Department of Natural Resources, Division of Parks and Recreation, Charleston 25305. Camping information.

WISCONSIN

Conservation Department, Box 450, Madison 53701. Camping information; canoe trails.

Clarkson Map Company, 725 Desnoyer Street, Kaukauna 54130. Maps and guidebooks published commercially; also camper's map and guide.

Wisconsin Association of Campground Owners, Box 6572, Milwaukee. Information on camping in privately operated campgrounds.

WYOMING

Travel Commission, 2320 Capitol Avenue, Cheyenne 82001. Camping information.

Bureau of Land Management, Department of the Interior, 318 Post Office Building, Lander 82520. Camping information.

Wyoming Campground Owners Association, Hyland Trailer Park, Cheyenne 82001. Information on camping in privately operated campgrounds.

CANADA

FEDERAL AGENCIES

Canadian Government Travel Bureau, 150 Kent Street, Ottawa, Ontario. Camping, canoe trip information.

Map Distribution Office, Department of Mines and Technical Surveys, Ottawa, Ontario. Topographical maps covering all of Canada. Free index map available. Specify area wanted.

ALBERTA

Government Travel Bureau, 1629 Centennial Building, Edmonton. Camping, canoe trip information.

Department of Lands and Forests, Technical Division, Edmonton. Provincial maps.

BRITISH COLUMBIA

Department of Travel Industry, Parliament Building, Victoria. Camping and canoe trip information.

Department of Lands and Forests, Director of Surveys and Mapping, Victoria. Provincial maps.

MANITOBA

Department of Tourism and Recreation, Tourist Branch, Room 408, Norway Building, Winnipeg 1. Camping and canoe trip information.

Department of Mines and Natural Resources, Director of Surveys, Winnipeg. Provincial maps.

NEW BRUNSWICK

Travel Bureau, Box 1030, Fredericton. Camping and canoe trip information.

Department of Lands and Mines, Fredericton. Provincial maps.

NEWFOUNDLAND AND LABRADOR

Tourist Development Office, Confederation Building, St. John's. Camping and canoe trip information.

Department of Mines and Resources, Director of Crown Land and Surveys, St. John's. Provincial maps.

NORTHWEST TERRITORIES

Tourist Office, 400 Laurier Avenue West, Ottawa 4, Ontario. Camping and canoe trip information.

NOVA SCOTIA

Travel Bureau, Department of Trade and Industry, Halifax. Camping information.

Department of Mines, Halifax. Provincial and county maps.

ONTARIO

Department of Tourism and Information, 185 Bloor Street East, Toronto' 5. Camping and canoe trip information.

Department of Lands and Forests, Surveys and Engineering Division, Toronto. Provincial maps.

PRINCE EDWARD ISLAND

Travel Bureau, Box 940, Charlottetown. Camping information.

QUEBEC

Department of Tourism, Fish and Game, 12 Ste. Anne Street, Quebec City. Camping and canoe trip information.

Department of Lands and Forests, Surveys Branch, Quebec City. Provincial maps.

SASKATCHEWAN

Tourist Development Branch, Power Building, Regina. Camping and canoe trip information.

Department of Natural Resources, Controller of Surveys, Regina. Provincial maps.

YUKON

Department of Travel and Publicity, Box 2703, Whitehorse. Camping and canoe trip information.